Advocating for Palestine in Canada

Histories, Movements, Action

Edited by
**Emily Regan Wills,
Jeremy Wildeman,
Michael Bueckert,
Nadia Abu-Zahra**

Fernwood Publishing
Halifax & Winnipeg

Development editing: Fiona Jeffries
Copyediting: Alicia Hibbert
Cover design: Evan Marnoch
Text design: Brenda Conroy
Printed and bound in Canada

Published by Fernwood Publishing
32 Oceanvista Lane, Black Point, Nova Scotia, B0J 1B0
and 748 Broadway Avenue, Winnipeg, Manitoba, R3G 0X3

www.fernwoodpublishing.ca

Fernwood Publishing Company Limited gratefully acknowledges the financial support of the Government of Canada, the Canada Council for the Arts, the Manitoba Department of Culture, Heritage and Tourism under the Manitoba Publishers Marketing Assistance Program and the Province of Manitoba, through the Book Publishing Tax Credit, for our publishing program. We are pleased to work in partnership with the Province of Nova Scotia to develop and promote our creative industries for the benefit of all Nova Scotians.

Library and Archives Canada Cataloguing in Publication
Title: Advocating for Palestine in Canada : histories, movements, action / edited by Emily Regan Wills, Jeremy Wildeman, Michael Bueckert and Nadia Abu-Zahra ; foreword by Libby Davies.
Names: Wills, Emily Regan, editor. | Wildeman, Jeremy, editor. | Bueckert, Michael, editor. | Abu-Zahra, Nadia, 1976- editor. | Davies, Libby, writer of foreword.
Identifiers: Canadiana (print) 20210259477 | Canadiana (ebook) 20210262281 | ISBN 9781773634760 (softcover) | ISBN 9781773634906 (EPUB) | ISBN 9781773634913 (PDF)
Subjects: LCSH: Arab-Israeli conflict—Foreign public opinion, Canadian. | LCSH: Palestine—Foreign public opinion, Canadian. | LCSH: Canada—Foreign relations—Palestine. | LCSH: Palestine—Foreign relations—Canada. | LCSH: Palestine—Press coverage—Canada. | LCSH: Arab-Israeli conflict—Press coverage—Canada. | LCSH: Public opinion—Canada. | LCSH: Palestinian Arabs—Civil rights.
Classification: LCC FC244.P19 A38 2021 | DDC 327.7105694—dc23

Contents

*To the seen and the unseen advocates
struggling for a better world.*

Foreword

Libby Davies

The movement for Palestinian human rights and self-determination has had its ups and downs in Canada, as outlined in this book, but overall, I have always seen it as a steady progression forward, a movement growing in strength and breadth despite formidable obstacles and challenges. Deeply committed activists from many diverse backgrounds have managed, remarkably, to maintain a level of activism and public awareness that has defied the odds, inspiring hope and possibility. The same has not always been the case in the political arena. I was elected as a member of parliament (MP) in 1997 until I left in 2015. During those eighteen years on the Hill, I was keenly involved in working for Palestinian recognition and rights. It was an experience in the latter years that sometimes left me in despair and turmoil, so different from my first years on the Hill, which had made me feel immensely positive about the work and interest of my fellow MPs on this critical issue.

If you talk to most activists today about their Palestine work, they will likely have personal stories about how hard it was, and still is in many ways, to crack the wall of silence and inaction on Palestine in the political sphere. It is a striking contrast to the incredible activism taking place in the community, on campuses, at faith centres and in the labour movement. This book addresses some of the challenges faced by the movement, what has been learned and what work is still to be done. The elephant in the room remains the sparse action, if not silence, from the elected, who on so many other issues are willing to speak out with aptitude and force and conviction. It bears examining why, on this issue, it has been so challenging to make them speak up.

I recall that in my earliest days on Parliament Hill there were many events on the Middle East — cultural, political and educational — that amplified the voices in the community and brought them into the halls of Parliament. This built a sense of solidarity and connectedness, as well as the idea that MPs could be strong allies and advocates for Palestine. I worked with many groups to plan and host a variety of functions aimed at fostering awareness, understanding and action for Palestinians. Some of these events would garner a high participation rate of MPs from different parties who were eager to hear guest speakers such as Norman Finklestein, Jeff Halper, Robert Fisk, Salman Abu Sita and Nahla Abdo. The events were engaging and informative, fostering dialogue and understanding. MPs heard about the human conditions in the occupied territories, the right of return, house demolitions, the wall, the assembly of road networks connecting settlements and the historical context. Often MPs would bring greetings from their political party, and local community members could openly engage with MPs. None of this seemed extraordinary at the time. After all, Parliament is meant to be the epitome of broad public discourse and exchange of views and the place for questioning Canada's role in the world. Most MPs belong to one or several international friendship associations and groups, and on many an evening it was not unusual to see competing events taking place, where MPs would dash from one event to another to be seen and noted. At a formal governmental level, Canada chaired the Refugee Working Group, which was part of multi-lateral Middle East peace process and seemed open to dialogue on issues like the right of return for Palestine refugees.

But that common, and in many ways comforting, scene began to change in the early 2000s, culminating with the election of Conservative Party leader Stephen Harper as Canada's prime minister in 2006. In tandem was a steady rise in the voices and lobby efforts by friends of Israel, making it clear that the public discourse and the openness of MPs to speak about the Middle East was about to dramatically change course. In the following years, an atmosphere of fear, censure and near-McCarthyism descended on the Hill like a shadow, with full effect. Attendance at events dwindled, and it was common to hear MPs say that even though they personally supported the issue of justice for Palestine, they were afraid to speak out for fear of being branded as antisemitic, or they may even face some level of censure from their party. It was a momentous downward slide. The Canada Palestine Parliamentary Friendship Association continued to exist, but only a mere handful of us remained active, and so we had to meet in someone's office to quietly confer about what we could do. If we did manage to organize an event and a guest speaker, we would be lucky to see a few faithful MPs attend. Fear is a powerful weapon. It shuts people down and debilitates open debate. We came to understand that the political blocks and the climate of fear were real, and they did much damage to open discussion and support for Palestine.

The uncritical pro-Israel rhetoric of the government was sharpening in tone and frequency simultaneously with the growing power and presence of pro-Israel lobbyists. Their message was chillingly clear: dare to speak out, dare to act, and you will feel the negative impact both personally and politically for doing so. I look back now in astonishment that even introducing petitions to do with Israel or the Middle East (a profoundly basic parliamentary procedure and daily occurrence just after Question Period) became an act of defiance that generated questioning and possible censure. That is when it became clear to me that the actions and words of MPs were being closely monitored and tracked by outside Zionist groups who would report our apparent misdemeanour to the party leadership. Things got worse. Organized and sophisticated work by pro-Israel groups was underway to host meetings and official conferences of MPs, with the goal of establishing definitions of antisemitism that were designed to choke free speech and silence criticism of harmful Israeli policies. There was a powerful alliance of government interests and outside groups working closely together on these initiatives. Combatting antisemitism and advocating for the rights of Palestinians are not mutually exclusive, despite what the pro-Israel lobby would have us believe. Both need to be part of a basic social justice framework. I cannot recall any other geographic area on the globe where basic discussion was so subject to fear and reprisal.

The attack on the World Trade Centre in 2001, and the growth of Islamophobia which followed, fuelled the politically motivated drive of liberal governments, resulting in hyper and discriminatory federal legislation to curtail civil liberties under the guise of protecting the security of Canadians. Subsequent legislation from Conservative governments targeted Canadians of Arabic background or Muslim faith as suspect. Community organizations that had previously received government funding, such as Palestine House, for community-based services, and Kairos Canada, for foreign aid to Palestinians, suddenly faced charges of wrongdoing and the termination of their funding. The dark and toxic political environment on Parliament Hill was now evident in the community too.

Despite these daunting challenges, work and advocacy continued on and off the Hill. I recall sitting in the House of Commons with a couple of other colleagues for hours and hours, even into days, to ensure that a unanimous consent motion could not be passed condemning the Boycott, Divestment and Sanctions movement (BDS). It was a game of cat and mouse, for as long as one of us was present to deny unanimous consent, the supporters of such a motion could not sneak it through. A small group of senators too, particularly Pierre De Bané, Marcel Prud'Homme and Pierre Claude Nolin, all now deceased, showed great courage to support Palestinian rights and the work of the Parliamentary Friendship Association. And on the outside, Canadians for Justice and Peace in the Middle East (CJPME) and Independent Jewish Voices (IJV) steadfastly kept up communication with MPs as much as they could to provide factual information, countering the growing anti-Palestinian propaganda and rhetoric.

Amazingly, a small group of MPs — three of us — visited the West Bank and Jerusalem in 2009, and two of us then continued to Gaza to witness the damage and destruction of Operation Cast Lead by the Israel Defence Forces (IDF). I recall so well that before we left, the Department of Foreign Affairs officials went to great lengths to tell us that if we "got into trouble" in Gaza they would do nothing to help us. Not that we anticipated any trouble, but it was a clear message that their usual policy of assisting MPs while travelling was off the table. Upon our return we tabled our report in Parliament, only to be met with hostility from pro-Israel MPs who wanted the report quashed. I also recall speaking in Parliament in dismay, responding to government initiatives to trash the Goldstone Report, the product of a UN fact-finding mission into human rights abuses during the 2008–09 Israeli assault on Gaza. "The Conservative attacks are reminiscent of McCarthyism and have no place in Canadian society," I had said. Unfortunately, my comments were not, even in hindsight, exaggerated.

The predominant perception in the Canadian Parliament during those years, as I detailed in my memoir *Outside In* (published in 2019), was that the Jewish community was of one mind when it came to supporting the policies of Israel and its occupation of Palestinian land and that no opposing view could be tolerated. Of course, this was not true then, and it certainly is not true today.

I am glad to say that the political environment with respect to the Middle East is improving these days, but it is still fragile and precarious. The courageous work that is being done in the community to foster education and factual discussion on this issue has been critical to sustaining links between the Palestine solidarity movement and individual MPs and political parties, creating more openness and comfort for MPs to speak out. There have been a number of organized visits for MPs to the occupied territories to see for themselves what is going on, separate from the regular visits organized by pro-Israel groups. In 2018, a multi-party delegation of eighteen MPs undertook an extensive visit to the West Bank. And on social media it is more common now to see MPs make statements in support of Palestinians and their rights. There are even instances where MPs and senators from different parties are willing to work together; for example, in May 2021, during Israel's latest assault on Gaza, twenty-four MPs and two senators from five political parties signed a joint letter calling for sanctions against Israel. It is also important to maintain pressure and encourage support within political parties themselves. Members can organize and bring forward resolutions at policy conventions to push their leadership to take a principled stance for Palestine. This was done successfully by grassroots members of the NDP in April 2021, adopting, by a significant majority, a resolution in support of a ban on trade with illegal settlements and an arms embargo on Israel. However, unless members and activists keep up the pressure, there is always a concern that the leadership may retreat to a more cautious and comfortable position.

Despite the gains made in recent years, MPs who speak out for Palestinian human rights still face unfounded charges of antisemitism and are often told they must be "balanced" in what they say. Balance is not an unworthy principle in general, but in this context, the idea of balance is promoted as a convenient political response to promote the notion that both sides are equal and both sides should have equal balance. Of course, this denies the history and reality of Israel's illegal occupation and its crushing of human rights. There are not two equal sides; there is an occupier and those who are occupied. In this context "balance" means upholding an unjust status quo.

This book clearly and forthrightly lays out the case for the growing strength of the pan-Canadian Palestinian solidarity movement and the need to make connections with people in elected office, especially at the federal level. It articulates the need for an honest and open discourse that must lead to Canadian actions in support of international law and human rights, whether at the UN, in the international community or within Canada.

Change is possible when we are engaged, when we build trust and when we create real space for debate. Our goal should be to continue to build the movement for Palestinian recognition, both inside the formal world of politics and within the broader public realm. To do so means understanding the barriers that exist and working hard to lobby and educate MPs both individually and (where possible) with political parties. It means working together with respect and in common purpose, even if there is some disagreement now and then.

We will always need to be vigilant and to push back on the censorship and political dogma that wants to shut down critical analysis and action. Parliamentarians must stand up to antisemitism and at the same time call for justice for Palestinians.

—Libby Davies, MP 1997–2015, author, *Outside In:*
A Political Memoir (2019, Between the Lines)

Acknowledgements

This collection was inspired out of a Canada and Palestine Research Symposium held at the University of Ottawa in February 2019, which explored Canada's historical and contemporary relationship with Palestine and the Palestinian people. That symposium was co-organized by Professor Michael Lynk (University of Western Ontario), Professor Reem Bahdi (University of Windsor), Professor Nadia Abu-Zahra (University of Ottawa), Dr. Jeremy Wildeman (then University of Bath) and Omar Burgan (labour rights researcher). Many of this book's chapters were first presented at the Symposium, and this book's authors participated as panelists, speakers or moderators. To bring these writings to publication, we are grateful to all who provided support and, in particular, the CJPME Foundation and the Canadian Union of Postal Workers.

We would like to acknowledge the support of Fernwood Publishing for making this book possible, including the brilliant editorial team and anonymous peer reviewers and, notably, our assiduous, thoughtful acquisitions editor Dr. Fiona Jeffries. This is a unique volume because it offers a sampling of the experiences and diverse voices of scholars, journalists and activists on Turtle Island who have been advocating for decades for justice-promoting policies toward Palestine.

Acronyms

2SLGBTIQ — Two-Spirit, lesbian, gay, bisexual, transgender, intersex, and queer

ADC — Arab Anti-Discrimination Committee

ANC — African National Congress

ANSAR — Arab Network of Students

AP — Associated Press

ASA — Arab Students' Association

BDS — Boycott, Divestment and Sanctions

C-FAR — Citizens for Foreign Aid Reform

CAJ — Canadian Association of Journalists

CBC — Canadian Broadcasting Corporation

CCPO — Coalition of Canadian-Palestinian Organizations

CIFTA — Canada-Israel Free Trade Agreement

CIJA — Centre for Israel and Jewish Affairs

CLC — Canadian Labour Congress

CJFE — Canadian Journalists for Free Expression

CJPME — Canadians for Justice and Peace in the Middle East

CPCCA — Canadian Parliamentary Coalition to Combat Antisemitism

CSAS — Canadian–South African Society

CUPE — Canadian Union of Public Employees

CUPW — Canadian Union of Postal Workers

EU — European Union

FPJQ — Quebec Federation of Professional Journalists

GUPS — General Union of Palestinian Students

HRC — HonestReporting Canada

HRTO — Human Rights Tribunal of Ontario

IAW — Israeli Apartheid Week

ICC — International Criminal Court

ICJ — International Court of Justice

ICRC — International Committee of the Red Cross

IHRA — International Holocaust Remembrance Alliance

IJV — Independent Jewish Voices Canada

JCPOA — Joint Comprehensive Plan of Action

MEWA — Middle Eastern Women's Association

NACC — North American Coordinating Committee

NECEF — Near East Cultural and Educational Foundation

NDP — New Democratic Party

NGO — non-governmental organization

OAS — Organization of Arab Students

OCHA — United Nations Office for the Coordination of Humanitarian Affairs

OPIRG — Ontario Public Interest Research Group

OPT — Occupied Palestinian Territory

PA — Palestinian Authority

PACBI — Palestinian Campaign for the Academic and Cultural Boycott of Israel

PAN — Palestine Advocacy Network

PFLP — Popular Front for the Liberation of Palestine

PLO — Palestine Liberation Organization

PSAC — Public Service Alliance of Canada

PSM — Palestine solidarity movement

QUAIA — Queers Against Israeli Apartheid

SAIA — Students Against Israeli Apartheid

SPHR — Solidarity for Palestinian Human Rights

SWOT — Strengths, Weaknesses, Opportunities, and Threat Analysis

TTC — Toronto Transit Commission

UJA — United Jewish Appeal

UN — United Nations

UNGA — United Nations General Assembly

UNISPAL — United Nations Information System on the Question of Palestine

UNRWA — United Nations Relief and Works Agency

Contributors

Editors

EMILY REGAN WILLS, PhD (The New School), is an associate professor of comparative and American politics in the School of Political Studies at the University of Ottawa. Her roots are in anti-war, feminist and queer liberation movements. She is the author of *Arab New York: Politics and Community in the Everyday Lives of Arab Americans* (NYU Press 2019).

JEREMY WILDEMAN, PhD (Exeter), is a fellow at the Human Rights Research and Education Centre, University of Ottawa. He is co-editor of the Special Issue Canadian Foreign Policy Journal *What Lies Ahead: Canada's Engagement with the Middle East Peace Process and the Palestinians* (2021). His doctoral research at the University of Exeter assessed the illiberal and colonial nature of contemporary Canadian foreign aid in the Occupied Palestinian Territory. In the 2000s, he co-founded and built a Palestinian-led non-governmental organization dedicated to youth and community development, called Project Hope, in the West Bank city of Nablus.

MICHAEL BUECKERT, PhD (Carleton), is vice-president at Canadians for Justice and Peace in the Middle East (CJPME), a national advocacy organization based in Montreal. He has a PhD in sociology with a specialization in political economy from Carleton University in Ottawa. His dissertation explored the Canadian opposition to boycott movements, and this research involved travel to Palestine and South Africa.

NADIA ABU-ZAHRA, DPhil (Oxon), is an associate professor at the University of Ottawa and holds the Joint Chair in Women's Studies at the University of Ottawa and Carleton University. She is co-author of *Unfree in Palestine: Registration, Documentation and Movement Restriction*. She co-facilitates with Emily Regan Wills the Community Mobilization in Crisis project, co-creating open educational resources with community mobilizers around the world.

Chapter Authors

NYLA MATUK is the author of two books of poetry: *Sumptuary Laws* and *Stranger*, and the editor of an anthology, *Resisting Canada*. Her poems have appeared in *The Poetry Review*, *The Walrus*, *The New Yorker*, and other journals and anthologies in Canada, the United States and the United Kingdom. She is the recipient of a Yaddo Fellowship and the Mordecai Richler Writer in Residence from McGill University.

SHERYL NESTEL, PhD (OISE/U of T), has been active in Palestinian rights movements in Canada, the United States and Israel-Palestine for over five decades. She served eleven years on the Steering Committee of Independent Jewish Voices Canada and is involved in their research program and other projects. She retired in 2012 from the Ontario Institute for Studies in Education, where her research and teaching focused on issues of race and racism in a transnational feminist and anti-colonial framework.

RANA NAZZAL HAMADEH is a Palestinian-Canadian artist and activist immersed in community organizing both on Turtle Island and in occupied Palestine. She holds an MFA in documentary media (Ryerson). Her photography, film and installation work draws on grassroots movements to offer creative challenges to settler-colonialism.

DIANA RALPH, MSW (Columbia), PhD (Regina) is a social worker, scholar, therapist and activist on a broad range of social justice and environmental issues. She is a retired associate professor of social work at Carleton University. She founded Independent Jewish Voices in 2008 and served on its Steering Committee until 2018. She has written two books, *Work and Madness* and *Open for Business/ Closed to People: Mike Harris' Ontario*, and a climate justice movie screenplay, *2084*. She is an observant Jew, a board member of her congregation, Or Haneshamah, and Canada's sole member on Reconstructing Judaism's Joint Israel Commission.

MICHAEL KEEFER, DPhil (Sussex), is professor emeritus at the University of Guelph, a former president of the Association of Canadian College and University Teachers of English and, for more than a decade, an active supporter of Independent Jewish Voices Canada (IJV). He has published widely on early modern literature and philosophy and on state crimes against democracy and Indigenous rights. On matters relating to Palestine, his work includes *Antisemitism Real and Imagined* (editor and co-author, 2010), *Hard Truths for Canada about Israel and Palestine* (2015), and essays "Criminalizing Criticism of Israel in Canada" (2014) and "Resisting McCarthyism: From the 'PC Wars' to the 'New Antisemitism'" (2016).

DAVIDE MASTRACCI is the managing editor at Passage. His work has been published widely in Canada and abroad. You can follow him on Twitter @DavideMastracci.

THOMAS WOODLEY has been involved with Canadians for Justice and Peace in the Middle East (CJPME) since it was established in 2004 and has been its president overseeing its remarkable growth since 2008. He has a BS-EE (Carnegie-Mellon), MS-EE (Stevens Institute of Technology) and MPA (Indiana University School of Public and Environmental Affairs), with a focus on public policy and public finance. He has worked in the federal government and NGO sector, having volunteered in Africa and the Middle East.

HASSAN HUSSEINI is a labour negotiator with a public sector union in Ottawa. He has been active in labour, social and international solidarity movements for the past thirty years. Hassan holds an MA (Carleton) in legal studies and is planning a return to academia next year to complete his PhD in Middle East politics.

Introduction

Nadia Abu-Zahra, Emily Regan Wills,
Jeremy Wildeman & Michael Bueckert

> We are like the
> wholeness of the sun
> the light sinks
> into the
> earth.
>
> *– From Turtle Island to Gaza*

Ojibwe and French-Canadian poet David Groulx writes of the shared experience of colonized peoples, extending this even further to the shared responsibilities of and toward all our relations (2019: 3.0). For many years, advocacy for and by colonized peoples has been mischaracterized as narrowly nationalist at best, and dangerously hostile at worst (Said 1979). Prejudices have dehumanized and discredited survivors' searches and struggles for dignity and justice (Maracle 2017).

When battling internal fear and insecurity, each of us is challenged to turn these toward motivation for solidarity with all others facing injustice, racism, colonialism and discrimination or marginalization of any kind. The personal struggle against fear can determine if we seek power and control over others or if we instead recognize not only our own fears but also the fears of others (Maté 2019; El-Bekai 2016; Jhally 1998 quoting Edward Said). This personal struggle is made even more difficult by efforts to divide and thereby weaken resistance to injustice (Choudry, Hanley and Shragge 2012). Solidarity cannot be presumed; it must be built (Desai 2021; Kelley 2019). This can be done through a shared vision or path, such as the one in the poem above.

This book is about those who have turned their inner fear into solidarity instead of control. It is about the highs and lows of these struggles. Those who advocate for Palestine as allies all have something that brought them to that advocacy. And Palestinians who advocate as allies with others do so in recognition of a shared path. Building community and healing from inner fears are mutual activities. As activist Harsha Walia says, "For me, as for many others, social movement organizing has been healing and empowering precisely because *within it* and *through it* I have found a means to redeem and liberate myself from all the injustices, categories, and assumptions laid on me" (2013: 274).

This book also explores what brings people to advocacy for Palestine on Turtle Island and how such advocacy is contingent on challenging far-reaching systems of injustice and structural violence (Matuk, this volume; Nestel, this volume; Walia 2020; Galtung 1990, 1985, 1975, 1969, 1964). It also explores how advocacy for Palestine is a canary in the coal mine, an early sufferer of what is coming for others. Through navigating advocacy for Palestine on Turtle Island, we investigate the production of fear through structures of racist hierarchies (Alexander 1983) and, as its counter, the extraordinary and life-affirming responses that build solidarity and healing.

Turtle Island/Canada and Palestine/Israel

Fusheeyea Mitre Tabasharini was born in 1864 to an Arabic-speaking family on a mountaintop in the eastern stretches of the Mediterranean coastline (Leney 1996). But at the age of 30, she left to never return. The father of her four children had died and, rather than accept her inheritance, she chose to emigrate (Leney 1996). Travelling alone, her voyage took her to Algonquin territory on Turtle Island. She was rejoined by her children and taught them the ways of their new home. She spoke Algonquin. She never learned English or French and creatively foiled efforts by the Hudson Bay Company's men to harm or hinder her relations with First Nations (Leney 1996).

White settlers on Turtle Island would rename parts as "Canada" and the "United States." The sovereignty of Indigenous Nations, with constitutional confederacy agreements, records of treaties, and decision-making processes (Sabzalian 2019; Sabzalian and Shear 2018; Horn-Miller 2013), came under attack by those same colonial structures. The populations of First Nations, Métis and Inuit were decimated through physical attack, movement restrictions, kidnapping of adults and children, biological warfare and enforced starvation (Paul 2006; Daschuk

2013; Truth and Reconciliation Commission of Canada 2015; Royal Commission on Aboriginal Peoples 1996). Ongoing settler-colonialism threatens Indigenous Nations on Turtle Island, as well as peoples elsewhere (McAdam [Saysewahum] 2015; Yellowhead Institute 2019). In the years between 2000 and 2020, the people of Iraq, Libya and Afghanistan, for instance, have been subject to invasions and bombardments by the Canadian military (Dobbin 2011; Engler 2013).

In this introduction and this book's conclusion, we use the term Turtle Island and Indigenous place names when referring to the lands and waters, and prioritize Indigenous sovereignty and futures (Maracle 2017). We recognize that the term Turtle Island is not universal among Indigenous Nations, yet is also widely used, and is our recognition, as settlers, of ongoing dispossession as well as sovereignty of Indigenous Nations (Coburn and Moore 2021). In this book, we use the term Canada to refer to advocacy engaging with the settler-colonial state and in communities of predominantly settlers. We also acknowledge that, with few exceptions, advocacy for Palestine on Turtle Island has not used Indigenous place names, and that until recently, and including in the chapters in this book, this continues to be the case. We are still in the midst of a struggle to educate ourselves. We do recognize that many persons refuse the exclusive binary conceptual form "settler/ Indigenous" with the idea that human mobility is possible without being settlers (Sharma 2020a, 2020b; Pete 2018; Sharma and Wright 2008). While welcoming "innovative radical possibilities of relationality" (Desai 2021: 14), and opposing "nationalist, racist politics of anti-mobility" (Sharma 2020b), we opt nevertheless to explicitly acknowledge the complicity with ongoing settler-colonialism, even if not a conscious aim, of newcomers or arrivants to Turtle Island (following the lead of Walia 2013 quoted above; see also Aikau et al. 2015; Byrd 2011; Razack 2015; Fujikane and Okamura 2008; Lawrence and Dua 2005; Thobani 2007).

Much has changed since the days when Tabasharini embarked on her months-long canoe journeys. She passed away on February 12, 1947. Nine months later, without any authority or jurisdiction to do so, the United Nations partitioned Palestine (Cattan 1973). Canada — particularly settlers from Britain — played a leading role (Kaplan 2009; Engler 2010). Close to one and a half million Palestinians were stripped of citizenship when members of the international community ceased to recognize their sovereignty (Abu-Zahra and Kay 2012). Today, ongoing settler-colonialism in Palestine threatens over 13 million Palestinians, as well as other nations. Tabasharini's homeland of Lebanon, for instance, was subject to Israeli military invasion in 1982 and months-long bombardment that displaced a quarter of the country's population in 2006 (Amnesty International 2006).

The irony of persecution is that, whether it emerges from fear or profit-seeking, it will invariably be justified as a form of protection. The language of defence, refuge, and even aid is put to the service of settler-colonialism, injustice, and systemic oppression (Gilroy 2006). Persecution is undeniable, but when does the survivor become the perpetrator? More importantly, when does the perpetrator awaken to the suffering they cause, and work to end it? When does the processing of fear result in solidarity instead of further harm?

The authors in this book examine moments of solidarity and the persecution that they face as they engage in that solidarity work. Universities, unions, faith groups and anti-imperialist and other left-wing movements have been major sites for organizing for Palestine, and advocates for Palestine have been able to find connections between the causes and ethics that motivate those spaces and claims for justice for Palestinians. The growth of these forms of solidarity shows the challenges of advocacy for Palestine, but it also shows the way that Palestinian liberation can be best understood as a part of a broader project of liberation from all forms of systemic injustice.

Building Solidarity and Healing

> From Palestine to Turtle Island, there is no justice on stolen land. —Students Against Israeli Apartheid (Nazzal Hamadeh, this volume)

Advocacy for Palestine on Turtle Island is "an anti-racist movement that challenges the violence of all forms of racism" (Nazzal Hamadeh, this volume). The resonance of the situation of Palestine and Palestinians is felt by so many on Turtle Island (Woodley, this volume). They include countless Jewish Canadians who feel alienated from part or all of the Zionist narrative that dominates Jewish community institutions on Turtle Island (Ralph, this volume); Québec sovereigntists who identify with Palestinians as a community denied sovereignty; critics of settler Canadian development assistance and foreign aid policy who are sceptical of policies towards Palestine/Israel; faith groups with community and spiritual ties in Nazareth, Al-Quds/Jerusalem, Bethlehem, Al-Khalil/Hebron, Haifa and throughout the region; anti-racist, anti-oppression and anti-colonial movements that perceive the same police and military tactics enacted against themselves as against Palestinians; and progressives and anti-militarists of all backgrounds who are critical of the globalized Israeli military-industrial complex and its link to global militarism. These connections present opportunities for greater advocacy and for Palestine to appear differently in the international collective imagination.

Advocacy groups for Palestine include those founded in the 1960s and 1970s, like the Arab Palestine Association, Canadian-Arab Friendship Society, Canadian Arab Federation, all on Wendat, Anishinaabe and Hodinöhsö:ni' territory (Toronto), and the Canada Palestine Association, in the unceded territories of the xʷməθkʷəy̓əm (Musqueam), Sḵwx̱wú7mesh (Squamish) and Səl̓ílwitulh (Tsleil-Waututh) Nations (Vancouver) (Labelle 2018: 174–75). In Mi'kma'ki (Nova Scotia) and the territories of the Nehiyaw, Denesuliné, Nakota Sioux, Anishinaabe, Niitsitapi and Métis (Alberta, Saskatchewan, Manitoba and Ontario), academics and others of Palestinian origin became active in this period, sharing stories of dispossession in Palestine, including Canada's role in that dispossession. Some of those mobilizing were conscious of the colonialism of which they were part on Turtle Island. In the 1970s, for instance, the Canada Palestine Association was a member of the Third World People's Coalition alongside Indigenous and Black rights advocacy groups, and actively opposed Indigenous leader Leonard Peltier's extradition to the United States (where he remains imprisoned today) (Desai 2021; Kawas 2020).

Moments of extreme injustice prompted further mobilization. In the wake of Israel's 1982 invasion of Lebanon, for example, Medical Aid for Palestine was established in Tio'tia:ke (Montréal), the National Council for Canadian Arab Relations and the Association of Arab Palestinian Canadians were founded in Algonquin territory (Ottawa), and the Near East Cultural and Educational Foundation (NECEF) was begun on Wendat, Anishinaabe and Hodinöhsö:ni' territory (Toronto). As people on Turtle Island watched Palestinians rise up (in Arabic, the Intifada) in the years 1987–93 and suffer a debilitating "bone-breaking" policy by Israel (such as smashing their elbows with rocks), further organizations formed, like Palestine House, Canadian Friends of Sabeel and the Canadian-Palestinian Educational Exchange. Again, in the same way that Stó:lō author and poet Lee Maracle had read Palestinian Mahmoud Darwish's poetry in 1976, trust-based solidarity was consciously fostered by First Nations with Palestinians (Kawas 2020; Walia 2003): Kanien'kehá:ka and other Hodinöhsö:ni' Nations related in their resistance in the 1990s with Palestinians' steadfastness (*sumud* in Arabic) or "self-reliance strategies delinked from the settler state" and the unarmed Intifada (Desai 2021: 7, citing Hill 2009).

Some settler Canadians, including foresighted government officials, sought more just approaches to Palestine than the policies that prevailed from the early twentieth century to the present. A supporter of Palestinian sovereignty in the 1940s, Elizabeth P. MacCallum was Canada's leading government expert on the Middle East (Newport 2014). Three decades later, Special Representative of the Government of Canada Respecting the Middle East and North Africa Robert L. Stanfield penned a report that would influence Prime Ministers Joe Clark and Jean Chrétien, as well as Foreign Affairs Minister Lloyd Axworthy (Robinson 2021). Canada recognized the Palestinian right to self-determination in 1989 (with widespread approval among public opinion; Wildeman 2021) and lent support to a "peace process" in the 1990s through a Middle East Working Group made up of twenty Canadian civil society organizations, including some of those mentioned above (Kingston 2007: 124). While these government responses admittedly fit within larger patterns to subdue and divert resistance to colonialism (Said 1995; Giacaman and Lønning 1998), they also demonstrate the capacity of advocacy to alter dominant discourses and the actions of those occupying positions of power.

Even though the heady years of 1993–2000 are mostly associated with international euphoria for peace in Palestine/Israel, the realities were far different: it was a period when Palestinian children and adults were shot, maimed or kidnapped and tortured in Israel's prison complex (Cook, Hanieh and Kay 2004) and colonization and movement restrictions intensified to a stranglehold (Abu-Zahra and Kay 2012). On Turtle Island, isolated voices spoke out, like Gaza-based psychologist Eyad El-Sarraj and James Graff, philosophy professor and co-founder of NECEF, in venues like the North American Coordinating Committee (NACC) for the United Nations Non-Governmental Organizations' Forum on Palestine. The forum was a consortium of labour, faith-based, feminist and civil rights groups and research institutes like the Centre d'études arabes pour le développement (United Nations 1994).

The voices of Graff and El-Sarraj were illuminating of a remarkable characteristic in much advocacy for Palestine on Turtle Island: both individuals spoke in support of healthy relations and justice, even when that meant criticizing those in power on Turtle Island and Palestine. In the 1994 UN NGO Forum on Palestine, El-Sarraj spoke of "60,000 Palestinian children in Gaza, below the age of 15 … suffering from some emotional problems that were the direct result of trauma at the hands of Israeli soldiers" (United Nations 1994). Over the subsequent two years, El-Sarraj was kidnapped three times, tortured and held for prolonged periods in solitary confinement by the Palestinian Authority (Martin Ennals Award for Human Rights Defenders 2021). Graff, meanwhile, spoke forcefully and tirelessly in El-Sarraj's support at subsequent UN NGO Forum meetings. Graff and El-Sarraj's worked to build solidarity and healing, "to break the cycle of violence that was being perpetuated from generation to generation" (United Nations 1994). They, as well as many others involved in advocacy for Palestine on Turtle Island, embodied Nazzal Hamadeh's (this volume) notion of "an anti-racist movement that challenges the violence of all forms of racism."

Healthy Relations and Advocacy

> Understanding the world through a Relationship Framework … we don't see ourselves, our communities, or our species as inherently superior to any other, but rather see our roles and responsibilities to each other as inherent to enjoying our life experiences. (Amadahy 2010, quoted in Walia 2012)

While the late 1990s were slower years in advocacy for Palestine, not least because of the diversion of resources and public and government attention to bolstering the "peace process," they were also important years to strengthen ties between decolonial movements on Turtle Island. The fruits of these efforts became evident in the year 2000 and after. With exceptions like El-Sarraj and Graff, few had analyzed the Oslo peace accords of the early 1990s and the peace process to understand that these were not about peace but rather about furthering colonialism (Said 1995, 1993; Giacaman and Lønning 1998). In September 2000, when Israeli soldiers stormed the holy site of Dome of the Rock and the Al-Aqsa mosque in Jerusalem, and when Israeli tanks bulldozed homes, people, and a swath of a refugee camp, many on Turtle Island were stunned and horrified. With deadly movement restrictions and international strategies of silencing (like those described in Mastracci, this volume), people on Turtle Island heard stulted news reports of rising death counts and incursions into the most private of Palestinian spaces. Students on university campuses across Turtle Island mobilized, along with some of the groups that had engaged in advocacy for Palestine over the previous four decades (Husseini, this volume). They built stronger alliances, issued public statements, held countless coalition-building and educational events, challenged dominant discourses, and took time to build healthy relations and spaces.

In 2002, several hundred protestors managed to cancel a speech by Benjamin Netanyahu, then a former Israeli prime minister, at Concordia University on Kanien'kehá:ka territory (Mallal and Addelman 2004). In the same year and region, Rachad Antonius, a professor of sociology at the Université de Québec à Montréal organized a visit to Palestine for a former Canadian justice minister serving as director of the organization Rights and Democracy. In 2004 at York University on Wendat, Anishinaabe and Hodinöhsö:ni' territory, Jewish-Canadian activist for Palestinian human rights, Dan Freeman-Maloy, was suspended for three years after leading a protest over Israel's treatment of the Palestinian people (Spurr 2004). The sudden punishment appeared disproportionate and procedures to contradict university policy. A lawsuit, against both the university and its president, ultimately went up to the Court of Appeal for Ontario and was refused to be heard by the Supreme Court. In the end, the parties came to a mutually satisfactory out-of-court settlement in 2007 and Freeman-Maloy was able to graduate. Activism at these and other universities culminated in the founding of Israeli Apartheid Week (IAW), in part to mobilize support for a worldwide Boycott, Divestment and Sanctions (BDS) campaign (Nazzal Hamadeh, this volume). IAW was "used as a model in developing Indigenous Sovereignty Week" (Desai 2021: 8).

The years 2000 and after witnessed the founding of Al-Awda, the Palestine Right to Return Coalition, the Coalition Against Israeli Apartheid, the Toronto Palestine Film Festival, Canadians for Justice and Peace in the Middle East, Students Against Israeli Apartheid, Students for Justice in Palestine, Students for Palestinian Human

Rights, Palestine Solidarity Collective, Faculty for Palestine, Labour for Palestine, University of Toronto Divest, Palestinian Youth Movement, Independent Jewish Voices, Just Peace Advocates, the Palestine Advocacy Network and the Palestinian Canadian Academics and Artists Network, among others. The first annual conference of Al-Awda was held in June 2003, on Wendat, Anishinaabe and Hodinöhsö:ni' territory (Toronto). In subsequent years, advocates for Palestine — Palestinian or otherwise — would support Kanien'kehá:ka at Kenhtè:ke (Bay of Quinte) (including in solidarity with the Wet'suwet'en), Kanonhstaton, Kanehsatà:ke and Kahnawà:ke (Ontario and Québec), Anishinaabe at Asubpeeschoseewagong (Grassy Narrows), Mitchikanibikok Inik (Barriere Lake), Kitchenuhmaykoosib Ininuwug (Big Trout Lake), the Secwepemc Nation at Skwelkwek'welt (Sun Peaks Resort) and Idle No More (Keefer, this volume; Desai 2021, Kilibarda 2009; Krebs and Olwan 2012; Walia 2003).

Strengthening relations toward long-term support is an ongoing activity that "means not just being present for blockades or in moments of crisis" (Walia 2012). While this has yet to be evidenced on a large scale, small steps are being made to expand connections between Palestine and Turtle Island through, for instance, learning exchanges and cultural engagement. In 2003, an educational initiative named Project Hope was founded by one of our co-editors to support international volunteers to Palestine from Turtle Island. By 2018, over 1,500 volunteer educators had lived and worked in the Palestinian city of Nablus, and tens of thousands of youth had benefitted from education programming.

In the years 2000–20, a Stó:lō former Chief joined the Freedom Flotilla (Kawas 2020; Jensen 2018), a Kanien'kehá:ka delegation travelled to Palestine, and "Indigenous land protectors wore kaffiyehs," flew Palestinian flags and participated in protests against the 2020 American "peace to prosperity" plan for Palestinian dispossession and repression (Desai 2021: 3–5, 7–8, 18). In 2004, the olive oil non-profit enterprise Zatoun was founded to further understanding of Palestinian culture and daily life; this was followed in 2009 by the establishment of Beit Zatoun (House of Olives) as a cultural centre, art gallery and community meeting space that hosted over 1,000 events. From Project Hope to Beit Zatoun, such initiatives became spaces for profounder mutual aid and support.

In each sector and sphere, this kind of mutual aid has continued to expand. Artists of different backgrounds collaborate in exhibitions and creations. Palestinian lawyers and law professors on Turtle Island have joined forces to both seek justice in Palestine — launching major initiatives to focus on rehabilitation, fair treatment and professionalism among justices — and on Turtle Island, supporting Indigenous legal struggles and challenges, such as those related to Idle No More. Feminist, labour, faith-based, civil rights, migrant rights, 2SLGBTIQ and gender justice, academic and liberatory institutions and movements continue to build stronger coalitions despite severe repression. Independent Jewish Voices (IJV), for instance, unites some twenty-five to thirty broadly progressive Jewish, Jewish/Muslim, Jewish/Arab and Jewish/Palestinian groups and in 2009 became the first Jewish organization in the world to almost unanimously endorse the Boycott, Divestment and Sanctions (BDS) campaign (Ralph 2021).

Labour unions on Turtle Island have strong ties with Palestinian labour unions, and these ties enable them to jointly organize worker-to-worker tours and maintain open lines of communication and mutual support. The Ontario wing of the Canadian Union of Public Employees in 2006 adopted a BDS position, followed by a growing number of labour councils and locals, as well as other national unions like the Canadian Union of Postal Workers (CUPW), Confédération des syndicats nationaux, Unifor and the Public Service Alliance of Canada (PSAC). The Canadian Union of Public Employees (CUPE) Ontario university workers' committee — an extension in many ways of ongoing campus activism — proposed in 2009 to extend the campaign to boycott any joint work with Israeli institutions that carry out military research. In 2021, the Canadian Labour Congress (CLC) adopted a position in support of an arms embargo on Israel, a ban on trade with settlements, promoting divestment from Israeli military and security companies and other measures. The influence of healthy relations and advocacy among labour unions has extended to political parties and their members who learn about colonialism on Turtle Island and in Palestine. The Green and New Democratic political parties have been endorsed by their members to adopt policies in favour of sanctions on Israel, such as an arms embargo.

Healthy relations and advocacy become not only a means but also an end toward demonstrating alternatives to unjust systems and racist hierarchies. What draws advocates together is not only a shared struggle — as there are differences; the struggle on Turtle Island predates that of

Palestine by some four hundred years — but more importantly, a shared vision, like that of Groulx's poem or of the Relationship Framework suggested by Amadahy. In this book we cannot cover all the facets of collective visions for the future, or of advocacy for Palestine on Turtle Island. We can only present brief vignettes of the systems of injustice that prevail to date, some elements of visions of possible futures and case studies of various sectors like the media, non-profits and postsecondary education. Our key finding, though, is that in transforming fear into solidarity, in seeing ourselves as in relation to one another, we can build those futures in the present.

Conclusion

Taken altogether, we learn from the chapters in this book that structures of racist hierarchies undermine refuge, liberation and freedom not only for some, but for all. They do this by inverting the perpetrator and survivor, causing real harm and, inevitably due to our interconnectedness, harming everyone. No marginalized group responds in a monolithic way, and a more enlightening route to understanding solidarity is to witness the shared aspirations for the future and how those aspirations are made real through consciously forging and practising healthy relations and advocacy (Desai 2021; Kelley 2019):

> We must reach worlds where people live freely with respect and dignity, without fear and without injustice … We must grow visionaries … We must act with humility. We walk on paths chipped at for centuries before us. We live in a world where what we know sits like a pebble on the shore of an ocean of what we don't know. (Hussan 2013: 280–81, 283)

In this book we wanted to open opportunities for conversations that can break through some of the challenges that advocates for Palestine face on Turtle Island in broadening analysis of the movement. Even though settler-colonialism and racism are global phenomena that have shaped the nature of world politics, they remain difficult targets to name for activists in particular. At times, the particularities of repression against advocacy for Palestine and social justice crowd out a clear view of the bigger picture. Finding ways to elucidate the connections between experiences of settler-colonialism globally — and more importantly, to share

visions for the future — offers paths toward healthy relations and healing. This book holds a particular value for those of us on Turtle Island
who are engaged in scholarship that aims towards transformation, and
is a way of inviting our contributors, and you, into a dialogue to share
thoughts, perspectives and visions.

References

Abu-Zahra, Nadia, and Adah Kay. 2012. *Unfree in Palestine: Registration, Documentation and Movement Restriction*. London: Pluto Press.
Aikau, Hokulani K., Arvin Maile, Mishuana Goeman, and Scott Morgensen. 2015. "Indigenous Feminisms Roundtable." *Frontiers: A Journal of Women Studies* 36, 3.
Alexander, Neville. 1983. "At Issue: Nation and Ethnicity." *Work In Progress* 28. <sahistory.org.za/sites/default/files/archive-files3/WpAug83.1608.2036.000.028.Aug1983.pdf>.
Amadahy, Zainab, and Cathryn Atkinson. 2010. "Community, 'Relationship Framework' and Implications for Activism." *Rabble.ca*, July 13. <rabble.ca/news/2010/07/community-%E2%80%98relationship-framework%E2%80%99-and-implications-activism>.
Amnesty International. 2006. *Lebanon: Deliberate Destruction or 'Collateral Damage?' Israeli Attacks on Civilian Infrastructure*. <amnesty.org/en/documents/MDE18/007/2006/en/>.
Byrd, Jodi. 2011. *Transit of Empire: Indigenous Critiques of Colonialism*. Minneapolis: University of Minnesota Press.
Cattan, Henry. 1973. *Palestine and International Law: The Legal Aspects of the Arab–Israeli Conflict*. London: Longman Group.
Choudry, Aziz, Jill Hanley, and Eric Shragge (eds.). 2012. *Organize! Building from the Local for Global Justice*. Oakland, CA: PM Press/Between the Lines.
Coburn, V., and M. Moore. 2021. "Occupancy, Land Rights and the Algonquin Anishinaabeg." *Canadian Journal of Political Science*, 1–18. <doi:10.1017/S0008423921000810>.
Cook, Catherine, Adam Hanieh, and Adah Kay. 2004. *Stolen Youth*. London: Pluto.
Daschuk, James. 2013. *Clearing the Plains: Disease, Politics of Starvation, and the Loss of Aboriginal Life*. Regina: University of Regina Press.
Desai, Chandni. 2021. Disrupting Settler-Colonial Capitalism: Indigenous Intifadas and Resurgent Solidarity from Turtle Island to Palestine. *Journal of Palestine Studies* 50, 2.
Dobbin, Murray. 2011. "Libya, Canada's Other Ugly War." *Counterpunch*, June 21. <counterpunch.org/2011/06/21/libya-canada-s-other-ugly-war/>.
El-Bekai, Samar. 2016. "Palestine: Via Dolorosa." In *Apartheid in Palestine: Hard Laws and Harder Experiences*, edited by Ageel, Ghada. Edmonton, AB: University of Alberta Press.
Engler, Yves. 2010. *Canada and Israel: Building Apartheid*. Black Point, NS: Fernwood Publishing.
___. 2013. "Canada's Secretive Role in Iraq." *Counterpunch*, March 29. <counterpunch.org/2013/03/29/canadas-secretive-role-in-iraq/>.
Fujikane, Candace, and Jonathan Y. Okamura (eds.). 2008. *Asian Settler Colonialism: From Local Governance to the Habits of Everyday Life in Hawai'i*. Honolulu: Uni-

versity of Hawai'i Press.

Galtung, Johan. 1964. "An Editorial." *Journal of Peace Research* 1.

____. 1969. "Violence, Peace and Peace Research." *Journal of Peace Research* 3.

____. 1975. "Three Approaches to Peace: Peacekeeping, Peacemaking and Peacebuilding." In *Peace, War and Defence — Essays in Peace Research*, Volume 1, edited by Johan Galtung. Copenhagen, Denmark: Christian Ejlers.

____. 1985. "Twenty-Five Years of Peace Research: Ten Challenges and Some Responses." *Journal of Peace Research* 22.

____. 1990. "Cultural Violence." *Journal of Peace Research* 3.

Giacaman, George, and Dag Jørund Lønning (eds.). 1998. *After Oslo: New Realities, Old Problems*. London: Pluto Press.

Gilroy, Paul. 2006. *Postcolonial Melancholia*. New York: Columbia University Press.

Groulx, David. 2019. *From Turtle Island to Gaza*. Edmonton: Athabasca University Press.

Hill, Gord. 2009. "From Gaza to Gustafsen: The Link between the Intifada and Indigenous Sovereignty in *Colonization and Apartheid*," posted by Ion Delsol, 26 September, video, 9:44, <youtube.com/watch?v=v8xvMoR4dXE&ab_channel=IonDelsol>.

Horn-Miller, Kahente. 2013. "What Does Indigenous Participatory Democracy Look Like? Kahnawa:ke's Community Decision Making process." *Review of Constitutional Studies* 18, 1.

Hussan, Syed Khalid. 2013. "Epilogue." In *Undoing Border Imperialism*, by Harsha Walia. Oakland, CA: AK Press.

Jensen, Kim. 2018. "'I Don't Think We Can Convert People with Talk' — Says Larry Commodore, First Nations Passenger on Gaza boat." *Mondoweiss*, August 13. <mondoweiss.net/2018/08/convert-commodore-passenger/>.

Jhally, Sut (Dir.). 1998. *Edward Said: The Myth of 'The Clash of Civilizations.'* <mediaed.org/transcripts/Edward-Said-The-Myth-of-Clash-Civilizations-Transcript.pdf>.

Kaplan, William. 2009. *Canadian Maverick: The Life and Times of Ivan C. Rand*. Toronto: University of Toronto Press.

Kawas, Marion. 2020. "Solidarity between Palestinians and Indigenous Activists Has Deep Roots." *The Palestine Chronicle*, February 18. <palestinechronicle.com/solidarity-between-palestinians-and-indigenous-activists-has-deep-roots/>.

Kelley, Robin D.G. 2019. "From the River to the Sea to Every Mountain Top: Solidarity as Worldmaking." *Journal of Palestine Studies* 48, 4.

Kilibarda, Kole. 2009. "Confronting Apartheid: The BDS Movement in Canada." *Upping the Anti: A Journal of Theory and Action*, 7. <uppingtheanti.org/journal/article/07-confronting-apartheid>.

Kingston, Paul. 2007. "Promoting Civil Society Advocacy in the Middle East and at Home: Non-Governmental Organizations, the Canadian International Development Agency, and the Middle East Working Group, 1991–2001." In *Canada and the Middle East in Theory and Practice*, edited by Paul Heinbecker and Bessma Momani. Waterloo: Wilfrid Laurier University Press.

Krebs, Mike, and Dana M. Olwan. 2012. "From Jerusalem to the Grand River, Our Struggles Are One: Challenging Canadian and Israeli Settler Colonialism." *Settler Colonial Studies* 2, 2.

Labelle, Maurice Jr. 2018. "Not So Nobel: Arab Perceptions of Lester B. Pearson and Canada." In *Mike's World: Lester B. Pearson and Canadian External Relations, 1963–68*, edited by Asa McKercher and Galen Roger Perras. Vancouver: UBC Press.

Lawrence, Bonita, and Enakshi Dua. 2005. "Decolonizing Antiracism." *Social Justice* 32, 4.

Leney, Peter. 1996. "Annie Midlige, Fur Trader." *Beaver* 76, 3.

Mallal, Samir, and Ben Addelman (directors). 2004. *Discordia* [Motion Picture.] Canada: National Film Board of Canada.

Maracle, Lee. 2017. *My Conversations with Canadians*. Toronto: Book*hug Press.

Martin Ennals Award for Human Rights Defenders. 2021. *Eyad El Sarraj: 1998 Laureate.* <martinennalsaward.org/hrd/eyad-el-sarraj/#film>.

Maté, Aaron. 2019. "Gabor Maté on the Misuse of Anti-Semitism and Why Fewer Jews Identify with Israel." *The Grayzone*, November 6. <thegrayzone.com/2019/11/06/gabor-mate-on-the-misuse-of-anti-semitism-and-why-fewer-jews-identify-with-israel/>.

McAdam, Sylvia (Saysewahum). 2015. *Nationhood Interrupted: Revitalizing nêhiyaw Legal Systems*. Vancouver: University of British Columbia Press.

Newport, Richard. 2014. "The Outsider: Elizabeth P. MacCallum, the Canadian Department of External Affairs, and the Palestine Mandate to 1947." PhD thesis, Carleton University.

Paul, Daniel N. 2006. *We Were Not the Savages: Collision between European and Native American Civilizations*. Black Point, NS: Fernwood Publishing.

Pete, Shauneen. 2018. "Meschachakanis, a Coyote Narrative: Decolonising Higher Education." In *Decolonising the University*, edited by Gurimder K. Bhambra, Dalia Gebrial and Kerem Nişancıoğlu. London: Pluto Press.

Ralph, Diana. 2021. *Question*. Email to Jeremy Wildeman, June 17.

Razack, Sherene H. 2015. *Dying from Improvement: Inquests and Inquiries into Indigenous Deaths in Custody*. Toronto: University of Toronto Press.

Robinson, Andrew N. 2021. "Talking with the PLO: Overcoming Political Challenges." *Canadian Foreign Policy Journal* 27, 1.

Royal Commission on Aboriginal Peoples. 1996. *Report of the Royal Commission on Aboriginal Peoples*. <bac-lac.gc.ca/eng/discover/aboriginal-heritage/royal-commission-aboriginal-peoples/Pages/final-report.aspx>.

Sabzalian, Leilani. 2019. "The Tensions Between Indigenous Sovereignty and Multicultural Citizenship Education: Toward an Anticolonial Approach to Civic Education." *Theory & Research in Social Education* 47, 3.

Sabzalian, Leilani, and Sarah Shear. 2018. "Confronting Colonial Blindness in Civics Education: Recognizing Colonization, Self-Determination, and Sovereignty as Core Knowledge for Elementary Social Studies Teacher Education." In *(Re)Imagining Elementary Social Studies: A Controversial Issues Reader*, edited by S.B. Shear, C.M. Tschida, E. Bellows, L.B. Buchanan, and E.E. Saylor. Charlotte, NC: Information Age.

Said, Edward W. 1979. *The Question of Palestine*. New York: Times Books.

___. 1993. The Morning After. *London Review of Books*, October 21.

___. 1995. *Peace and Its Discontents: Essays on Palestine in the Middle East Peace Process*. New York: Vintage.

Sharma, Nandita. 2020a. *Home Rule: National Sovereignty and the Separation of Natives and Migrants*. Durham, NC: Duke University Press.

___. 2020b. "Against National Sovereignty: The Postcolonial New World Order and the Containment of Decolonization." *Studies in Social Justice* 14, 2.

Sharma, Nandita, and Cynthia Wright. 2008. "Decolonizing Resistance, Challenging Colonial States." *Social Justice* 35, 3.

Spurr, Ben. 2004. "Suspended York U Student Sues for $850K." *The Varsity*, October 18. <thevarsity.ca/2004/10/18/suspended-york-u-student-sues-for-850k/>.

Thobani, Sunera. 2007. *Exalted Subjects: Studies in the Making of Race and Nation in Canada*. Toronto: University of Toronto Press.

Truth and Reconciliation Commission of Canada. 2015. *Honouring the Truth, Reconciling for the Future: Summary of the Final Report of the Truth and Reconciliation Commission of Canada*. <nctr.ca/records/reports/>.

United Nations. 1994. *Eleventh North American ngo Symposium on the Question of Palestine*. Palestinian Rights (DPR) Publication. <unispal.un.org/DPA/DPR/unispal.ns f/0/658859BB57BB9BE5852561E20054AC0B>.

Walia, Harsha. 2003. "Resisting Displacement, North and South: Indigenous and Immigrant Struggles." Colours of Resistance Archive. <coloursofresistance.org/388/ resisting-displacement-north-and-south-indigenous-and-immigrant-struggles/>.

___. 2012. "Decolonizing Together: Moving Beyond a Politics of Solidarity to a Practice of Decolonization." *Briarpatch*, January 1. <briarpatchmagazine.com/articles/view/ decolonizing-together>.

___. 2013. *Undoing Border Imperialism*. Oakland, CA: AK Press.

___. 2020. *Border and Rule: Global Migration, Capitalism, and the Rise of Racist Nationalism*. Black Point, NS: Fernwood Publishing.

___. 2021. "Assessing Canada's Foreign Policy Approach to the Palestinians and Israeli-Palestinian Peacebuilding, 1979–2019." *Canadian Foreign Policy Journal* 27, 1.

Yellowhead Institute. 2019. *Land Back: A Red Paper*. Toronto: Yellowhead Institute. <redpaper.yellowheadinstitute.org/>.

Part I

Systems of Injustice

Chapter 1

The Elephant in the Room

Nyla Matuk

A place called "Palestine" featured in my catechism classes — scenes in watercolour illustrated the New Testament stories the nuns taught in my French Catholic school. I was not French Canadian or Christian, and the Jésus of Nazareth I learned about had Aryan features and a kind-looking beard. He wore long robes and leather sandals. In the east end of Ottawa, in the 1970s, I learned about a place called the "Middle East" from the evening news. I spoke French at school all day and at home switched to English with my parents. At night, on the phone, my father spoke a little Arabic to his relatives; my mother, who was from New Delhi, spoke Hindi to hers. Since my father was Palestinian, and the place in the catechism was Palestine, I once asked my mother, was it possible to make the case to my class that I was like Jesus too? Palestinian?

The question led to the first experience of the suppression of my identity that I can recall. It came from inside my own home, circa 1974 — my mother answered my question by telling me not to reveal to anyone that I, or my father, was Palestinian. I do not remember exactly how my mother expressed this, but it was an admonition, and however she expressed it, she conveyed that it was a highly charged, dangerous thing to claim to be Palestinian. She was anxious about it: I was not to speak of this to anyone. As my parents' marriage frayed and finally ended, the "Palestinian" appellation was added to her qualification of my father: the designation for an identity with an unknown but dark underpinning. The place he came from was both a mystery imbued with violence I knew from TV, yet also known to anyone who knew where Jesus walked; where other elements of the Bible could be found — a manger, a carpenter's shop, the banks of the Dead Sea. The land of Jesus's miracles and the city of Jesus's passion, faith, death and resurrection was also the city of my father's birth and upbringing, like that of centuries of Matuks.

The Challenge of Being Palestinian in Canada

Using autobiographical anecdotes and historical accounts, in this essay I canvass my personal history as a Canadian of Palestinian descent and the challenges I faced growing up with an identity that I felt compelled to conceal because of a culture of hostility that was actively promulgated against us by the Canadian state. Relating a personal history located in the colonial-Canadian context of the late twentieth century up to the present, I describe some of the anti-Palestinian racism that constituted and constitutes an intrinsic feature of my Canadian life. There I discovered that anti-Palestinian racism is pervasive among the highly educated, in the media and among professional-class settler Canadians. I have found they display an active incuriosity and obliviousness to internal Canadian settler-colonization and the support that Canada gives overseas to a fellow European settler-colony that was also established by the British Empire, but in that case in historic Palestine: the Israeli state.

Growing up, I held no loyalty or sense of belonging to any nationality or ethnicity. This was likely the result of a simultaneous pressure to shun my Palestinian identity and assimilate as a settler in the Canadian state, which stood in opposition to belonging to a Palestine where I could, or would, find meaningful family stories, geographies of significance, familial attachments to local histories, people, places and a history of resistance to displacement and elimination by a colonial state. It is my belonging to *that place* and the collective memory of its people, as well as the belonging engendered through my father's memories and photographs, where I find meaning. Conversely, I have failed to find a meaningfully and morally purposeful identity in Canada, the place my parents chose to settle in, as they escaped destructive colonial incursions in Palestine and India.

Claiming a Canadian identity felt a lot less authentic than taking up the identities of either parent, yet both of their identities seemed farfetched and exotic in 1970s east-end Ottawa. The framing nation-state stories of Anglophones and Francophones that inform Canadian history may hold significance for many Canadians, but not for me. There was nothing germane to me that I could hew from the material conditions of this land nor, obviously, from the places where most white Canadians traced their histories — Scotland, Ireland and England, for instance, or Germany, Ukraine or France. Here, Indigenous Peoples had been glossed over in my school textbooks if mentioned at all; reproductions of their possessions or pilfered items like canoes and even tipis were displayed in the decorous, imperious glass cases and halls of the Museum of Civilization in Ottawa (at that time called the "Museum of Man") along with dinosaur skeletons and Bronze Age remains. They were mystified and fetishized in an official Story of Man.

The best word to describe this unanchored situation, as presented by imperial history, for me, is "depersonalized." Any attempt I made to blend in with white friends at school was met with an incurious or perplexed attitude when it came to discussing my provenance. The topic was mostly avoided, perhaps easily so during a time when identity was not as pronounced as it is today. The French Canadian and Catholic commemorations, masses and traditions were aligned with my classmates' home lives and histories, but not mine. For me, life as a child was about feeling excluded from recurrent customs while carrying no particularly recognizable, rooted personal history or claim to those customs. Maybe it did not help to live with parents of two different cultures. In addition, although my mother was from India, her lineage is traced to Afghanistan and Bokhara, in the country now called Uzbekistan. Both her lineages immigrated to India. The cultural chasm between my parents was deep, not only because they were both strangers to North America but because each had chosen to live with someone also estranged from it. There was neither a shared culture between them nor a rooted connection to the wider culture in which they lived. Because Islam is such an eclectic religion and they were not particularly religious, it did not act as connective tissue either.

While there are countless reasons to feel depersonalized or out of place, it is not the same as becoming aware of a deliberate erasure of Palestinian identity in the wider culture or the sometimes deliberate, sometimes subconscious practices of self-erasure. I have felt and done both. And none of this erasure, which is racism, is a fraction of the danger and pain Palestinians must withstand on their land undergoing fragmentation, colonization and unchecked military violence and occupation. The diaspora experience of anti-Palestinian racism is a kind of aftershock of the colonial violence done to the people on the land and the Palestinians in nearby refugee camps. The fact that diaspora Palestinians, too, belong to the land places them in the crosshairs of the ongoing dispossession and eliminationist policy of Israel and its agents and allies working outside the territory. If Palestinians "inside" are incarcerated, tortured and killed with impunity, their mobility prevented or heavily controlled, their identities monitored, their surnames catalogued, their national consciousness and efforts toward liberation prohibited, their property and land destroyed, confiscated or given to Jews; Palestinians "outside" are demonized, erased and even sued for defending their very identity and reminding the world of the dispossession of indigenous Palestinians from their own land. They are also otherwise oppressed by the policies enacted by sister settler-colonial and/or imperial colonizer states such as Canada, France, the United States, England and Australia. As a result of wanting to ignore these unhappy truths, it took me a long time to come to terms with carrying "a name that raises eyebrows," as the writer Lila Abu-Lughod has characterized Palestinian identity (Nashashibi 2014: 31). Yet once I opened my eyes to the particular denial and erasure that constitutes anti-Palestinian racism, it was difficult to look away.

Growing Up Palestinian in Canada

I do not exist in the fraught condition of exile but at a distance from it. I was born in Winnipeg. I do not speak Arabic. When I first encountered keffiyehs and Palestinian flags in the 1980s, they seemed only slightly familiar to me. As an English literature student at McGill University, I started to read the war of letters volleyed back and forth between Jewish Zionists and anti-Zionists in the *McGill Daily*. Divesting from South Africa was also front and centre. At Concordia University, the Concordia Collective for Palestinian Human Rights brought visiting speakers like Robert Fisk and Norman Finkelstein to Montreal. I read *After the Last Sky* (Said 1986) and *The Question of Palestine* (Said 1979), which gave me a clearer explanation of the sensation of floating depersonalization that I had felt. When I mentioned activism on campus to my father, he got on edge:

"Do NOT get involved."
Me: "Why?"
"You will be blacklisted."
Me: "Who's going to blacklist me? What does that even mean?"

He would refuse to say more. I assumed he was paranoid, an over-protective father speaking out of a McCarthy-era mindset. Yet I was wrong to dismiss his warning. As Edward Said's father said to him a few hours before dying, "I'm worried about what the Zionists will do to you. Be careful" (Said 1999: 117). As I wrote this essay, decades after my father's warning, I discovered that at McGill a blocklist of students who actively support Palestine liberation has been compiled for decades. An essay about the blocklist published in May 2021 reports it has served as a way to terrorize these students (McGill Students for Palestinian Human Rights 2021). But the experience of diaspora Palestinians is varied. The journalist Sharif Hikmat Nashashibi says that because the diaspora is over seventy years old, it has developed multiple identities separate from those inside Palestine. "There are those who claim that the passion felt for Palestine," Nashashibi writes, "particularly by those in the diaspora, is a construct of parental indoctrination. This is as preposterous as it is offensive ... the conduct of Israeli troops stirred me to research my origins, homeland and people, and champion their cause for freedom and human rights" (2014: 282). It occurred to me that Palestinians in the diaspora of a certain generation, while having lived through McCarthyism in the 1950s, are also socialized inside a colonized register, and colonization is locatable in people as much as it might be visible in built and natural environments. My father remembers that his time at the St George's School, run by the British, was replete with racism against the Palestinian children and favouritism toward the European ones; he remembers the teachers' harsh words reserved for Palestinians. And having left Palestine for the United States as a young man compounded his internalized colonialism: there are all kinds of Palestinian cultural and historic details I mention to him that simply do not register. Every Palestinian of that generation onwards has been affected directly by the Nakba of 1948 and the ongoing Nakba on Palestinians in Palestine ripples out to Palestinians around the world.

As an undergraduate, I remember visiting high school friends living in Ottawa. They had invited a few people over for drinks, including the brother of a mutual high school friend — I had not met the brother before, and the high school friend was not at the party. The friend's brother had just returned from a trip to Israel — possibly one of the "Birthright" trips, free trips to Israel for Jewish young adults to support their connection to Israel — and when he found out I was Palestinian, proceeded to ask, in all seriousness, why I was not wearing a hijab, working with an assumption that Palestinians are all religious Muslims. He then started to indulge a parody of a Hebrew accent, repeating the phrase, "the dirty Arabs." Although he might have sounded like he was parodying an Israeli Jew, my hijab-free lifestyle took him aback and seemed to make him nervous: I did not fit the profile of the fearsome Palestinian he may have been taught to hate. I left the party disturbed and angry.

At McGill, in a graduate seminar on editorial scholarship, I had another such encounter. The seminar took place in dedicated rooms in the basement of the Redpath Library, a years-long enterprise to finish several volumes of the diaries, letters and works of the eighteenth-century novelist Fanny Burney. Usually I would work there alone, and one afternoon, for some reason, the topic of Palestine/Israel arose while I was sharing a large worktable with a professor. He was not young, perhaps late middle-aged. "Well, I'm on the side of the Jewish people on that one," he declared and, using a detailed version of Winston Churchill's infamously racist phrase "higher grade race" (Suarez 2020), went on to say, "If you look at history, the Jews have made far greater contributions to culture and civilization than the Arabs." Needless to say, 1991 seems like another era in terms of acceptable speech. I would not even have known where to begin to report this racist remark uttered during class time by a professor directly to a student; and I did not dare tell him about my background after that, for fear of humiliating him or suffering a lower mark. It seemed bewildering to me at that age that a fully tenured professor at a top institution would hold such views, seemingly oblivious to the history of Western imperialism. In the case of Palestine, it appeared that boldly Orientalist views were readily indulged.

That was not the last time that Israel was fully normalized or justified to me while I sat helpless in an academic classroom. In 2008–09, I attended the University of Toronto to take courses for credit toward an application to a master's program in public policy. An energetic American Jewish professor, younger than me, taught the requisite political science research methods course. He would draw examples from political contexts to illustrate the principles of probability and other quantitative analysis methods. In a bright, chirpy voice, he frequently used voting numbers from the Knesset to feed into a probability equation in order to determine which factions might form the government, which might band together to form a coalition and so on. He could have been speaking about any other government cabinet — it was entirely normalized — but these lectures took place during Operation Cast Lead on Gaza in 2008.

On December 27 of that year, Israel launched a massive twenty-two-day military assault on the Palestinian Territory. The ferocity of the attack was unprecedented in the more than six decades of oppression against Gaza, most of whose population are refugees from nearby villages in what is now considered Israel. The assault killed approximately 1,400 Palestinians, most of them civilians (IMEU 2012). In the aftermath of the offensive, a UN-appointed fact-finding mission found strong evidence of war crimes and crimes against humanity committed by both the Israeli military and Palestinian militias (UNHCR 2009). Investigations by human rights groups such as Amnesty International (2009) and Human Rights Watch (2009) came to similar conclusions.

Operation Cast Lead is morbidly infamous for Israel's use of white phosphorus munitions in densely populated urban areas of Gaza, and it was internationally criticized (IMEU 2012). Despite the commission of such atrocities on a territory already under a punishing, punitive blockade collectively punishing everyone inside, this professor in Toronto seemed to think it was perfectly acceptable to natter on nonchalantly about Israel, its governing body and even its politicians who gave those military orders in classroom discussions, while the violence itself was taking place. It was hard to imagine this kind of *blasé* attitude applied in other contexts but was recognizable behaviour from my earlier years at McGill. The professor's clearly favourable opinion of Israel meant that no student would dare point out these moral transgressions in class without fear of a mark being lowered. The elephant in that room was my Palestinian identity.

The way in which he could so freely refer to a statecraft that has always been in the service of ensuring demographic control, ethnonationalism and apartheid suggests that he is afflicted with a troubling combination of denial and brainwashing. In fact, Canadian culture always seems ready to look the other way or chalk up Israel's actions against the Palestinians to a complicated "conflict" between two state actors. As Nahla Abdo has noted, to call the expulsion of Palestinians an "ethnic cleansing" creates a condition of *racialization of indigenous people*, thereby conferring a *fait accompli* status to the settler-colonial state — as if Palestinians are an ethnicity among living others there, when in fact they are being removed from the land to which they belong (Abdo 2020).

The combined weight of years of silence from Western mainstream media, a fear of being falsely labelled an antisemite, the argumentative

Zionists popping up here and there with their threats of blocklisting and my own natural tendency to avoid confrontations all had a chilling effect not only on me declaring my identity, but even in exploring a facet of interiority in which belonging to Palestine on personal and political terms was an incontrovertible moral stand. Thus, self-censorship and erasure, an oft-cited condition of anti-Palestinian racism, was a burden of my writing life. As I write this in 2021, I am still not entirely sure that an application for a writing residency fellowship in Canada or the United States would be hurt if the project description was about Palestine. I am still pondering if there is a way to avoid that self-censorship and send in an application anyway.

For many years, I managed to avoid making Palestine a subject of my creative work. Either the focus of my work was subconsciously avoidant of the topic or else I was genuinely busy and curious with other avenues of research holding my attention. But here and there, prior to the bombardment of Gaza in the summer of 2014, it emerged. I had a conversation with a novelist friend around 2012 in connection with another major round of violence on Gaza at that time. I do not remember many details except the feeling of being ill-equipped to argue with him: he was highly educated, a successful novelist and newspaper columnist. He insisted to me that the fictional biblical connection warranted colonial Zionist claims. Even though he knew as little about the colonial history of the place at the time as I did, he was a lot more confident in advancing his reactionist argument, since he knew he could get away with it by arguing with the consensus, itself the product of Israeli propaganda. He knew there was no danger in arguing the Zionist case, even though the Zionist case, whose secular roots enabled the operationalization of settler-colonial takeover, is indefensible in the liberal post-colonial world. Whatever he said that day if applied to any other national group would be tantamount to condoning genocide, and it was even more despicable that his argument rested on fictional Bible stories.

In the summer of 2014, as I watched in horror in real time on Twitter, Israel relentlessly attacked Gaza again, killing 2,202 civilians including 526 children (B'Tselem 2016). At the height of the bombardment, Israel killed one child an hour (Defence for Children International-Palestine 2016). In one high-profile instance among countless familial tragedies, four boys from the Bakr family were targeted and killed as they played soccer on the beach (Abunimah 2014). Gaza was severely decimated and declared unliveable even as Israelis pitched lawn chairs from their hilltop settlements to watch and cheer the bombardment of the besieged territory (Levinson 2009). I do not remember what I tweeted from the account I held at that time, but it attracted the ire of a poet acquaintance, a Jewish American who lives in Toronto. After a volley of arguments on Twitter, we agreed to start a correspondence to discuss the Palestine/Israel issue. Predictably, he sent me articulate liberal Zionist commentators; I sent whatever I could find on the history of the aggression on Palestinians. Finally, he asked, "Why are you so worked up about this? Do you know anyone who lives in Gaza?" To which I answered that my father's family is Palestinian. My poet acquaintance was so removed from the idea of a person of real Palestinian heritage that it did not occur to him why I might be so upset.

It was disturbing for me to realize he thought it strange anyone should be "so upset," given that we saw the bodies of children having to be preserved in ice cream freezers (Bloom and Spillet 2014), the story of a man with the remains of his three-year-old son in a plastic bag (Beaumont 2014) and years of stories in which Israel delayed or attacked Palestinian Red Crescent ambulances rushing to hospitals with wounded civilians (Voice of America News 2009). I remember now, five years after that incident, I sat across a café table from this same poet, who had shown up at a poetry reading which friends of mine — two Jewish anti-Zionist poets — had invited me to read. I wondered if he found it curious that we should know each other. I was taken aback when, in the midst of our chat at the table before the readings, he drew from his wallet a business card for the King David Hotel in Jerusalem. He simply took it out of his wallet and said, "Oh I wonder what this is doing here." Yet it was not so unusual to realize that I, a native daughter of the land where the infamous King David Hotel stood, should not have visited there yet by age 49; but that he, an American Jew, would have visited several times, with an option to live in the city where that hotel is located. Up to that point, my only encounter with the hotel was an old black and white photo from the front page of a newspaper in my father's collection of photos from his youth, covering the hotel's 1946 bombing.

One must remember that no young person in Gaza — whose population is mostly made up of people under age forty — would have seen their native land beyond the encircling gates: not Jerusalem and the Al Aqsa Mosque or the Dome of the Rock; nor Haifa, just up the coast; nor the Dead Sea or the beauty and wonder of the ancient city of Ariha (Jericho); nor the South Al-Khalil (Hebron) hills. The control of Palestinian movement is entrenched in a system of identification cards, military checkpoints and travel permits that are usually denied. Yet this American poet who posts his endorsement of Jews supporting Black Lives Matter (BLM) except, as he noted, for BLM's anti-Zionist creed, has likely visited such places more than once.

Anti-Palestinian Racism in Canada

There is an ongoing campaign spearheaded by Independent Jewish Voices (IJV), called "Stop the JNF: End Tax Breaks for Colonization," that lobbies the Canada Revenue Agency to revoke the charity status of the Jewish National Fund (JNF) (Stop the JNF Canada n.d.). The JNF has played a very active role in the destruction of Palestinian villages, the demolition of Palestinian homes and the illegal confiscation of Palestinian land for ethnically exclusionary Jewish use. As Nestel notes in Chapter 2, it is an active agent of Palestine's ongoing settler colonization. It is therefore disturbing to find large signs for donations for the JNF along Toronto's Bathurst Street, along with advertisements for Israel Bonds inside nearby bus shelters. Those bonds provide a massive influx of investment from Canada and elsewhere into Israel (Mushell 2015), which further allows Israel to afford the costs of its ongoing settler colonization of Palestinian lands.

Several years ago, a Toronto-area friend who is an activist started a campaign asking the Toronto Transit Commission (TTC) to remove the advertisements for the bonds. Her organization also tried to buy advertising space on the TTC to show the map of Palestine's territorial shrinkage due to Israeli colonization. This ad has been placed on public transit in Vancouver, where a campaign was launched on August 27, 2013, at the Vancouver City Centre SkyTrain station on the Canada Line, and on buses throughout the TransLink system (Palestine Awareness Coalition 2013). Yet, the TTC refused to let the ad be placed, while Israel Bonds continued to be advertised.

Most people do not understand that, as the Palestinian-American comedian Amer Zahr recently noted, Israel has literally taken Palestine *akhaduha mafroosheh*, "fully furnished" (Zahr 2020). They would not give the Israel Bonds advertisements a second thought or certainly not in the way a Palestinian would. Because of their role in the ongoing colonization of Palestinian lands and the erasure of my people from them, the presence of the JNF and Israel Bonds signs raising funds in support of that process seem tantamount to a coordinated system of hate against my people. They constitute an active form of erasure of my family, my ancestors and our places of memory and material effects; they stand for the theft of the land to which Palestinians will always belong and represent the material means of the ongoing Nakba, which is genocide. Where my great-grandmother's cottage once stood in the hills south of Al-Khalil, settlers protected by the Israeli army are burning down Palestinian olive groves.

Most of the people whose anti-Palestinian racism stands out as particularly harmful in Canada include highly educated scholars, professional writers, journalists, newspaper columnists, clergy and the like. I attended the 2014 street protests in Toronto during the onslaught of Israeli violence on Gaza with a popular leftist Canadian newspaper columnist. As we were talking, she blurted out, "but it's wrong to say that Zionism is racism." She stated it to me with great confidence. Anyone who has read the diaries and accounts of Zionist founders and leaders knows that a vital part of the plan for establishing a Jewish state — an ethnonationalist one — was the premeditated removal of the native inhabitants of the land; this idea of the "transfer" of the indigenous Arab population was also detailed in the British Peel Commission of 1937 with a view to establishing a European colony (Masalha 1992; Khalidi 2019). Another writer insisted to me repeatedly that it was not advisable to use the word "apartheid" to describe the situation because the word was "divisive" and therefore not useful. This highly educated critic and poet, clearly not having examined the list of over sixty-five Jim Crow–type laws in Israel (Adalah 2017), was nonetheless confident in his insistence to me that using that word was misleading.

The real life encounters I have had with anti-Palestinian racism certainly meet their match in online activity. A middle-aged poet and novelist of my acquaintance posted an article on Facebook about a rocket attack from Gaza. That attack was met with the usual disproportionate violence from Israel. She asked her audience, "Surely Israel has the right to defend itself?" The Facebook post on my timeline advocated for a state of violence, expressed in terms of self-defence. It tacitly approved of continuously colonizing the land through land confiscation and military occupation against a defenceless population by an advanced and nuclear

Western military power. The person who posted the article is a member of my own writing community in Canada; she has never interacted with anything I have said in this regard on Palestine/Israel.

Anti-Palestinian racism, when it is not coming from Zionists, is cobbled together through some combination of Zionist historical narrative and contemporary Israeli propaganda, in combination with the sheer laziness of media commentators who could not be bothered to decolonize their viewpoints by engaging with a Palestinian narrative or Palestinian media or by interviewing Palestinian scholars. As Davide Mastracci describes in this volume, mainstream Canadian media's refusal to cover Israeli violence, segregationist laws, home demolitions, murders and so on solidifies the laziness of using non-Palestinian points of view. This has helped Israel enjoy widespread and institutionalized impunity while committing violations of international law on an ongoing basis (Ruebner 2020). Meanwhile, the media reports on violence only when an Israeli is attacked and not on the systemic violence of the military occupation and colonization of Palestinian land.

That the state was created by force of arms and imperial violence is simply erased from public view, as is the racist Partition Plan. None of it is exposed outside of scholarly work and so these ridiculous statements on the rights of self-defence of a state are uttered and documented as unquestionably fact, on the side of justice, and loudly pronounced in full confidence without remorse. It is as if Palestinians do not exist, or exist in such abstract, remote terms, that a revisionist history justifying the need for a state to protect oppressed Jews in Europe is fiercely defended despite its outsized distortion of ideological roots, as mendacious as any number of nineteenth-century arguments for European colonial domination.

Conclusion

When I pointed out that the dates sold at my local Noah's Health Food store in Toronto should be boycotted because they are produced on land that is illegally occupied by settlers, the store manager told me the policy is to "give customers a choice," as if that "choice" was somehow a way of making the whole cretinous practice of stealing land a matter of opinion and consumerism. Palestinians, who are subject to racism both inside and outside Israeli rule, do not consider supporting military occupation and settlements on occupied territory to be a matter of consumer choice. They are colonial injustices which are recognized as illegal under international law (United Nations Human Rights Office of the High Commissioner 2021).

In July 2020, the Palestinian-Dutch supermodel Bella Hadid faced censorship by Instagram for posting a photo of her father's United States passport showing his place of birth listed as "Palestine" (Al Jazeera 2020). She accompanied the image with a note professing her pride in being Palestinian. Instagram removed the photo and sent Hadid a note declaring that her post "violated community standards." We know Facebook, which owns Instagram, has subcontracted an Israeli organization to monitor both platforms in an effort to "combat racism" (Nassar 2020). We know this monitoring has led to the removal of hundreds of Palestinian content pages and news services with Bella Hadid's advertisement of the word "Palestine" (7amleh: The Arab Center for Advancement of Social Media 2021).

It was hard to believe Instagram's apology after Hadid complained publicly about the censorship. They claimed that for her own security, they did not allow passport numbers to be exposed. It was an ironic replica of the State of Israel's excuses for front-line violence perpetrated against the Palestinian people: a question of security. It was a reminder how even when we build up courage to speak out, we still face innumerable barriers to expressing ourselves as Palestinians. Our identity is the elephant in the room.

References

7amleh: The Arab Center for Advancement of Social Media. 2021. *The Attacks on Palestinian Digital Rights: Progress Report, May 6–19, 2021.* May 21. <7amleh.org/storage/The%20Attacks%20on%20Palestinian%20Digital%20Rights.pdf>.

Abdo, Nahla. 2020. "Systemic Racism in the U.S. and Israel: Analogies and Differences." *Socialist Bullet,* August 11. <socialistproject.ca/2020/08/systemic-racism-the-us-and-israel/>.

Abunimah, Ali. 2014. "Children Die Playing Football, in Taxi with Grandma, as Israel Bombs Gaza for the Tenth Day." *Electronic Intifada*, July 16. <electronicintifada.net/blogs/ali-abunimah/children-die-playing-football-taxi-grandma-israel-bombs-gaza-tenth-day>.

___. 2018. "Snipers Ordered to Shoot Children, Israeli General Confirms." *Electronic Intifada*, April 22. <electronicintifada.net/blogs/ali-abunimah/snipers-ordered-shoot-children-israeli-general-confirms>.

Adalah: The Legal Center for Arab Minority Rights in Israel. 2017. "The Discriminatory Laws Database." September 25. <adalah.org/en/content/view/7771>.

Al Jazeera. 2020. "Instagram Apologises to Supermodel Bella Hadid Over Removed

Post." July 9. <aljazeera.com/news/2020/7/9/instagram-apologises-to-supermodel-bella-hadid-over-removed-post>.

Amnesty International. 2009. "Israel/Gaza: Operation 'Cast Lead': 22 Days of Death and Destruction." July 2. <www.amnesty.org/en/documents/mde15/015/2009/en/>.

B'Tselem. 2016. "50 Days: More than 500 Children: Facts and Figures on Fatalities in Gaza, Summer 2014." July 20. <https://www.btselem.org/press_releases/20160720_fatalities_in_gaza_conflict_2014>.

Beaumont, Peter. 2014. "A Father Opens a Plastic Bag: 'This Is My Son,' He Says, Killed by an Israeli Shell." *Guardian*, July 18. <theguardian.com/world/2014/jul/18/father-gathers-body-dead-son-two-plastic-bag-gaza-shelling>.

Bloom, Dan, and David Spillet. 2014. "Gaza's Dead Children Are Kept in Ice Cream Freezers." Daily Mail.com, August 3. <dailymail.co.uk/news/article-2714575/Humanitarian-crisis-Gaza-half-million-homeless.html>.

Defense for Children International-Palestine. 2016. "Submissions on Behalf of Child Victims and Their Families Pursuant to Article 19(3) of the Article." International Criminal Court, March 16. <d3n8a8pro7vhmx.cloudfront.net/dcipalestine/pages/5380/attachments/original/1585917296/CR2020_01074.PDF>.

Human Rights Watch. 2009. "White Flag Deaths: Killings of Palestinian Civilians During Operation Cast Lead." August 13. <hrw.org/report/2009/08/13/white-flag-deaths/killings-palestinian-civilians-during-operation-cast-lead>.

IMEU (Institute for Middle East Understanding). 2012. "Operation Cast Lead." January 4. <imeu.org/article/operation-cast-lead>

Khalidi, Walid. 2019. "The Hundred Years' War on Palestine: A Keynote Lecture by Rashid Khalidi." Columbia Global Centers, December 14. <soundcloud.com/columbiaglobalcenters/the-hundred-years-war-on-palestine-a-keynote-lecture-by-rashid-khalidi>.

Levinson, Charles. 2009. "Israelis Watch the Fighting in Gaza from a Hilly Vantage Point." *Wall Street Journal,* January 8. <wsj.com/articles/SB1231366613816062175>.

Masalha, Nur. 1992. Expulsion of the Palestinians: The Concept of Transfer in Zionist Political Thought, 1882–1948. Washington, DC: Institute for Palestine Studies.

____. 2019. Palestine: A Four Thousand Year History. London: Zed Books.

McGill Students for Palestinian Human Rights. 2021. "A Blacklist Is Terrorizing Pro-Palestine Students at McGill." <mcgillsphr.medium.com/a-blacklist-is-terrorizing-pro-palestine-students-at-mcgill-8708f525b533>.

Murphy, Maureen Clare. 2021. "How Human Rights Watch Favours Israel." *Electronic Intifada*, August 4. <electronicintifada.net/content/how-human-rights-watch-favors-israel/33721>.

Mushell, Ari. 2015. "The Danger of Israel Bonds." *Times of Israel*, September 3. <blogs.timesofisrael.com/the-danger-of-israel-bonds/>.

Nashashibi, Hikmat Sharif. 2014. "Fostering Palestine." In *Being Palestinian: Personal Reflections on Palestinian Identity in the Diaspora,* edited by Yasir Suleiman. Edinburgh: Edinburgh University Press.

Nassar, Tamara. 2020. "Facebook Appoints Israeli Censor to Oversight Board." *Electronic Intifada*, May 26. <electronicintifada.net/blogs/tamara-nassar/facebook-appoints-israeli-censor-oversight-board>.

Palestine Awareness Coalition. 2013. "Disappearing Palestine." October 10. <palestineawarenesscoalition.wordpress.com/media/>.

Ruebner, Josh. 2020. "Congress Enables Israeli Impunity at ICC." *Electronic Intifada*, May 15. <electronicintifada.net/blogs/josh-ruebner/congress-enables-israeli-impunity-icc>.

Said, Edward. 1999. *Out of Place: A Memoir.* New York: Vintage Books.

Stop the JNF Canada. n.d. .

Suarez, Thomas. 2020. "Winston Churchill's Racist Legacy in Palestine." *Electronic Intifada*, June 18. <electronicintifada.net/content/winston-churchills-racist-legacy-palestine/30481>.

UNHCR (UN Human Rights Council). 2009. *Report of the United Nations Fact-Finding Mission on the Gaza Conflict.* Paras. 365–92, UN Doc. A/HRC/12/48, September 25. <un.org/Docs/journal/asp/ws.asp?m=A/Hrc/12/48>.

United Nations Human Rights Office of the High Commissioner. 2021. "Occupied Palestinian Territory: Israeli Settlements Should Be Classified as War Crimes, Says UN Expert." July 9. <ohchr.org/en/NewsEvents/Pages/DisplayNews.aspx?NewsID=27291&LangID=E>.

Voice of America News. 2009. "UN, Red Cross Protest Israeli Attacks on Ambulances 2002-03-20." October 26. <voanews.com/a/a-13-a-2002-03-20-21-un-66278957/540429.html>.

Zahr, Amer. 2020. "Fully Furnished/Akhaduha Mafroosheh." July 3. <youtube.com/watch?v=UX8oChavStk>.

Chapter 2

Zionist Loyalty and Euro-Jewish Whiteness

Untangling the Threads of a Lethal Complicity

Sheryl Nestel

European Jewish whiteness in North America has been on the anti-racist agenda at least since James Baldwin published an article entitled "Negroes Are Anti-Semitic Because They're Anti-White" in the *New York Times* on April 9, 1967. Baldwin wrote the article during a period characterized by profound anger and upheaval in many racialized communities, an increasingly militant movement for African American rights and the rise of an explosive tension in New York City between the predominantly Jewish United Federation of Teachers and African Americans fighting for community control of failing schools. The firing of many teachers, large numbers of whom were Jewish, contributed to the public debate on the question of what was deemed "Black Anti-semitism" (Hentoff 1970).

Baldwin, one of the twentieth century's most astute commentators on race, argued that Black antipathy towards Jews stemmed not from any historic tradition of anti-Jewish hatred but from a resentment of how European Jews in the United States, once vilified and racialized, had embraced assimilation into a white majority culture and civic structure which had at first enslaved and then demonized, brutalized and systematically excluded Blacks from equal participation in American life. Jews had seemingly made the choice to embrace the designation of whiteness but were also seen to have deployed the Jewish experience of oppression and genocide in order to demonstrate to racialized others the unlimited possibilities of American meritocratic democracy.

In his article, Baldwin righteously flipped this focus on "Black Anti-Semitism" into an examination of Jewish whiteness, a topic whose relevance, for a variety of reasons, has persisted for the last fifty years. What is disturbing in the most recent discussions are the numerous attempts to disavow European Jewish whiteness by claiming that histories of oppression and genocide make Jewish racial dominance an impossibility (Burton 2018). This claim seems to be substantiated by a repugnant resurgence of antisemitism in North America. The most egregious of these white supremacist attacks against American Jews were the murders at the Tree of Life Synagogue in Pittsburgh in 2018, the deadly shooting at Chabad Poway in 2019 and chants by tiki torch-toting, Nazi insignia-wearing marchers in Charlottesville, Virginia, who, during a Unite the Right rally in 2017, chanted, "Jews will not replace us" (Hein 2017). We might ask why, if Jews of European origin are targeted by white supremacists, are they then seen as racially privileged? What I argue is that Jews must be understood as simultaneously under attack *and* as the beneficiaries of racial privilege. What I wish to demonstrate here is that recent racist attacks on Jews notwithstanding, the fervent anti-Palestinianism of the mainstream Jewish community[1] and the role played by many Jewish communal organizations in denying Israel's history of ethnic cleansing and its suppression of Palestinian human rights works to secure European Jewish whiteness in the United States, Canada and across the globe.[2]

The Racial Repositioning of North American Jews

There is an abundance of rich and innovative scholarship on Jewish racial repositioning in the United States in the twentieth and twenty-first centuries. Among the topics that have been explored are cultural loss and cultural adaptation (Kranson 2017), socioeconomic advantage and racial mobility (Brodkin 1998; Jacobson 1998; Goldstein 2006), new spiritual iterations of Jewishness and Judaism in the American context (Magid 2013), the shifting racial meanings of Jewish embodiment (Gilman 1991), the impact of Western gender normativity on the whitening of European Jews (Boyarin 1997) and numerous other issues related to the transformation of Jewish racial identity.

In contrast to a fairly substantial body of scholarship on Jews and whiteness in the United States, there is almost no comparable literature in Canada. As Canadian cultural studies scholars Michelle Byers and Stephanie Tara Schwartz explain, there is a "lack of interrogation within Jewish studies of the constitution of Jewish identity within problematic colonial tropes like multiculturalism [and] there is no (or very little) scholarship in the area of critical Jewish studies and/or cultural studies" (2013: 72). The intellectual conservatism of mainstream Jewish organizations and their institutional involvement in major Canadian Jewish studies departments might explain the relative absence of work which applies a critical race lens to Canadian Jewish identity. Another possible explanation for this gap is what Stef Creps calls a "gaping disciplinary divide that has long separated Jewish and postcolonial studies" (2013: 78). As Brian Cheyette argues, "Ethnic studies in the United States … from which much postcolonial scholarship grew, emerged at a moment of Third World solidarity with the Palestinians. This in turn led to sharp academic, political and cultural divisions between ethnic and Jewish studies and postcolonial and Holocaust studies" (2018: 1239). It can be argued that, with a few exceptions, this dynamic has played out in Canadian academia as well.[3]

As Joshua Alston argues in his work on Jewish positionality within British settler societies, "The practicalities of settlement projects, with their intense interaction with non-white others, allowed Jews by comparison to become the bearers of white supremacy, rather than the racialized objects of it" (2019: 65). In the absence of critical Canadian scholarship on Jews and racialization, where can we look for documentation of this "intense interaction" and what can it tell us about how Jewish identity emerges in and through the racialized other? Fictional accounts can shine a light into those spaces where the lives of white Canadian Jews and those of their racialized counterparts intersect. As Sarah Phillips Casteel notes in her singular work on Jewishness and Canadian Caribbean identity, "If the figure of the Jew in North American and European literatures more generally is typified by its racial ambiguity, this ambiguity may be traced across numerous black diasporic texts as well" (2005: 114). Casteel focuses her analysis on African Caribbean Canadian author Austin Clarke's *The Meeting Point*, the first volume of his *Toronto Trilogy*. Published in 1967, Clarke's novel examines the relationship between prosperous European Jewish immigrants and their African Caribbean domestic employees. In the book, Clarke explores the racial animus towards Caribbean immigrants of the novel's Jewish characters while at the same time acknowledging and exploring Jewish racial anxiety and indeterminacy. As Casteel explains:

If Jews are not white in the eyes of the Wasp [*sic*] establishment, they console themselves that at least they are whiter than the Caribbean immigrants they employ. As Jews, they exhibit a sense of marginality with regard to whiteness but a sense of whiteness and belonging with regard to blackness … consolidating their claim to whiteness at the expense of … Caribbean immigrants. (2005: 122)

While it is important to note that the vast majority of Canadian Jews are of European origin, racial diversity within the Canadian Jewish community is growing. Immigration, intermarriage, conversion and adoption are increasingly challenging the notion of Jews as a uniformly white demographic group. Meanwhile, those who identify as Jews of colour have become increasingly vocal about their experiences of racism within Jewish institutions (Rose 2019). As author and filmmaker Rebecca Pierce (2020) has argued, "Jews of colour encounter this systemic 'sense of normative whiteness' on a regular basis in the everyday experience of having our Jewish identity questioned." Increased recognition of the presence of racialized Jews in Canada is critical to revealing and eliminating their experiences of racism and exclusion;[4] it also serves to correct the popular perception that Jews are a racially homogenous group. However, the political trajectory of Canadian Jews towards white racial status nonetheless continues apace, given how the overwhelmingly majority of the community has European origins.

Zionism, Racism and Jewish Whiteness

While a comprehensive critical analysis of European Jews' transformation in Canada from a suspect and deeply racialized immigrant population to a successful white ethnic minority still remains to be written, we can cautiously speculate on the outline of this transition. Broadly speaking then, in Canada European Jews have integrated into a structurally white supremacist social order in a way which has served to highlight the racist differentiation of Indigenous Peoples and racialized immigrants from European white settlers. Contemporary Jewish racial identity then must be understood in the context of other immigrations and diasporas which emerged in the post-Holocaust/anti-colonial era. However, to fully understand the transition of European Jews in Canada to racial "respectability," we must also understand the impact of the State of Israel and Zionism on this process.

Perhaps no event has contributed more to the institutional and ideological transformation of the Canadian Jewish community than the Israeli victory in the 1967 Six Day War. As historian Harold Troper explains,

> [It] spurred the building of a full-time professionally organized Canadian Jewish lobby effort on behalf of Israel and issues of Jewish concern and precipitated a papering over of long-festering rifts in the Jewish community so as to give the outward appearance of unity. (2010: 170)

The victory also transformed the way in which Canadian Jews viewed themselves. Reform Rabbi Gunther Plaut observed at the time that "proud identification with the valor and courage of the Israelis gave the [Canadian] Jews a new image, not the least in their own eyes" (Troper 2010: 163). The Six Day War consolidated Jewish identification with the triumphalist Zionist settlement project and allowed Jews to become "a normal white group with its own settler and national projects ... [and] offered a model for transcending Jewishness itself, with the urban degenerate diaspora Jew emerging to become the Zionist sabra or the secular frontiersman, restoring a supposedly inadequate Jewish masculinity" (Alston 2019: 65). Writing about the United States context, in the wake of the war Zionism became what Shaul Magid has called an "American Jewish dogma," which bound together Jewish victimhood during the Holocaust and the necessity of Jewish emotional, political and financial support for the Israeli state, while rendering non- or anti-Zionism an unspoken heresy (2014: 239). This dogmatic viewpoint was adopted equally in Canada, within the broader North American diasporic Jewish community.

Support for Israeli settler-colonialism has also been a key factor in the whitening of diasporic Jewish communities in North America, even as Jews experience horrific and murderous antisemitic attacks. Moreover, the most extreme expressions of loyalty to Zionism and opposition to Palestinian self-determination frequently make use of a white Western narrative which portrays Palestinians/Muslims/Arabs as violent, barbaric, irrational, patriarchal and homophobic (Goldberg 2009). Such portrayals claim to link the biblical Philistines to the contemporary inhabitants of modern-day Palestine. As Theo David Goldberg argues, contemporary Palestinians have been identified as the direct kin of biblical Philistines, "conceived in the representational struggles as blood thirsty and warmongering, constantly harassing modern-day Israelites, debauched and lacking in liberal culture" (2009: 26). Ironically, Jewish anti-Palestinian racism further serves to affirm the civilized disposition of European Jews while reproducing and reactivating those racist conceptual models that had been used historically to persecute and decimate European Jewish communities (Anidjar 2003).

Much diasporic Jewish support for Israel has involved a deep denial of the country's historical record of Palestinian dispossession and its contemporary regime of violence, control and discursive deception. The debate as to whether Israel is a racist and/or apartheid society is an ongoing one and many Jews and Israelis adamantly disavow the charge (Anti-Defamation League n.d.). It seems prudent then to reiterate here the many ways in which the Israeli state and its founders created and currently maintain a racist regime. Several foundational European Zionist thinkers, however ideologically disparate, tended to utilize the same discourses of race as had been employed to denigrate and ultimately exterminate Jews in the modern European societies in which they lived. Zionist writers advocated the transformation of Jewish bodies into ones that more comfortably reflected European norms. Male Jews were seen as weak and feminine, a characterization that led to the Zionist championing of the new "muscle Jew," who would build and, importantly, be rebuilt by working the land in historic Palestine (Presner 2007; Boyarin 1997). Reflected in this notion is a certain spirit of enterprise associated with traits such as "energy, will, ambition, the ability to think and see things through" and so on — attributes perceived to be lacking in non-white bodies (Dyer 1997). Eugenicist health regimes targeted the supposed cultural and biological primitivity of Jewish non-European immigrants from Arab countries (Hirsch 2009), known as Mizrahi, while racist Israeli settlement policies led to these immigrants being deposited in the years after the establishment of the State of Israel in far-flung and vulnerable border locations with little infrastructure and few resources (Yiftachel 1998). In some cases, the infants of Mizrahi immigrants were seized from their parents and offered for adoption to European Jewish families (Madmoni-Gerber 2009), a trauma which has yet to be fully acknowledged or resolved in Israel.

While a belief in the inherent cultural and corporeal inferiority of Mizrahi Jews permeated Zionist settlement policy after the establishment of the Jewish state, classic Zionism viewed all diasporic Jewish bodies as biologically fragile and in need of regeneration. For some Zionist ideologues, the entire Jewish diaspora was regarded as a degenerate space in need of dissolution (Falk 2006). The promotion of Zionism as central to transformation of the Jew entails embracing elements of self-hatred and internalization of the disparaging notions of Orientalism that were applied by Europeans to both Jews and Arabs.

The turning point of the Zionist project was the expulsion of more than 750,000 Palestinians in 1948 — the result of an ethnic cleansing plan that had been formulated well before that time and which included the destruction of more than five hundred Palestinian villages as well as several fully documented massacres of Palestinians (Masala 2018; Sa'adi and Abu-Lughod 2007; Pappé 2006; Morris 1987). Those Palestinians who managed to remain inside the new Jewish state's borders were, until 1966, ruled by a military government which denied them national and civil rights and which even conducted a 1956 massacre in which forty-eight Palestinians were killed for returning after work to their village of Kafr Qasim, unaware of a hastily imposed curfew (Robinson 2013). Further expulsions and village demolitions followed the 1967 war, which saw many a half million Palestinians flee to Jordan, Syria and Egypt, never to return (Segev 2007).

Abigail Bakan observes that the aftermath of the 1967 Arab-Israeli war brought "changes in the legitimacy of Zionism in Western hegemony, and dramatically marked transitional moments in the ascent of Jews into whiteness by permission" (2016: 262). Israel's victory in the 1967 war granted diaspora Jews what might be deemed "identity by proxy" whereby Jews shed their historically ascribed character as a racialized and feminized collectivity through their identification with a militarily powerful, highly masculine and decidedly white and Western Israeli Jewish society (Kaplan 2018). As noted above, Zionism became a form of secular religion for many Jews in the West who had shed significant spiritual, cultural and political traditions, including time-honoured modes of worship, the use of Yiddish and involvement in working-class and left-wing politics to be accepted into white settler societies (Goldstein 2006). What followed was a cultural transformation of Jewish diasporic life wherein Israeli culture and politics pre-empted local diasporic cultural development.

Is Israel a Racist Society?

As Ronit Lentin has argued, "Israel's lifelong project, though ultimately a function of constructing Jewish insecurity, is an ongoing project of racial branding, of setting apart as racially distinct, and of enabling the guiltless extinction of a whole group at least politically if not physically" (2018: 27). These goals have been pursued utilizing a variety of technologies, including the seizure of Palestinian land without compensation and Jewish settlements on Palestinian land in direct contravention of international law (Sfard 2018); a deeply discriminatory water control regime in the West Bank and Gaza (Hever 2014); the testing of weapons and policing tactics on Palestinians and the export of these to oppressive political regimes which work to control racialized and otherwise unruly populations (Halper 2015); the second-class status of Palestinian citizens of Israel and their unequal access to basic resources such as electricity, water and education (Ehrenreich 2016); the degradation of population health for Palestinians both inside Israel and in the West Bank and Gaza (Rothschild 2017); the Separation Wall, separate roads for Jewish settlers and Palestinians, the Israeli Nation State Law securing Jewish political dominance, the right of return for Jews only and the reduction of Gaza to conditions of bare life (Finkelstein 2018); laws against commemorating the Nakba; the separate legal system in the occupied territories which convicts 99 percent of Palestinians charged (Erakat 2020); and the ongoing travesty of the Jewish National Fund (JNF), which restricts the use of land it controls to Jews and has been involved in the destruction of Palestinian villages, including those of Bedouin in the Negev/Naqab desert (Amara, Abu-Saad and Yiftachel 2012). In addition, recently enacted racist immigration and asylum policies have impacted non-Jews who have sought refuge in the Jewish state, including notably, African asylum seekers who have endured brutalization, imprisonment and forced repatriation (Orr and Ajzenstadt 2020). Despite all of this, many mainstream Jewish organizations continue to defend Israel as "the only democracy in the Middle East."

Canadian Jewish Communal
Leadership and Support for Racism

There is both implicit and explicit support for Israel's racist policies by many mainstream Jewish institutions in Canada. Israeli legislators may enact these policies and Jewish Israeli soldiers may carry them out, but

Jewish organization worldwide collude with this travesty of justice by coming to Israel's defence. Jews in Canada are nominally presided over by a Jewish communal leadership that adheres unerringly to the dictates of Israel's government. The disappearance of even a semblance of communal diversity and political variety accompanied the wildly undemocratic hijacking of the Canadian Jewish Congress by a group of wealthy and powerful philanthropists (Freeman-Maloy 2006). Transformed into the Committee for Israel and Jewish Affairs (CIJA) in 2011, it shares a political agenda with right-wing ideologues in B'nai Brith Canada and the Canadian Friends of Simon Wiesenthal Centre for Holocaust Studies, groups that ostensibly support human rights for all but have been loyal proxies for the Israeli state and ardent purveyors of anti-Muslim and anti-Palestinian rhetoric. Moreover, these groups have consistently refused to condemn the unabashedly Islamophobic Jewish Defense League, which has allied itself with such white supremacist groups as the Soldiers of Odin, the English Defense League, and Patriotic Europeans Against the Islamicisation of the Occident (PEGIDA).

These groups exert a significant influence over Jewish religious, cultural and educational institutions in Canada, helping guarantee through funding and other means that Jewish loyalty to Israel will be reproduced and reinforced. Some of the more egregious positions taken by CIJA include backing the move of the United States embassy from Tel Aviv to Jerusalem, a position known to be flatly rejected by Canadians (Bueckert et al. 2020); support for cancelling the Joint Comprehensive Plan of Action (JCPOA) accord with Iran, which is meant to block its development of a nuclear weapons program in return for allowing it to re-enter the international community; and defending the killing and maiming of protesters during the Great March of Return in Gaza 2018–19. These groups also supported the extradition of Lebanese Canadian sociologist Hassan Diab to France on charges of terrorism, even though the charges were refuted when Diab was recently cleared after spending more than three years in solitary confinement in a French jail (CIJA 2014; B'nai Brith 2014). CIJA also opposed Bill M-103, which called for collecting data on hate crimes and for studying ways to end systemic racism and religious discrimination, including Islamophobia. CIJA objected to the use of the word "Islamophobia," calling it "misleading, ambiguous and politically charged" (CIJA 2017). A group of right-wing pro-Israel advocacy groups held a conference in Toronto in September of 2017 in which Bill M-103 was characterized as the beginning of the imposition of Sharia law in Canada (Zhou 2017). Finally, the organ of the Jewish community, the weekly *Canadian Jewish News,* published articles zealously defending Israeli policies written by such virulently conservative pro-Israel Jewish writers as journalist Barbara Kay and academic Gil Troy, while at the same time refusing to publish articles that offered anything other than minor criticisms of the Jewish state.

Stonewalling Dissent in the Jewish Community

Reflecting the dogmatic approach identified by Magid in the United States Jewish community, where non- or anti-Zionism was rendered unspoken heresy, the wall of silence that has been built by the institutional Canadian Jewish community around Israel's violations of Palestinian national and human rights disallows not only non- or anti-Zionist speech but fails to engage even with the most credible and considered scholarly challenges to Zionist thinking. By contrast, Hannah Arendt reminds us that to hold different opinions and to be aware that others may think differently shields us from a "God-like certainty which stops all discussion and reduces social relationships to those of an ant heap. A unanimous public opinion tends to eliminate bodily those who differ, for mass unanimity is not the result of agreement but an expression of fanaticism and hysteria" (Bernstein 2018: 41).

Indeed, the stonewalling of public critique of Israel has been quite aggressively pursued against Jews and non-Jews alike. We continue to witness attacks on students, academics and community activists upon whom the considerable weight of the Zionist advocacy apparatus has been applied (Jewish Voice for Peace 2015). Recently, the International Holocaust Remembrance Alliance working definition of antisemitism, which holds that harsh criticism of the Jewish state constitutes antisemitism, was adopted by the Canadian government after strenuous lobbying by mainstream Canadian Jewish organizations. There is a vigorous drive by pro-Israel Jewish institutions in Canada to have the definition adopted by provincial legislatures, city councils, police forces, universities and other public institutions. While it is unclear how this policy will be applied or if can withstand a legal challenge, it threatens to create a major crisis for scholars, campus and community activists and others working for the cause of justice for Palestinians (Sachs 2019).

Jewish dissent on this issue has been stifled through a campaign of shaming and defamation in which those who protest are roundly condemned, and indeed frightened into silence through the threat of excommunication from the Jewish community. I have watched people I know come in disguise to demonstrations for justice for Palestinians because they fear being identified by their families, community members or work colleagues. Ferocious insults are often flung at Jewish Palestine solidarity activists who express their views publicly.[5] Personally, I endured months of attacks on my qualifications as an academic by figures in the mainstream Jewish community (and was even condemned in the Ontario Provincial Legislature) after supervising a master's thesis that articulated an anti-Zionist critique of the March of the Living, a program which conducts guided trips to the sites of European extermination camps (Sztainbok 2011). I have been called a *kapo,* referring to Jews who loaded into the crematoria the bodies of those exterminated by the Nazis. I have also been branded "self-hating" even though I regularly celebrate Shabbat and Jewish holidays, belong to a synagogue, sent my three children to Jewish day school and spent fifteen years of my life living in the Jewish state. While these are the kinds of insults that we have come to expect from those on the Jewish right, similar sentiments have been expressed by mainstream Jewish organizations and the liberal Zionist camp.

In 2017, I attended the conference of JSpaceCanada, which calls itself "Canada's Progressive Zionist Voice." Following a panel on inclusion and exclusion in the Jewish community, I rose to ask why such a discussion did not include voices such as those of the pro-Palestinian group Independent Jewish Voices Canada, of which I am a member and which includes both non- and anti-Zionist members. After pondering this for a few seconds, the chair of the panel — an avowed Zionist and well-known anti-hate activist — responded unashamedly by asking rhetorically, "Would I invite a Nazi to sit on the panel?" What can be understood then from this unnerving response? By invoking the Nazi genocide in relation to anti-Zionism the speaker demonstrated that an anti-Zionist position, even when espoused by Jews, is seen as a genocidal stance and one which situates not only Palestinians but also Jews who support them as an existential threat to the Jewish people.

Support for Israel then is the litmus test not only of one's belonging to the Jewish people but of one's membership in the family of civilized nations. As Santiago Slabodsky (2014) argues, Jews, once decried as bar-

barians, now find themselves on the other side of the equation. Despite the long and relatively peaceful history of Jewish life in Islamic countries, Israel and Jews worldwide are now seen as immutably "Western" and "civilized," and any attack on Israel represents an assault not only on world Jewry but on the West itself.

Certainly, support for the Palestinian struggle by many on the Jewish left threatens that tenet of Jewish whiteness which positions Jews as the curiously redeemed repository of all that is good about the West. As Canadian sociologist Morton Weinfeld argues, Jews in Canada are now "true insiders" (2018: 270). Palestinians, on the other hand, are grievously represented as a culture of death and genocidal intention, a ploy which anthropologizes and depoliticizes the Israel/Palestine conflict and makes it appear hopelessly intractable. For Jews to ally with the Palestinian struggle then is to invite the re-racialization of diasporic Jewry, a fate which Jewish communities have resisted at least since the end of World War II. Moreover, representing the conflict as cultural rather than political renders those who uncritically support Zionism and the Jewish state unable to acknowledge human suffering outside of a Western paradigm. By this logic, when Jews express support for the Palestinian struggle what they do is endanger Jewish positioning as a whitened model minority. Thus, pro-Palestinianism is not tolerated by an institutional Jewish community which strives for acceptance in white settler societies like Canada, which are incontrovertibly racist in both their colonial histories and contemporary exclusionary postures and structures.

Victimhood as Refuge

What elusive process prevents Jews on the right and the left, but especially on the liberal left, from recognizing and acknowledging Israel's ongoing dispossession of and violence against Palestinians? The desire to secure victim status plays a significant role in this process. Victimhood, it seems, has become the most widely embraced identity for Jews in Israel and elsewhere. For many Jews, the open wound of the Holocaust is a constant reminder of the precarity of Jewish existence even in the safest countries where Jews reside. The Holocaust plays a decisive role in Zionist politics and is deployed, in historian Ian Lustick's words, as a "template for Jewish life" (2019: 37). As Lustick argues, this template has had its largest and most destructive effect on the capacity of masses of Israeli Jews to empathize enough with Palestinian Arabs to deal effectively with their demands and discontent. The basic syllogism holds that all enemies are Nazis and all Arabs or Muslims are enemies, so Arabs and Muslims are Nazis, effectively disqualifying them as objects of humane concern … To the extent that Arabs and Muslims are automatically seen as Nazis or are expected to act as Nazis and to the extent that gentiles are always liable to "revert to type" as anti-Semites, then every problem faced by Israel is most convincingly portrayed as potentially another Holocaust. (2019: 51)

Within this logic, Jewish victimhood is inevitable, and any measures that must be taken to prevent another Holocaust can be justified. An ethnocentric Jewish state in Israel/Palestine is seen as the ultimate antidote to the precariousness of Jewish existence. Consequently, support toward a state which grants equal rights for all residents is seen as support for genocide.

Claims to a trans-historical victim status may serve to shield us as Jews from becoming accountable for the suffering caused by the Zionist project. Historical trauma is seen by many as embedded in the Jewish DNA (Lehrner and Yehuda 2018). It is difficult, if not impossible, for most Jews to hold the status of victim and victimizer in the same conceptual frame. Challenges to our identity as victims threaten basic assumptions about the essential status of the Jew. If this version of the Jew as eternal victim is to survive as justification for Israeli violence and dispossession, any challenges to it must be silenced. Loyalty to the Jewish state and the Zionist vision comes to be seen as a matter of life or death. However, we Jews must critically examine the discourse of eternal victim status and begin to see it not as our genetic inheritance but as a produced response used unashamedly for political ends by those with the will and the power to do so. Jews must confront the politicization of the victim narrative and wrest it away from its use to maintain Palestinian wretchedness. Yes, we Jews have been victimized and we currently face renewed and very worrisome threats. These circumstances must not, however, serve as an excuse to dehumanize, victimize and brutalize others.

Where then do Jews of conscience, to use Marc Ellis' (2004) useful term, turn for direction? Many Jewish activists refer to Jewish sources as guideposts to ethical thinking and action. These are helpful and allow us to mobilize Jewish tradition in the fight for justice. However, this strategy has its limitations. As Judith Butler argues in her important critique of Zionism, *Parting Ways,* if we work only within Jewish critiques of Zionism, we reimpose a Jewish framework on the conflict. If we are to strive for cohabitation, Butler argues, then we must engage with the frameworks and critiques of those with whom we want to live in peace (Butler 2012). As diasporic Jews, we have a long history of encounter with the "other" and should hopefully possess the conceptual and experiential resources to imagine a political ethos which embraces the notion of cohabitation.

Conclusion: Which Side Are You On?

In a recent book, Houria Bouteldja (2016) offers Jews a path through this thorny dilemma. Bouteldja, a Muslim Tunisian French activist, defines herself as one of the "wretched of the interior" — that is, racialized migrants from the Global South who continue to experience colonial treatment in supposedly post-colonial times and places. Bouteldja challenges Jews to undo a deadly and illusory loyalty to a form of ethnonationalism that requires constant boundary maintenance through an intentional fictionalization of histories, an ironic valorization of notions derived from a European racial supremacist past and present, and the deployment of state violence disguised as self-defence.

Bouteldja poses to Jews a question that we recognize from struggles past: Which side are you on? And, speaking in a decidedly anti-colonial register, she pulls no punches:

> In fact, it's true, you were really chosen by the West. For three cardinal missions: to solve the white world's moral legitimacy crisis, which resulted from the Nazi genocide, to outsource republican racism, and finally to be the weaponized wing of Western imperialism in the Arab world. Can I allow myself to think that in your heart it is the part that loves the white world that pushed you to sign this deal with the devil? This is how, in the span of fifty years you went from being pariahs, to being on the one hand dhimmis of the republic to satisfy the internal needs of the nation state and on the other, Senegalese riflemen to satisfy the needs of western imperialism … You have given up on depriving white people of their throne and, instead, pledged your allegiance to them. (2016: 56)

Bouteldja challenges Jews to divest themselves of the illusion of full belonging and reclaim histories of co-existence, such as that of La Convivencia in medieval Spain, and legacies of shared struggle, such as that of the pre-war Socialist Jewish Labour Bund. She excoriates us for trading our religion, our history and our memories for a colonial ideology, for abandoning our secular identities and for despising our historic languages of Yiddish and Arabic. "In only fifty years," she exclaims, "it is as if sorcerers had put a spell on you. Is Zionism yet another name for your capitulation?" (2016: 57).

Bouteldja also understands the Holocaust as conjoined with imperial conquest and dispossession — an understanding that should force us to rethink the exclusivist meaning of the Holocaust and to turn "Never Again" into "Never Again for Anyone." She implores Jews to join networks of resistance that challenge not only the criminality of the West but also the complicities of our own communities in oppressive regimes and practices. She is not singling out Jews with this critique but applying it broadly to all those caught in the doubly untenable trap of Western white supremacy wherein our positioning in matrices of both oppression and dominance are confusing if not completely confounding. In other words, Bouteldja urges Jews to reject the temptations of racial repositioning and its requirement that Jews demonstrate allegiance to racist and colonial modes of thought and action rather than siding with the oppressed. Moreover, she proposes that through shared struggle and "revolutionary companionship" we can begin to understand the ways in which we are implicated in both furthering and hindering each other's paths to liberation.

I suspect that Palestinian American scholar Edward Said would have appreciated Houria Boutildja's work and it is fitting here to end with his words:

> It is inadequate to only affirm that a people was dispossessed, oppressed or slaughtered, denied its rights and its political existence, without at the same time doing what Fanon did during the Algerian War, affiliating those horrors with the similar afflictions of other people ... This does not mean a loss in historical specificity, but rather it guards against the possibility that a lesson learned about oppression in one place will never be forgotten or violated in another place or time. (Said 1986: 44)

Notes

1. I use the term "mainstream" to designate those Jewish organizations that are affiliated with the Centre for Israel and Jewish Affairs, the United Jewish Appeal and other explicitly Zionist communal organizations. It is important to note that just 47 percent of Canadian Jews are affiliated with a Jewish communal institution other than a synagogue (Brym, Neuman and Lenton 2019). Nonetheless, Jewish lobby groups such as CIJA and B'nai Brith consistently claim to represent the entire Jewish community.
2. It is important to emphasize that Jewish opinions on Israel/Palestine are non-monolithic and constantly in flux. Recent evidence belies the existence of unconditional support for Israel among Canadian Jews. See, for example Diana Ralph in this volume. See also Brym, Neuman and Lenton (2019). This poll conducted by Environics in conjunction with the University of Toronto and York University reports that 44 percent of those polled believe the current Israeli government is not making a sincere effort to bring about peace. This survey is analyzed in Ralph, this volume.
3. See, for example, Corey Balsam (2011).
4. For a comprehensive overview of scholarship on Moroccan Jews in Canada, see Cohen and Schwartz (2016). See also Train (2013).
5. See, for example, Fogel (2019).

References

Alston, Joshua. 2019. "The Loyal Jews of the British Empire: Jewish Settlers in Canada, South Africa and Australia, 1917–50." Unpublished master's thesis, University of Leiden.

Amara, Ahmad, Ismael Abu-Saad, and Oren Yiftachel. 2012. *Indigenous (In)justice: Human Rights Law and Bedouin Arabs in the Naqab/Negev*. Cambridge, MA: Harvard University Press.

Anidjar, Gil. 2003. *The Jew, the Arab: A History of the Enemy*. Stanford, CA: Stanford University Press.

Anti-Defamation League. n.d. *Response to Common Inaccuracy: Zionism Is Racism.* <https://web.archive.org/web/20200831081818/adl.org/resources/fact-sheets/response-to-common-inaccuracy-zionism-is-racism>.

B'nai Brith International. 2014. "B'nai B'rith Praises Canadian Supreme Court for Extradition of Suspect in 1980 Paris Synagogue Bombing." November 14. <bnaibrith.org/press-releases/bnai-brith-praises-canadian-supreme-court-for-extradition-of-suspect-in-1980-paris-synagogue-bombing>.

Bakan, Abigail. 2016. "Race, Class, and Colonialism: Reconsidering the 'Jewish Question.'" In *Theorizing Anti-racism: Linkages in Marxism and Critical Race Theories*, edited by Abigail Bakan and Enakshi Dua. Toronto: University of Toronto Press.

Baldwin, James. 1967. "Negroes Are Anti-Semitic Because They're Anti-White." *New York Times*, April 9. <archive.nytimes.com/www.nytimes.com/books/98/03/29/specials/baldwin-antisem.html?_r=1>.

Balsam, Corey. 2011. "The Appeal of Israel: Whiteness, Anti-Semitism and the Roots of Diaspora Zionism in Canada." Unpublished master's thesis, Ontario Institute for Studies in Education of the University of Toronto.

Bernstein, Richard J. 2018. *Why Read Hannah Arendt Now?* Cambridge: Polity Press.

Bouteldja, Houria. 2016. *Whites, Jews and Us: Towards a Politics of Revolutionary Love.*

South Pasadena, CA: Semiotext(e).

Boyarin, Daniel. 1997. *Unheroic Conduct*. Berkeley: University of California Press.

Brodkin, Karen. 1998. *How Jews Became White Folks: And What That Says about Race in America*. New Brunswick, NJ: Rutgers University Press.

Brym, Robert, Keith Neuman, and Rhonda Lenton. 2019. 2018 *Survey of Jews in Canada*. <environicsinstitute.org/docs/default-source/project-documents/2018-survey-of-jews-in-canada/2018-survey-of-jews-in-canada---final-report.pdf?sfvrsn=2994ef6_2>.

Bueckert, Michael, Thomas Woodley, Grafton Ross, et al. 2020. "No Double Standards: Canadians Expect Greater Impartiality vis-à-vis Israel." Part 2 of a national opinion survey of Canadians conducted June 5–10, 2020. Survey conducted by EKOS Research Associates, co-sponsored by Canadians for Justice and Peace in the Middle East, Independent Jewish Voices Canada, and United Network for Justice and Peace in Palestine-Israel. <www.cjpme.org/survey2020_r2>.

Burton, Nyla. 2018. "White Jews: Stop Calling Yourselves 'White-Passing.'" *Forward*, July 2.

Butler, Judith. 2012. *Parting Ways: Jewishness and the Critique of Zionism*. New York: Columbia University Press.

Byers, Michele, and Stephanie Tara Schwartz. 2013. "Theorizing Multicultural Jewish Identity in Canada." In *Critical Inquiries: A Reader in the Study of Canada*, edited by Lynn Caldwell, Darryl Leroux, and Carrianne Leung. Black Point, NS: Fernwood Publishing.

Casteel, Sarah Phillips. 2005. "Experiences of Arrival: Jewishness and Caribbean-Canadian Identity in Austin Clarke's *The Meeting Point*." *Journal of West Indian Literature* 14, 1/2 (November).

Cheyette, Bryan. 2018. "Postcolonialism and the Study of Anti-Semitism." *American Historical Review*, October.

CIJA (Centre for Israel and Jewish Affairs). 2014. "Press Release: The Centre for Israel and Jewish Affairs Commend the Supreme Court of Canada for Upholding Hassan Diab Extradition." November 13. <cija.ca/hassan-diab-extradition/>.

___. 2017. "CIJA's Position on M-103." February 2. <https://web.archive.org/web/20170312051842/cija.ca/m103/>.

Cohen, Yolande, and Stephanie Tara Schwartz. 2016. "Scholarship on Moroccan Jews in Canada: Multidisciplinary, Multilingual, and Diasporic." *Journal of Canadian Studies/Revue d'études canadiennes* 50, 3.

Creps, Stef. 2013. *Postcolonial Witnessing: Trauma Out of Bounds*. New York: Palgrave Macmillan.

Dyer, Richard. 1997. *White*. New York: Routledge.

Ehrenreich, Ben. 2016. *The Way to the Spring: Life and Death in Palestine*. New York: Penguin Press.

Ellis, Marc. 2004. *Toward a Jewish Theology of Liberation: The Challenge of the 21st Century*. Waco, TX: Baylor University Press.

Erakat, Noura. 2020. *Justice for Some: Law and the Question of Palestine*. Stanford: Stanford University Press.

Falk, Raphael. 2006. *Zionism and the Biology of the Jews*. Switzerland: Springer.

Finkelstein, Norman. 2018. *Gaza: An Inquest into Its Martyrdom*. Oakland: University of California Press.

Fogel, Shimon. 2019. "Counter-Jewish Anti-Zionists by Keeping Israel on the Seder Table." *Canadian Jewish News* April 18.

Freeman-Maloy, Dan. 2006. "AIPAC North: 'Israel Advocacy' in Canada." <https://web. archive.org/web/20150127050625/http://www.notesonhypocrisy.com/node/19>.

Gilman, Sander. 1991. *The Jew's Body*. New York: Routledge.

Goldberg, David Theo. 2009. *The Threat of Race: Reflections on Racial Neoliberalism*. Oxford: Wiley-Blackwell.

Goldstein, Eric. 2006. *The Price of Whiteness: Jews, Race and American Identity*. Princeton and Oxford: Princeton University Press.

Halper, Jeff. 2015. *War Against the People: Israel, The Palestinians and Global Pacification*. London: Pluto Press.

Hein, Joe. 2017. "Recounting a Day of Rage, Hate, Violence and Death." *Washington Post*, August 14. <washingtonpost.com/graphics/2017/local/charlottesville-timeline/>.

Hentoff, Nat. 1970. *Black Anti-Semitism and Jewish Racism*. New York: Schocken.

Hever, Shir. 2014. "Economic Cost of the Occupation to Israel." In *The Impacts of Lasting Occupation: Lessons from Israeli Society*, edited by Bar-Tal, Daniel and Izhak Schnell. Oxford: Oxford University Press.

Hirsch, Dafna. 2009. "'We Are Here to Bring the West, Not Only to Ourselves:' Zionist Occidentalism and the Discourse of Hygiene in Mandate Palestine." *International Journal of Middle East Studies* 41, 4.

Jacobson, Matthew Frye. 1998. *Whiteness of a Different Color: European Immigrant and the Alchemy of Race*. Cambridge, MA: Harvard University Press.

Jewish Voice for Peace. 2015. *Stifling Dissent: How Israel's Defenders Use False Charges of Anti-Semitism to Limit Debate Over Israel on Campus*. <jewishvoiceforpeace.org/wp-content/uploads/2015/09/JVP_Stifling_Dissent_Full_Report_Key_90745869.pdf>.

Kaplan, Amy. 2018. *Our American Israel: The Story of an Entangled Alliance*. Cambridge, MA: Harvard University Press.

Kranson, Rachel. 2017. *Ambivalent Embrace: Jewish Upward Mobility in Postwar America*. Chapel Hill: University of North Carolina Press.

Lehrner, Amy, and Rachel Yehuda. 2018. "Cultural Trauma and Epigenetic Inheritance." *Development and Psychopathology* 30.

Lentin, Ronit. 2018. *Traces of Racial Exceptionalism: Racializing Israeli Settler Colonialism*. London: Bloomsbury Academic.

Lustick, Ian. 2019. *Paradigm Lost: From Two-State Solution to One-State Reality*. Philadelphia: University of Pennsylvania Press.

Madmoni-Gerber, Shoshana. 2009. *Israeli Media and the Framing of Internal Conflict: The Yemenite Babies Affair*. New York: Palgrave-Macmillan.

Magid, Shaul. 2013. *American Post-Judaism: Identity and Renewal in a Postethnic Society*. Bloomington: Indiana University Press.

___. 2014. "Butler Trouble." *Studies in American Jewish Literature* 33, 2.

Masala, Nur. 2018. *Palestine: A Four Thousand Year History*. London: Zed Books.

Morris, Benny. 1987. *The Birth of the Palestinian Refugee Problem, 1947–1949*. New York: Cambridge University Press.

Orr, Zvika, and Mimi Ajzenstadt. 2020. "Beyond Control: The Criminalization of African Asylum Seekers in Israel." *International Review of Sociology* 30, 1.

Pappé, Ilan. 2006. *The Ethnic Cleansing of Palestine*. Oxford: Oneworld Publications.

Pierce, Rebecca. 2020. "Jews of Color and the Policing of White Space." *Jewish Currents*, May 29. <jewishcurrents.org/jews-of-color-and-the-policing-of-white-space>.

Presner, Todd Samuel. 2007. *Muscular Judaism: The Jewish Body and the Politics of Regeneration*. New York: Routledge.

Robinson, Shira. 2013. *Both Citizens and Strangers in Citizen Strangers: Palestinians and* the Birth of Israel's Liberal Settler State. Stanford, CA: Stanford University Press.

Rose, Alex. 2019. "Being a Jew of Colour: Finding Acceptance and Inclusion." *Canadian Jewish News*, April 24.

Rothschild, Alice. 2017. *Condition Critical: Life and Death in Israel/Palestine*. Washington, DC: Just World Books.

Sa'di, Ahmad H., and Lila Abu-Lughod. 2007. *Nakba: Palestine, 1948, and the Claims of Memory*. New York: Columbia University Press.

Sachs, Jeffery. 2019. "Canada's New Definition of Anti-Semitism Is a Threat to Campus Free Speech." *University Affairs*, September 10.

Said, Edward. 1986. *After the Last Sky: Palestinian Lives*. New York: Pantheon Books.

___. 1999. *Out of Place: A Memoir*. New York: Vintage Books.

Segev, Tom. 2007. "The June 1967 War and the Palestinian Refugee Problem." *Journal of Palestine Studies* 36, 3 (Spring).

Sfard, Michael. 2018. *The Wall and the Gate: Israel, Palestine and the Legal Battle for Human Rights*. New York: Metropolitan Books.

Slabodsky, Santiago. 2014. *Decolonial Judaism: Triumphal Failures of Barbaric Thinking*. New York: Palgrave Macmillan.

Sztainbok, Vannina. 2011. "When Neo-Con Politicians, Media Attack Academics: Interview with Sheryl Nestel." *Rabble,* Jan. 26.

Train, Kelly. 2013. "Am I *That* Jew? North African Jewish Experience in the Toronto Jewish Day School System and the Establishment of Or Haemet Sephardic School." *Diaspora, Indigenous, and Minority Education* 7, 1. <doi.org/10.1080/15595692.2012.742055>.

Troper, Harold. 2010. *The Defining Decade: Identity, Politics, and the Canadian Jewish Community in the 1960s*. Toronto: University of Toronto Press.

Weinfeld, Morton. 2018. *Like Everyone Else but Different: The Paradoxical Success of Canadian Jews*. McGill-Queen's Press.

Yiftachel, Oren. 1998. "Nation Building and the Division of Space: Ashkenazi Domination in the Israeli 'Ethnocracy.'" *Nationalism and Ethnic Politics* 4, 3.

Zhou, Steven. 2017. "Zionist Groups in Canada Are Jumping on the 'Creeping Sharia' Bandwagon." *BuzzFeed News*, Nov. 15.

Chapter 3

Singled Out

South Africa, Israel and Accusations of Unfair Criticism

Michael Bueckert

A t a town hall in St. Catharines, Ontario, in January 2019, Canadian Prime Minister Justin Trudeau made a case for treating certain criticisms of Israel as antisemitic.[1] After an audience member requested that he retract his previous condemnation of the Boycott, Divestment and Sanctions movement (BDS), Trudeau instead doubled down on his opposition, warning of a relationship between antisemitism and "undue criticism" of Israel. "When you have movements like BDS that single out Israel, that seek to delegitimize and in some cases demonize," Trudeau said, "we have to recognize that [these things] aren't acceptable" (Maloney 2019). Far from a unique response, Trudeau was referencing a popular framework developed by Natan Sharansky (2004) called the "3D test" or the "three Ds of antisemitism," which specifies that criticism of Israel can be considered antisemitic if it involves demonization, double standards or delegitimization. Israel's supporters frequently rely on this framework to evaluate the language and activism of Israel's critics, often pointing to it as evidence that Palestinian solidarity movements have crossed the line. When asked about BDS again a few months later, Trudeau specifically referenced the "3Ds" as a form of antisemitism applied "against the state of Israel" (*Global News* 2019).

One problem with Sharansky's framework, however, is that its own standards (the 3Ds) closely resemble the accusations levelled by other countries, including the former apartheid regime of South Africa, when faced with criticism themselves. If the framework can be applied to the discourse surrounding countries other than Israel, this may suggest that its explanatory power is weak and that it may be describing a dynamic other than antisemitism. In this chapter, I demonstrate this problem by comparing the claims of the 3Ds framework to the rhetoric of supporters of South Africa in the 1970s and 1980s, who consistently complained that the country was subject to unfair criticism from the anti-apartheid movement. The intent of this particular study is not to explore the similarities between the systems of oppression of the two countries, nor to evaluate in detail whether the framework of "apartheid" is applicable to Israel, even though it is increasingly and credibly understood in this way (see B'Tselem 2021; Human Rights Watch 2021; Ageel 2015; Soske and Jacobs 2015; Pappé 2015). Rather, the purpose here is to reveal the similarities in how South Africa and Israel have responded to criticism.

First, I discuss the origins of the 3D framework in the conversations around the "new antisemitism" in the early 2000s. Second, I draw primarily upon archival research of pro–South African propaganda to demonstrate how the friends of South Africa believed that the country was being demonized, "singled out" for criticism and held to a double standard, and who warned that South Africa's enemies posed an existential threat to the country itself. I conclude that the rhetorical parallels between the two cases suggest that the 3D framework is not a sufficient or reliable tool to evaluate antisemitism. In fact, it has merely codified the same rhetoric that was made by supporters of South Africa, turning the language of isolated regimes or pariah states into evidence that their opponents are motivated by antisemitism. I further suggest that these parallels in how South Africa and Israel have responded to their critics are rooted in their shared perspectives and experiences as settler-colonial states whose apartheid practices have made them targets of intense criticism and popular pressure on the world stage.

The New Antisemitism and the 3D Test

Morton Weinfeld, McGill professor of sociology and historian of the Jewish community in Canada, concluded in 2005 that most "traditional indicators" of antisemitism — for example, anti-Jewish attitudes, degree of income or education, and the exclusion of Jewish Canadians from business or social networks — "suggest that Canadian antisemitism has been declining since the 1950s and is relatively low by comparative standards" (Weinfeld 2005: 41; Brym, Shaffir and Weinfeld 2010). The exception to this trend is the increasing numbers of reported antisemitic incidents, including harassment, although this may be a result of better reporting practices (Brym, Shaffir and Weinfeld 2010: vi–vii; Brym 2019: 5). Despite this, Weinfeld (2005: 41) warns that there is still a "palpable concern" that antisemitism is a "real and growing danger," and Brym, Shaffir and Weinfeld (2010: vii–viii) claim that "in [the] place" of traditional forms of antisemitism "we witness growing attacks on Israel and Israeli policies, including the spread of Israel Apartheid Week on Canadian university and college campuses."

This claim that anti-Israel and anti-Zionist sentiments are driving a new resurgence in antisemitic activity has been repeatedly articulated by scholars and Zionist activists since the early 2000s. This was a period in which criticism of Israel was growing, largely in response to the Israeli crackdown against the Second Intifada, leading to key events, including the debates over Zionism as racism associated with the 2001 United Nations Durban conference and high profile demonstrations on Canadian campuses against pro-Israeli speakers. Irwin Cotler, a human rights lawyer, former Liberal federal cabinet minister and Canada's special envoy on combatting antisemitism, described this new trend in alarming terms:

> What we are witnessing today — which has been developing incrementally, almost imperceptibly, and sometimes indulgently, for some 30 years now — is a new, virulent, globalizing and even lethal anti-Jewishness reminiscent of the atmospherics of the 1930s, and without parallel or precedent since the end of the Second World War. This new anti-Jewishness overlaps with classical antisemitism, but is distinguishable from it. (Cotler 2004)

The "new antisemitism," as it is often called, is distinguished from classical antisemitism in that it no longer discriminates against individual Jews but is instead "aimed at the Jewish state" (Sharansky 2004) and therefore constitutes an assault on "the right of the Jewish people to live as an equal member of the family of nations" and discrimination "against Jews as people" rather than as individuals (Cotler 2004). According to David Matas (2005: 196), human rights lawyer and consul to B'nai Brith Canada, this phenomenon sits alongside Holocaust denial as one of the two main forms of antisemitism today and is "by far the greater threat to the Jewish community."

Supporters of the "new antisemitism" thesis are quick to clarify that there is a distinction between antisemitism and the legitimate criticism of Israeli policy (excluding criticism of the constitution of Israel itself), but precisely drawing this line has been notoriously difficult and subject to considerable debate. "In fact," write Brym, Shaffir and Weinfeld (2010: viii), "one of the challenges for Diaspora Jews involves distinguishing criticism of Israeli policies, anti-Zionism, and antisemitism." There is a general feeling that much criticism of Israel is ultimately motivated by antisemitic attitudes, which is difficult to parse out; even though "many critics of Israel are not anti-Semites," it would be "disingenuous" to claim that antisemitism does not play a role in "generating or sustaining anti-Zionist sentiment and action" (Brym, Shaffir and Weinfeld 2010: viii). Therefore, some authors have decided that criticism of Israel can be considered antisemitic when it becomes excessive — a determination which is of course entirely up for interpretation. For example, Matas (2005: 38) argues that when "extremely inflammatory language" is directed towards the State of Israel, this is "by implication" accusing the Jewish community itself of being "complicit in those crimes." Taking a somewhat different line of argument, Weinfeld (2005: 46) asserts that when criticism is "harsh," "one-sided" and has no "constructive purpose," then it is "indeed antisemitic in its consequences, and possibly in motive." Regardless of intentions, then, there may be antisemitic consequences of criticizing Israel in too strong terms, although those consequences are never spelled out.

In an attempt to overcome these ambiguities, Sharansky (2004) developed a conceptual framework for ostensibly distinguishing between legitimate criticism of Israel and antisemitism, known as the "three D's of antisemitism" or the "3D test." Following this method, any given criticism towards Israel is evaluated against 3Ds: 1) demonization, as when "Israel's actions are blown out of all sensible proportion"; 2) double standards, as when Israel is "singled out" or criticism is "applied selectively"; and 3) delegitimization, that is, when "Israel's fundamental right to exist is denied." If the criticism of Israel in question is determined to meet any of these criteria, then it is deemed antisemitic and therefore illegitimate.

The 3D test has proven to be tremendously popular and is promoted as a resource by organizations including the Anti-Defamation League and the Centre for Israel and Jewish Affairs. The same language is also used by liberal Zionist organization JSpaceCanada (n.d.), which opposes "any claims that question Israel's right to exist, and reject[s] attempts to vilify, demonize or delegitimize the State of Israel." The framework was codified by the US State Department in 2010 (State Department 2010), and its key elements were incorporated into the International

Holocaust Remembrance Alliance (IHRA)'s working definition of anti-semitism, which was adopted by the Trudeau government in 2019, followed by the provincial governments of Ontario in 2020 and Quebec in 2021. Promoting their government's decision to adopt the IHRA working definition, Liberal MPs Anthony Housefather and Michael Levitt (2019) explicitly pointed to "delegitimization, demonization, and double standards" as features of antisemitic rhetoric as defined by the IHRA.

The significant problems with the "new antisemitism" thesis are discussed elsewhere in this book, notably by Ralph in Chapter 5 and Keefer in Chapter 6. It is worth adding here that its central claim — that anti-Israel or anti-Zionist activity is driving a resurgence in antisemitism — does not have an empirical basis. According to Brym and Lenton (2021: 6), the "emerging consensus" among researchers on this topic is that there is relatively low overlap between anti-Israel and anti-Jewish attitudes. In fact, a public opinion poll conducted by EKOS in 2020 (Bueckert et al. 2020: 21) found evidence of the opposite: "Rather than seeing a correlation between criticism of Israel and otherwise antisemitic views … those who were most likely to see criticism of Israel as legitimate [including a boycott of Israel or comparisons with apartheid South Africa] were also the most likely to say that statements about Jewish-Canadians [such as the idea that Jews control the media] were antisemitic," and vice versa. While antisemitic attitudes can be found across the political spectrum, there appears to be more tolerance for those views among Israel's supporters than there is among its critics.

Even if there was a strong empirical or theoretical basis for the claims that anti-Israel sentiment is associated with antisemitic attitudes, however, the 3D test framework would still not be as useful as its popularity suggests. While it promises guidance, the framework does not solve the basic problem at hand — the chosen criteria are still subject to considerable interpretation and debate as matters of opinion and can easily be (mis)applied to any incident of criticism. As we will discover in the following sections, eerily similar complaints were made by supporters of apartheid South Africa in the 1970s and 80s, who believed that South Africa was being criticized entirely unfairly and who accused their critics of demonization, double standards and delegitimization against the country. This suggests the criticism that Israel receives may not be unique after all but is like that experienced by other states.

Demonization

South Africa's supporters frequently complained that the country was subject to an entirely negative and one-sided point of view, at odds with reality and poisoning the possibility of constructive debate. Glenn Babb, the notorious South African Ambassador to Canada from 1985–87, often criticized the "exaggerated rhetoric" used against South Africa,[2] arguing that the country was being "vilified" in a public debate full of "dismal ignorance."[3] Babb was unhappy that any good intentions by South Africans would be met with cynicism and "continuous sniping" and that people never gave the government any credit for its reforms, but instead had a "tendency to look at South Africa through glasses which will always make it look as though it was ill-intentioned towards the people it was governing."[4] Babb accused the government of being in an "incestuous relationship" with "anti-South Africa" groups and the African National Congress (ANC), who together were supposedly manufacturing an unfriendly attitude towards South Africa in Canada — Babb referred to them as the "the anti-South Africa industry."[5] His successor, Ambassador J.H. De Klerk, fretted publicly that the policy of the Canadian government was "self-righteous," "myopic and misguided," and "based on information gleaned from an alarmingly biased press."[6]

Bias was a common accusation from South Africa's supporters. In "Who's Behind the South African Crisis?," a 1985 pro-apartheid cartoon by Vic Lockman which was distributed in Canada by the far-right Canadian League of Rights, it was suggested that the common portrayal of apartheid as an "especially vile" form of discrimination was due to the failure of the "biased liberal media" to "present the full and honest facts."[7] South Africans have "responded negatively" to the attention they have received, wrote John Shingler, a South African expat, McGill professor and director of the Canadian–South African Society (CSAS), for they "see it as distorted and one-sided, and an over-simplification out of touch with the nitty-gritty of daily life. And they are right" (1984: 532). John Chettle, the North American director of the South Africa Foundation (an independent anti-sanctions group representing South African businesses) addressed the 1983 Annual General Meeting of the CSAS with a speech intending to correct "inaccuracies and misapprehensions" about the situation in South Africa, which he described as "entirely normal":

Which is to say that it is full of anxiety, irritation, recrimina-

tion and doubt. This is not a passing phase in South Africa. It is
something like a permanent condition. South Africans, having
a wonderful climate, magnificent scenery, beautiful women and
fine wines have only one other thing to bicker about, and that is
politics, and they do it with an enthusiasm which other peoples
reserve for weather, women and wines.[8]

The country's supporters argued that one-sided and anti–South
African attitudes were preventing reasonable conversation from taking place. As J.H. De Klerk lamented, the debate over South Africa was
characterized by "wildly emotional responses" rather than "rational
analysis."[9] Chettle (1972: 184) wrote about the "McCarthyism of the left"
on university campuses, which did not allow for positive views on South
Africa to be expressed, and complained about the "academic intoler-
ance" in the African Studies Association, which had been taken over by
"semi-militants." Shingler (1984: 536) similarly argued that debates had
become "unbalanced," "one-dimensional" and "wholly negative," and
that in this way South Africa itself had become "tainted" as a country,
making it impossible to take a "moderate" position or to oppose economic measures against South Africa:

> The result is that the vocabulary of the debate can be abusive
> and shrill. Those who adopt a moderate tone, or who try to see
> different aspects of this many-sided picture, or who travel to
> South Africa, become "fascists," "racists" and "agents of BOSS."

In this environment, any groups defending or connected to South Africa
were deemed illegitimate; Shingler (1984: 536) complained that ostensibly independent groups like the South Africa Foundation were often
"accused of receiving funds from the South African government and
denounced as an 'overseas agent of apartheid.'" In essence, the country
itself had been demonized, making any association toxic. Similarly, the
director general of the South Africa Foundation wrote of his frustrations that "anything that smacks of government funding is immediately
tainted and attacked as propaganda of an 'illegitimate' or 'racist' government" (de L. Sorour 1987: 182).

Double Standards

In 1969, South African propagandist Eschel Rhoodie (1969: 90, 113) railed against the "outrageous" and "crude double standard" that was applied against South Africa, claiming that activists had adopted a "hypocritical and self-righteous attitude towards South Africa in which the merits of South Africa's policies are completely lost." For Rhoodie, the negative attention his country received was almost without precedent: "Not since World War II (perhaps never in peace time) has any country been subjected to such a barrage of vehemently hostile criticism and so many attempts to force a change in its domestic policy, as in the case of South Africa" (1969: 82). This same case was made years later in the opening editorial of a glossy 1987 pro-apartheid magazine called "South Africa: Nation on Trial" (a special edition of the US-based Family Protection Scorecard): "South Africa bashing has become a national sport ... South Africa is judged by double, triple, and even quadruple standards. Many of these are highly subjective, intellectually inconsistent, biased, racist, and downright arrogant."[10]

Accusations of double standards were common, as South Africa's defenders argued that criticism against the country was being applied selectively, while anti-apartheid activists ignored other human rights abusers. This sentiment was also expressed by Babb in a backgrounder released by the Embassy, where he noted the "selectivity" with which "the world singles South Africa out as a special case."[11] For Shingler (1984: 530), this selectivity was an injustice and even a form of discrimination against white South Africans:

> I think that to single out South Africa on the grounds either of the violation of civil liberties or of institutionalized racial discrimination is a kind of inverted racism, on the basis of which South African whites are required to expiate a collective guilt for the accumulated wrongs committed during the past five centuries of western hegemony.

South Africa's supporters believed that the amount of attention the country received was irrational. As Babb wrote, the Canadian government had an "obsession" with South Africa.[12] Michael Christie, the general manager of the South Africa Foundation, wondered, "Why does a friendly country, with a history not dissimilar, come to preoccupy so intensely a great power like the United States?"[13] Similarly, Lockman's comic urged Americans not to "rashly cast off a valuable friend to satisfy the ravings of a radical minority!"[14] Worst of all was alleged hypocrisy of the United Nations, which they perceived to be unfairly targeting South Africa — and saw themselves to be in the same situation as Israel:

> To add to the confusion there is the position in the United Nations. There a ruthless majority has broken the charter to enforce its own will, and has threatened Israel with precisely the same illegal sanctions that have been visited on South Africa. To make matters worse they have used precisely the same rhetoric, and made precisely the same charges against Israel that they have previously made against South Africa. It has been enough to raise a thought, horrifying to some, that there may be as little justification in the charges against South Africa as in those against Israel. (Chettle 1975: 103)

South Africa's supporters accused their critics of focusing on apartheid while ignoring injustice elsewhere. To highlight this alleged hypocrisy, Glenn Babb made a highly publicized visit in 1987 to Peguis Indian Reserve (now Peguis First Nation) in Manitoba, with the intention of drawing attention to the problems faced by Indigenous communities, which, he claims, "were in many ways a lot worse than the black population of South Africa." Reflecting on that visit, he says that the idea behind it was to show that racial discrimination "was a universal problem in the world, not just in South Africa" (2017). Babb also argues that while boycotts against South Africa received a lot of publicity because the country was an "easy target," there was no attention paid to other countries' human rights abuses:

> You could feel comfortable with yourself, pat yourself on your shoulder and say "Yes, we are taking a moral stand about South Africa," but then you'd begin to wonder, where was the moral stand about China? And where was the moral stand about the caste system in India? Where was the moral stand about the invasion of Hungary? The moral stand about Stalinism? None of that ever came into the public, it was suppressed and kept under wraps, it was too delicate a measure. But [about] South Africa you could say what you liked. (Babb 2017)

Babb says it was "painful to be accused of things which in the end, had nothing by comparison to the other immoral public iterations in the rest of the world" (2017).

The complaint against "double standards" was expressed in many other forms. Lockman's comic criticized "Liberal do-gooders," asking, "Why don't they picket communist tyrants?"[15]; right-wing columnist Doug Collins asked if anti-apartheid activists have ever "organized a defence fund for the millions of Soviet citizens clapped into GULAG without trial?"[16]; and the *Hamilton Spectator* questioned the Canadian government's "double standard for Africa" of opposing apartheid while supporting African dictators.[17] Citizens for Foreign Aid Reform (C-FAR), an Ontario-based group run by white nationalist Paul Fromm, was furious when Prime Minister Mulroney announced trade restrictions on South Africa but not against "Marxist Nicaragua, genocidal Ethiopia" or the "unspeakable Soviet Union" and called the policy a "Tory betrayal."[18] C-FAR adapted its article into an advertisement titled "Mulroney's South African Sanctions Cost Jobs!" that was published by major newspapers, including the *Globe and Mail* and the *Ottawa Citizen* in November 1985; it lambasted Mulroney's "one-sided 'get-South Africa' threats" and "hypocritical" sanctions, and asked why Canada didn't boycott Tanzania or the USSR.[19]

While allegations of hypocrisy largely took an anti-communist or anti–Soviet Union ideological line, South Africa's defenders occasionally drew upon other examples. During a public forum on South African censorship in 1988, an event which was sponsored by the Canadian government and held at Ottawa City Hall, one audience member raised a question about why Canada and the United Nations would focus on South Africa while Israel was currently amidst a crackdown on Palestinian protestors (e.g., the First Intifada):

> What is this maniacal preoccupation with South Africa at the moment? I mean, 200 Palestinians are being shot to death in the streets on the West Bank you know. I hope [you] will use the same kind of energy to bring inequities in Israel to the general public.[20]

This quote is ironic considering the tendency of Israel's supporters today to suggest that an inappropriate amount of attention is being paid to Israel, even claiming that this is indicative of antisemitism on the part of Israel's critics. In fact, as we will see below, Israel and South Africa at the time shared a close and covert relationship (Polakow-Suransky 2011).

Delegitimization

Friends of South Africa believed that the anti-apartheid movement was aiming much further than a change in the country's racist policies — if successful, their demands would lead to violent overthrow or total destruction. "There is a war going on," warned conservative journalist Peter Worthington, "not against apartheid, but against South Africa itself."[21] Shingler expressed this same sentiment when he claimed that the criticism made against South Africa was "no longer of apartheid *as a policy,* but of South Africa *as a society.*"[22]

In this way, supporters felt they had to defend the legitimacy of the state, and of white South African society, which they believed to be facing an existential threat. As Chaliand (1985: 1) wrote in *South Africa International,* "South Africa — white South Africa — is a state, like Israel, whose survival is threatened in the long term, which is the situation for no other country in the world. Any defeat would be final." Canadian businessperson Conrad Black, rejecting calls to stop investing in South Africa in 1979, affirmed that white South Africans have a "perfect right to self-preservation" and said they should be "commended for having the collective pride and motivation to defend themselves" (quoted in Pratt 1997: 45–46). However, few would openly support the notion that apartheid South Africa had a positive right to exist, as such, and the idea of white self-determination was rarely advanced for an international audience in explicit terms. Instead, the more subtle underlying claim of most pro–South African propaganda was that white South Africans had a negative right to maintain things the way they were, or at least to adopt reforms on their own terms, if simply to prevent their own demise. In this way, the pro–South African lobby was adept at mobilizing an implicit idea of white self-determination as threatened by African and Marxist barbarism.

As international pressure grew upon South Africa to extend equal democratic rights to all, the country's defenders insisted that this was impossible, and they tried to prove this by pointing to neighbouring African countries. South African Ambassador J.H. De Klerk warned against pursuing a "majority rule" or "a simple one person one vote system" in South Africa, due to the "cataclysmic failure" of such constitutions in Africa.[23] Family Protection Scoreboard's South Africa issue claimed that the idea that "One man, one vote is the solution" was actually a media distortion, and that "it's impossible to name one African country where this has worked."[24] A former president of the South Africa Foundation, Jan S. Marais, argued that calls for "majority rule" amounted to judging South Africa by "Western standards while her conditions are largely determined by factors found throughout Africa: the poorest and most backward of all the continents":

> Black South Africans wryly ask which African country they should emulate as a model of majority rule government. Surely not Tanzania, whose ruler, Julius Nyerere, heads one of the world's 25 poorest nations, with no sign of democratic rule in sight? And what about Machel's Mozambique (not enough food, little development, no vote); or Cuban-occupied Angola; or starving Chad; or inflation-ravaged Nigeria, where the cost of living is double that of South Africa?[25]

While these arguments were sometimes framed within the problem of ethnic diversity in South Africa,[26] *Toronto Sun* columnist McKenzie Porter put this argument more directly when he argued that the real problem was "the inability of native blacks to govern well a modern state."[27]

Often these warnings would be quite graphic and apocalyptic. Lockman's comic argued that democracy failed elsewhere in Africa because "Western liberals" had "forced 'democratic elections' on people ill equipped for self rule!" and warned that democracy in South Africa would lead to dictatorship and famine.[28] Babb warned the *Ottawa Citizen* that "we can't afford a bloodbath,"[29] and Worthington accused anti-apartheid activists of wanting "bloodshed and an overthrow of the system at any price."[30] In a full page article for the *Globe and Mail* titled "The good side of white South Africa," Kenneth Walker wrote that one person, one vote "is a recipe for slaughter in South Africa," and that "if a bloodbath does occur, ill-informed churchmen, do-gooders, hypocrites who judge the Third World [sic] by a Western moral code, naive politicians and an irresponsible media will all have helped pull the trigger."[31] Once again, it was Porter who offered the most openly racist version of this argument, as published by the *Calgary Sun* in 1981:

> Left-lib denunciations of South African policy spring from the illusion that all men are equal. If the whites of South Africa enfranchised the primitive black majority, social chaos would

ensue. Within a decade the only civilized nation on the African continent would collapse.[32]

This apocalyptic vision would often feature the Soviet Union quite prominently as the agent of South Africa's destruction. "Goaded south by Soviet Agents, black Communist hordes would invade from the primordial North," wrote Porter on the prospect of ending apartheid, and "soon all Africa would groan under the Russian jackboot."[33] The Western Canadian Society of South Africa warned that the country was a bulwark against the Soviet Union, and its fall would threaten the West; therefore, "for the survival of all democracies we must support South Africa in their struggle against communist conquest."[34] Yet, the most striking image comes from Lockman's comic in a panel on the "Soviet encirclement of South Africa"; here the artist presents an image of a giant bear with a hammer-and-sickle, moving down from the African continent upon frightened South African factories and mines who are completely surrounded, and declaring "We shall drive South Africa into the Sea!"[35]

Conclusion: The Protest of Pariahs

If the rhetoric of Israel's supporters seems remarkably similar to the arguments used to defend apartheid South Africa, it is quite clearly not because the criticism of South Africa was also motivated by antisemitism or, for that matter, anti-white racism. Instead, the similarities are likely related to their shared histories as settler-colonial and apartheid states, desiring to be accepted among "Western" nations yet finding themselves subject to intensive isolation campaigns on the international stage.

Such similarities between South Africa and Israel extend beyond discussions of the contemporary BDS movement. Following the Six Day War in 1967, when Israel extended its control over the occupied Palestinian territories, South Africa and Israel began to see themselves as sharing a common experience as strategically important states that were being unfairly singled out by their critics. The reaction in South Africa to the Six Day War, as expressed in publications of the ruling National Party and the South African Jewish community, was a widespread understanding that the two countries had shared destinies and a common "struggle for existence" (Polakow-Suransky 2011: 46–47). For South Africans, Israel's victory was inspirational in that it proved the ability of small countries to "act vigorously in [their] own interest," and it even "gave an unexpected boost to the very doctrine of apartheid itself":

> Israel has no stomach for the inclusion of a large Arab population within its permanent political boundaries. To remain a predominantly Jewish State is regarded as an essential guarantee of security and survival. During Dr. Verwoerd's funeral oration, while all South Africa listened, the speaker had prophetically said as much by likening the Republic of Israel, equally encircled, equally laborious, equally concerned with the blessings of peace, equally determined to persevere. (De Kiewiet 1970: 3–4)

In the war's aftermath, this idea of shared interests led to growing bilateral relations between the countries, even as Israel's Labor party was officially denouncing the apartheid regime; this period included the 1968 formation of the Knesset's Israel–South Africa Friendship League and secret cooperation between officials throughout the 1970s on security and a joint nuclear program. South African Prime Minister Vorster's highly publicized trip to Israel in 1976 was followed by much warmer relations with Begin's Likud government after 1977, whose ethnonationalist ideology brought the countries deeper into a "shared worldview" (Polakow-Suransky 2011: 53–54, 89, 110). This process mirrored the growing relationship between the African National Congress and the Palestinian Liberation Organization, as well as an emerging paradigm among African countries that "white rule in Southern Africa constituted a neo-imperial historical phenomenon of the same type as … Zionism" (Miller 2016: 85). Cooperation between Israel and South Africa well until the end of the 1980s was thus grounded in their shared self-perception of victimhood and their outsider status as "pariah states" (van Vuuren 2017: 452–53, 468–85).

Perhaps it is because of this shared experience and self-perception that the rhetoric from South Africa and its supporters can fit comfortably within the framework of the "three D's of antisemitism." Even if the terminology used was not always identical, South Africa's supporters insisted that criticism of the country was unfair, in a manner that is consistent with the allegations of demonization, double standards and delegitimization. Of course, there are important differences between how these allegations operate in these two cases — whereas very few people would have upheld Afrikaner self-determination as an important value to protect, the idea of Jewish self-determination as manifested in the State of Israel has a great deal of public support and sympathy, in part due to religious reasons (for example, Christian Zionism), as well as a response to the long history of anti-Jewish discrimination, violence and genocide. Therefore, Israel's "right to exist" possesses a certain moral legitimacy that South Africa never had and to which many people consciously give precedence over the realization of Palestinian rights. Relatedly, the experience of antisemitic attitudes and violence within Western societies gives plausibility to the argument that criticism of Israel may be *motivated* by racism, whereas arguments that opposition to South Africa might be based on anti-white racism, to the extent that these were ever offered, were not convincing.

What this comparative analysis shows, however, is that the 3D test is inadequate, as are the various frameworks which have adopted its standards, including the IHRA definition of antisemitism. In effect, Israel's supporters have bundled together a number of rhetorical strategies — ones which are not unique to criticism of that country but have been used by other pariah states — and have codified them in a framework that is supposed to prove antisemitism. The problem is not just a lack of precision but the standards themselves, which are claims about a lack of fairness. It is self-evident that any country facing significant criticism will draw upon similar claims. Absurdly, it also suggests that criticism of a state should be understood as equivalent to discrimination against minorities, and that each should be addressed by governments in the same way.

If the 3D framework is not useful for challenging racism, its basic conceit may undermine human rights initiatives — it adopts rhetoric that has been historically used to justify racist and oppressive regimes, and uses it as a weapon against its critics, accusing them of being racist for criticizing Israel. In fact, the IHRA definition of antisemitism has been widely interpreted as a direct threat to pro-Palestinian activists and the right to dissent, precisely because it conflates antisemitism with criticism of Israel in a way consistent with the 3D framework. For this reason, the IHRA has been strongly opposed by a wide range of civil society actors, including the BC Civil Liberties Association (BCCLA 2019), the Canadian Labour Congress (CLC 2020), the Canadian Federation of Students (CFS 2020), the Ontario Confederation of University Faculty Associations (OCUFA 2020), more than 650 Canadian academics (IJV

2020) and more than 140 Jewish faculty in Canada (*Canadian Dimension* 2021), and the New Democratic Party (NDP) has expressed concerns that the IHRA "could be a threat for people who legitimately denounce grave human rights abuses by the government of Israel against Palestinians" (quoted in Forrest 2019).

Finally, the framework also clearly imposes unreasonable and ahistorical conditions upon activism. Today, the very fact that the BDS movement focuses its attention on Israel (and not Syria, for example), is regularly used as evidence that BDS is antisemitic. When this line of argument was levelled towards the South African anti-apartheid movement, however, it simply was not convincing, perhaps because "singling out" a country is inherent to the nature of targeted human rights campaigns — and especially campaigns which are initiated by movements in said country, such as the African National Congress or the Palestinian BDS National Committee. Ironically, supporters of the 3D test are demanding standards that are not applied to any other social movement. Moreover, both states have singled themselves out as exceptional, boasting of being ostensibly the only democracies in backwards regions surrounded by autocratic regimes. These grandiose claims have made it easy for critics to point out the failures of South Africa and Israel to live up to their stated values, while also aggravating the self-perception of these states that they are being held to a double standard. In this case, however, what is perceived as a "double standard" is just the application of a universal anti-apartheid standard to a country which refuses to be held accountable.

Notes

1. This chapter is adapted from several components in my PhD thesis: Michael Bueckert, "Boycotts and Backlash: Canadian Opposition to Boycott, Divestment and Sanctions (BDS) Movements from South Africa to Israel," unpublished PhD dissertation, Carleton University, 2020. A short blog post with an earlier version of the arguments in this chapter was previously published under a Creative Commons licence on the website *Africa Is a Country*, as "When is it antisemitic to criticize Israel?" March 26, 2019 <https://africasacountry.com/2019/03/when-is-it-antisemitic-to-criticize-israel>.
2. Laurie S. Wiseberg and Harry Scoble Human Rights Internet Collection, University of Connecticut Libraries Archives and Special Collections, Storrs, CT (hereafter WSC), Box 444, Folder 10, Glenn Babb, "Blind Spots I have Observed in Canada," *Influence Magazine*, February-March 1987.
3. WSC, Box 444, Folder 10, "South African Ambassador outlines history of apartheid," newspaper clipping, *Kemptville Weekly Advance*, March 5, 1986.

4. wsc, Box 444, Folder 10, "Freedom in South Africa: Envoy, banned editor differ," newspaper clipping, *Globe and Mail*, April 23, 1986.
5. wsc, Box 444, Folder 10, Glenn Babb, "Blind Spots I have Observed in Canada," *Influence Magazine*, February-March 1987.
6. wsc, Box 444, Folder 10, J.H. De Klerk, "Speaking Notes for address to Rotary [Hamilton, Ontario]," South African Embassy press release, March 25, 1988.
7. wsc, Box 452, Folder 5, Vic Lockman, "Who's Behind the South African Crisis?" cartoon, June 10, 1985. According to marginalia, this comic was mailed as a supplementary section with "On Target" and "cis," publications of the Canadian League of Rights.
8. Fonds Maurice Sauvé, Library and Archives Canada, Ottawa (hereafter fms), Box 140, Folder 1, John Chettle, "Speech to Annual General Meetings of the Canadian — South African Societ, Montreal and Toronto," October 17 and 20, 1983.
9. wsc, Box 444, Folder 10, "South African Ambassador outlines history of apartheid," newspaper clipping, *Kemptville Weekly Advance,* March 5, 1986.
10. wsc, Box 444, Folder 20, Editorial note by David W. Balsiger in *South Africa: Nation on Trial*, Family Protection Scoreboard South Africa Special Edition, 1987.
11. wsc, Box 444, Folder 10, Glenn Babb, "Press Communique issued by the South African Ambassador," September 13, 1985.
12. wsc, Box 444, Folder 10, Glenn Babb, "Blind Spots I have Observed in Canada," *Influence Magazine*, February–March 1987.
13. wsc, Box 444, Folder 20, Michael Christie, "Immorality of Disinvestment," in *South Africa: National on Trial*, Family Protection Scoreboard South Africa Special Edition, 1987.
14. wsc, Box 452, Folder 5, Vic Lockman, "Who's Behind the South African Crisis?" cartoon, June 10, 1985.
15. wsc, Box 452, Folder 5, Vic Lockman, "Who's Behind the South African Crisis?" cartoon, June 10, 1985.
16. wsc, Box 452, Folder 5, Doug Collins, "Fund Folk Folly," *West Side Week*, December, 7 1986.
17. fms, Box 177, Folder 19, "Double standard for Africa [editorial]," newspaper clipping, *Hamilton Spectator,* August 17, 1981.
18. wsc, Box 452, Folder 5, Citizens for Foreign Aid Reform, "Mulroney's Trade Restriction on South Africa: The Tory Betrayal," *c-far Newsletter*, Number 138, August 1, 1985.
19. wsc, Box 452, Folder 5, "Mulroney's South African Sanctions Cost Canadian Jobs!" Advertisement sponsored by Citizens for Foreign Aid Reform, published in the *Globe and Mail*, November 13, 1985, and the *Ottawa Citizen*, November 28, 1985.
20. wsc, Box 452, Folder 4, Transcript, "Public Forum on South African Censorship and Propaganda" [issue 1, tape 1, page 40], Department of External Affairs, Ottawa City Hall, August 2, 1988.
21. anc Canada Mission, anc Archives, University Library, University of Fort Hare, Alice, Eastern Cape (hereafter anc), Box 28, Folder 64, Peter Worthington, "Forward," *The ANC Method: Violence. The Liberation Struggle in South Africa* [booklet accompanying documentary], September 1987.
22. John David Shingler Fonds, McGill University Archives, Montreal, Quebec, MG 4225, Box 3, Memo from John Shingler to John Chettle (South Africa Foundation), page 42, August 1982. Emphasis in original.
23. wsc, Box 444, Folder 10, J.H. De Klerk, "Speech by Ambassador JH De Klerk,

McPhail Memorial Baptist Church Dinner, National Press Club," communique of the Embassy of South Africa in Ottawa, September 14, 1990.

24. wsc, Box 444, Folder 20, David W. Balsiger, "News Media Distortions Exposed," in *South Africa: National on Trial,* Family Protection Scoreboard South Africa Special Edition, 1987.

25. wsc, Box 444, Folder 10, Jan S. Marais, *The New South Africa: A Unique Opportunity,* August/September 1982.

26. wsc, Box 444, Folder 10, Jan S. Marais, *The New South Africa: A Unique Opportunity,* August/September 1982.

27. fms, Box 140, Folder 1, McKenzie Porter, clipping of untitled column, *Toronto Sun,* January 23, 1984.

28. wsc, Box 452, Folder 5, Vic Lockman, "Who's Behind the South African Crisis?" cartoon, June 10, 1985..

29. wsc, Box 444, Folder 10, "South Africa: Its ambassador to Canada tells his government's side," newspaper clipping, *Ottawa Citizen,* September 14, 1985.

30. wsc, Box 444, Folder 10, "ANC says video by Canadian journalist resembles S. African govt. propaganda," newspaper clipping, *Ottawa Citizen,* October 3, 1989.

31. wsc, Box 444, Folder 10, Kenneth Walker, "The good side of white South Africa," newspaper clipping, *Globe and Mail,* December 2, 1986.

32. fmsc, Box 177, Folder 19, McKenzie Porter, "It's an illusion," clipping of column, *Calgary Sun,* October 6, 1981.

33. fmsc, Box 177, Folder 19, McKenzie Porter, "It's an illusion," clipping of column, *Calgary Sun,* October 6, 1981.

34. ANC, Box 28, Folder 64, Letter from Western Canadian Society of South Africa to "Friends of South Africa," September 16, 1987.

35. wsc, Box 452, Folder 5, Vic Lockman, "Who's Behind the South African Crisis?" cartoon, June 10, 1985.

References

Ageel, Ghada (ed.). 2015. *Apartheid in Palestine: Hard Laws and Harder Experiences.* Edmonton: University of Alberta Press.

Anti-Defamation League. n.d. "Response to Common Inaccuracy: Israel Critics Are Anti-Semites." <https://web.archive.org/web/20180629155644/adl.org/resources/fact-sheets/response-to-common-inaccuracy-israel-critics-are-anti-Semites>.

B'Tselem. 2021. "A Regime of Jewish Supremacy from the Jordan River to the Mediterranean Sea: This Is Apartheid." January 12. <btselem.org/publications/fulltext/202101_this_is_apartheid>.

Babb, Glenn. 2017. Interview with the author, April 26.

bccla (British Columbia Civil Liberties Association). 2019. "The bccla Opposes the International Campaign to Adopt the International Holocaust Remembrance Association (ihra) Definition of Antisemitism." June 18. <bccla.org/our_work/the-bccla-opposes-the-international-campaign-to-adopt-the-international-holocaust-remembrance-association-ihra-definition-of-antisemitism/>.

Brym, Robert. 2019. "Antisemitic and Anti-Israel Actions and Attitudes in Canada and Internationally: A Research Agenda." *Patterns of Prejudice* 53. <doi.org/10.1080/0031322X.2019.1614295>.

Brym, Robert, and Rhonda Lenton. 2021. "Antisemitism, Anti-Israelism and Canada in Context." Online advance draft, to be published in *Critical Perspectives on Jewish*

Identity, Israel-Diaspora Relations, and Antisemitism, edited by Robert Kenedy, Uzi Rebhun and Carl Stephan Erlich. New York: Springer. Online version: <academia. edu/44808306/Antisemitism_anti_Israelism_and_Canada_in_context>.

Brym, Robert, William Shaffir, and Morton Weinfeld. 2010. "Introduction to the Wynford Edition." In *The Jews in Canada*, second edition, edited by Robert Brym, William Shaffir, and Morton Weinfeld. Don Mills, ON: Oxford University Press Canada.

Bueckert, Michael, Thomas Woodley, Grafton Ross, et al. 2020. "Canadians Reject Branding Criticism of Israel as Antisemitic." Part 3 of a national opinion survey of Canadians conducted June 5–10, 2020. Survey conducted by EKOS Research Associates, co-sponsored by Canadians for Justice and Peace in the Middle East, Independent Jewish Voices Canada, and United Network for Justice and Peace in Palestine-Israel. <www.cjpme.org/survey2020_r3>.

Canadian Dimension. 2021. "Jewish Faculty in Canada Against the Adoption of the IHRA Working Definition of Antisemitism." Open letter. April 9. <canadiandimension. com/articles/view/jewish-faculty-in-canada-against-the-adoption-of-the-ihra-working-definition-of-antisemitism>.

Canadian Jewish News. 2019. "Canadian Government Adopts IHRA Definition." June 25. <cjnews.com/news/canada/canadian-government-adopts-ihra-definition-of-anti-semitism>.

CFS (Canadian Federation of Students). 2020. "CFS Supports IJV's Definition of Antisemitism." February 26. <cfs-fcee.ca/cfs-supports-ijvs-definition-of-antisemitism/>.

Chaliand, Gérard. 1985. "French Impressions of South Africa II." *South Africa International* 14, 1.

Chettle, John. 1972. "Foreign Reports: Washington." *South Africa International* 2, 3.

___. 1975. "Foreign Reports: Washington." *South Africa International* 6, 2.

CLC (Canadian Labour Congress). 2020. Tweet. March 6. <twitter.com/CanadianLabour/status/1235992781635629057?s=20>.

Cotler, Irwin. 2004. "Identifying the New Anti-Semitism." Feb. 28. <aish.com/jw/s/48892472.html>.

De Kiewiet, Cornelis Willem. 1970. "The World and Pretoria." *South Africa International* 1, 1.

De L. Sorour, J. 1987. "Director General's Report." *South Africa International* 17, 4.

Forrest, Maura. 2019. "There's a Debate over Canada's New Definition of Anti-Semitism, and It Might Sound Strangely Familiar." *National Post*, June 27. <nationalpost.com/news/politics/theres-a-debate-over-canadas-new-definition-of-anti-semitism-and-it-might-sound-strangely-familiar>.

Global News. 2019. "Trudeau Says Canada Believes in a Two State Solution with Israel and Palestine." [Video.] April 16. <globalnews.ca/video/5175006/trudeau-says-canada-believes-in-a-two-state-solution-with-israel-and-palestine>.

Hilf, Rudolph. 1987. "Consensus Politics — an Answer to South Africa?" *South Africa International* 18, 1.

Housefather, Anthony, and Michael Levitt. 2019. "Housefather & Levitt: Why Canada's Adopting the IHRA Definition of Anti-Semitism." *Canadian Jewish News*, June 25. <cjnews.com/perspectives/opinions/housefather-levitt-why-canadas-adopting-the-ihra-definition-of-anti-semitism>.

Human Rights Watch. 2021. *A Threshold Crossed: Israeli Authorities and the Crimes of Apartheid and Persecution.* Report, April 27. <hrw.org/report/2021/04/27/threshold-crossed/israeli-authorities-and-crimes-apartheid-and-persecution>.

IJV (Independent Jewish Voices Canada). 2020. "Open Letter from 650+ Canadian Academics Opposing the IHRA Definition of Antisemitism." February 27. <ijvcanada. org/open-letter-from-canadian-academics-opposing-the-ihra-definition-of-antisemitism/>.

JSpaceCanada. n.d. "Where We Stand." <jspacecanada.ca/where-we-stand/>.

Maloney, Ryan. 2019. "Trudeau Says He Will 'Continue to Condemn the BDS Movement' at St. Catharines Town Hall." *Huffington Post Canada*, January 16. <huffpost.com/ archive/ca/entry/trudeau-bds-movement_a_23644306>.

Matas, David. 2005. *Aftershock: Anti-Zionism and Antisemitism*. Toronto: Dundurn Group.

Miller, Jamie. 2016. *An African Volk: The Apartheid Regime and Its Search for Survival*. New York: Oxford University Press.

OCUFA (Ontario Confederation of University Faculty Associations). 2020. "OCUFA Opposes Ontario Government Circumventing Democracy and Public Debate on Bill 168." October 28. <ocufa.on.ca/press-releases/ocufa-opposes-ontario-government-circumventing-democracy-and-public-debate-on-bill-168/>.

Pappé, Ilan (ed.). 2015. *Israel and South Africa: The Many Faces of Apartheid*. London: Zed Books.

Polakow-Suransky, Sasha. 2011. *The Unspoken Alliance: Israel's Secret Relationship with Apartheid South Africa*. New York: Vintage.

Pratt, Renate. 1997. *In Good Faith: Canadian Churches Against Apartheid*. Waterloo, ON: Wilfrid Laurier University Press.

Rhoodie, Eschel. 1969. *The Paper Curtain*. Johannesburg: Voortrekkerpers.

Sharansky, Natan. 2004. "3D Test of Anti-Semitism: Demonization, Double Standards, Delegitimization." *Jewish Political Studies Review* 16.

Shingler, John. 1984. "Canadian Universities and South Africa." *South Africa International* 14, 4.

Soske, Jon, and Sean Jacobs (eds.). 2015. *Apartheid Israel: The Politics of an Analogy*. Chicago: Haymarket Books.

Van Vuuren, Hennie. 2017. *Apartheid Guns and Money: A Tale of Profit*. Johannesburg, South Africa: Jacana Media.

Weinfeld, Morton. 2005. "The Changing Dimensions of Contemporary Canadian Antisemitism." In *Contemporary Antisemitism: Canada and the World*, edited by Derek J. Penslar, Michael R. Marrus, and Janice Stein. Toronto: University of Toronto Press.

Part II

Insights for Possible Futures

Chapter 4

Israeli Apartheid Week
Popular Dissent, Creative Intervention

Rana Nazzal Hamadeh

On March 8, 2020, Angela Davis delivered the keynote address for the sixteenth annual Israeli Apartheid Week (IAW) at the University of Toronto, the campus where the global movement was started sixteen years earlier. Sharing her vision of abolition and internationalism, Davis spoke about the fundamental indivisibility of struggles against injustice everywhere:

> The important activism and advocacy of Students Against Israeli Apartheid, Students for Justice in Palestine, BDS activism and others throughout this region are helping to transform the landscape of the campaign for solidarity with Palestine and, in the process, is strengthening our struggles against racism and our overall quest for social justice. These organizations, these and other organizations and activists, are a part of a strong global community of people who understand that their stance against the occupation of Palestine is linked to progressive movements against racism, misogyny, xenophobia, assault on the environment and all efforts to make this planet a better place for us all. (UofT Divest)

This iteration of IAW took place in exceptional circumstances: following a series of moves by the United States to bolster Israeli apartheid through the "Deal of the Century" and at the onset of an unprecedented global pandemic. Even with many events moving online, IAW 2020 was successfully held in hundreds of cities around the world. Virtual events traversed continents to draw connections between militarization, logics of carcerality and white supremacy and resistance to the Israel–United States annexation plan. In her keynote, Davis thanked IAW organizers for their many years of insistence on drawing connections between international movements. Indeed, IAW has become not only a propelling force for the Palestinian liberation movement but an annual space for the building of coalitions and the sharing of solidarity between international movements.

IAW is a largely decentralized annual event united by a shared goal: to raise awareness about Israeli apartheid and settler-colonialism and to respond to the Palestinian call for Boycotts, Divestments and Sanctions (BDS). The week has grown to be held on hundreds of campuses and in cities across the world and has facilitated a massive transformation in popular discourse on Palestine and Israel, popularizing the apartheid analysis and enabling the success of numerous campaigns to divest from Israeli apartheid. It has also enabled us to explore the ways that our liberation is tied to one another. As the Palestinian-American attorney Ahmad Abuznaid said on Palestinian solidarity with Black communities, our experiences "do exist at the crossroads of oppression, but our experiences also exist at the crossroads of justice and liberation" (ADC 2020).

I have been involved in IAW for over a decade — as an organizer, a speaker and an attendee. I participated in IAW for the first time in 2009 while I was a high school student in Ottawa, coordinating with the organizing group Students Against Israeli Apartheid (SAIA) at Carleton University to engage other young students in the Palestine solidarity movement. After spending time living and organizing in the Palestinian West Bank, I attended Carleton and became heavily involved in organizing IAW on the campus between 2012 and 2017 and have been connected with IAW organizers at Ryerson University and University of Toronto since 2019. I came to this work as someone impacted directly by the apartheid policies supported implicitly or explicitly by the Canadian state and its institutions, but also as someone wishing to strengthen my analysis and build alongside other communities on the path to justice. Speaking from insight into the unique challenges facing those who assert Palestinian rights in Canada, this chapter looks at what makes IAW a transformative part of the movement for Palestinian rights in Canada and beyond. I explore how IAW is a comprehensive global movement and draw on my experiences with SAIA Carleton to emphasize patterns of repression faced by IAW organizers on campuses across the country. Although attacks on IAW and BDS have been unremitting, the past sixteen years of growth and creative interventions are a testament to the resilience of this movement.

Name and Shame:
The Apartheid and Settler-Colonial Analysis

The first objective of IAW is to raise awareness about Israel's apartheid policies and ongoing settler-colonialism. This analysis is cemented in its very name, Israeli Apartheid Week. The term "apartheid" is not used to provoke or captivate, but it is a legal term which describes a systemic form of discrimination and domination found in many of the policies enacted by Israel's regime. Apartheid is not only prohibited in international law but classified as a crime against humanity by the 1973 International Convention on the Suppression and Punishment of the Crime of Apartheid and the 1998 Rome Statute of the International Criminal Court. The Convention and the Rome Statute, recognized by governments worldwide, together offer a clear definition of apartheid, and since 2007 authorities in the UN have increasingly used the term to describe Israeli practices (Dugard and Reynolds 2013: 869, 878–81). The work of international legal and human rights scholars to apply this legal definition to the case of Israel has confirmed what Palestinians already knew: that the institutionalized racist policies of the Israeli state constitute apartheid. Not surprisingly, the Israel and Zionist lobby has taken issue with this association, fearing that the moral consensus that South African apartheid was wrong would spread to the Israeli context. According to the senior vice-president of the Centre for Israel and Jewish Affairs (CIJA), the largest pro-Israel lobby group in Canada: "The comparison of contemporary Israel to the state sanctioned system of racial separation and degradation in apartheid South Africa is an historical lie of massive proportions, designed only to set the foundation for Israel's demise" (Shear 2013). Historian Catherine Chatterley of the Canadian Institute for the Study of Anti-Semitism similarly claimed that "pro-Palestinian activists" fabricated the notion of Israeli apartheid "to delegitimize the State of Israel by comparing it to racist South Africa" (quoted in IJV Canada 2019). However, many prominent South African leaders have been vocal about how their visits to occupied Palestine provoked painful memories of apartheid, and the South African government has decried Israeli policies as reminiscent of apartheid since the early 2000s (Dugard and Reynolds 2013: 868). A 2009 legal study commissioned by the Government of South Africa confirmed that the Israeli occupation amounted to "a colonial enterprise which implements a system of apartheid" (Tilley 2009: 13), and in a 2017 report prepared for the UN, Richard Falk and Virginia Tilley wrote: "Beyond a reasonable doubt ... Israel is guilty of policies and practices that constitute the crime of apartheid as legally defined in instruments of international law" (191). In short, the apartheid analysis was applied to Israel long before the launch of IAW, and the legal evidence proving its applicability continues to grow (e.g., Davis 1987; Shah 1997; Bisharah 2002; Davis 2003).

The apartheid analysis has also furthered a deeper understanding of the colonial reality of Zionism and enables historical and contemporary links to be drawn to other peoples' struggles. From the beginning, IAW events built an understanding of Zionism as settler-colonialism, and this work is significant because it also allows us to forge links with other Indigenous struggles and envision liberation beyond the confines of international law. This understanding is bolstered by the work of Palestinian scholars such as Nadera Shalhoub-Kevorkian (2014), Yara Hawari (Hawari, Plonski and Weizman 2019) and Noura Erakat and Tareq Radi (2016), who have contributed to the growing body of work that explores Zionism as a settler-colonial structure. The primary pursuit of settler-colonialism is land, requiring the disappearance of Indigenous Peoples to clear the land for settlement. Over the last century, the majority of Palestinians have been forcibly expelled from their lands, prevented from returning and replaced exclusively by Jewish Israeli settlers. If we understand Israel as a settler-colonial project, then we understand that it must be challenged through decolonization and not merely the pursuit of equal rights in law. Liberation must include the return of Palestinian refugees to their lands and homes and the dismantling of colonies as well as all military and civil institutions of religio-racial Jewish supremacy. As Tuck and Yang explain, "Decolonization specifically requires the repatriation of Indigenous land and life. It is not a metonym for social justice" (2012: 21). The Palestinian-American human rights attorney Noura Erakat elaborates:

> Striving to dismantle the legal barriers to inequality without addressing the territorial dimensions of the Palestinian struggle is not enough. Palestinian citizens of Israel originally from Ikrit and Kufr Bir'im, for example, do not just want better education, health care, and job opportunities within the state, they seek to return and rebuild their demolished villages. (2019: 231–32)

For those of us familiar with the Palestinian experience, there is nothing unique about the assertion that Israel's regime amounts to a system of racial segregation, but the way that IAW catapulted the notion of Israeli apartheid into popular discourse was indeed groundbreaking. As more and more university students and their communities are invited into the movement for Palestinian rights through IAW, they are introduced to richer understandings of the issue that go beyond slogans and media snippets, and they are provided with a clear mechanism for taking action: the boycott movement.

A Pathway to Action:
Responding to the Palestinian Call for BDS

The second aim of IAW is to build support for the Palestinian campaign for BDS. In 2004, the Palestinian Campaign for the Academic and Cultural Boycott of Israel (PACBI) was launched by several Palestinian associations representing academics, intellectuals, artists, educators and more. A year later and just months after the first IAW took place, the broader call for Boycotts, Divestments and Sanctions (BDS) was initiated by Palestinian civil society, including political parties, unions, NGOs and coalitions representing "the three integral parts of the people of Palestine: Palestinian refugees, Palestinians under occupation and Palestinian citizens of Israel" (Palestinian Civil Society 2005). BDS was a direct response to the decades-long and ongoing failure of the international community to hold Israel accountable for its crimes, and as Hassan Husseini explains in Chapter 9, BDS would bolster the effectiveness of campus activism in exposing and challenging Israeli crimes. Through the specific tactics of boycotts, divestments and sanctions, BDS gives individuals (including consumers, academics and artists) as well as members of institutions (including universities and churches) a means to mount pressure on Israel until it complies with international law and Palestinian rights. Inspired by the South African anti-apartheid boycott movement, the BDS movement has three demands: end the occupation and colonization of all Arab lands; recognize the rights of the Arab-Palestinian citizens of Israel to full equality; and respect the right of Palestinian refugees to return to their homes (Palestinian Civil Society 2005). As a grassroots call, BDS has been taken up by unions, academic associations and institutions around the world.

To understand the effectiveness of this movement, one only need look at the aggressive counter-mobilization against BDS by Israel and its advocates. Israel has dedicated tens of millions of dollars to a global anti-BDS response and has passed laws against BDS that bar the entry into Israel (and by extension, Palestine) of anyone who promotes it (Baroud and Rubeo 2018). The apartheid state has also invested heavily in public relations campaigns like Brand Israel, which was established in 2005 — the same year as IAW and BDS. Produced by the Israeli Foreign Ministry, Brand Israel sent writers, theatre companies, exhibitions and artists abroad to beautify Israel's image in the West. The campaign tried to bolster Israel's reputation in the United States and Europe as liberal, cosmopolitan and Western, in direct contrast with the supposedly backward, violent and unenlightened Arab and Islamic countries surrounding it (Puar 2011). More troubling, Israel has been pushing for anti-BDS legislation that suppress the right to boycott; in the United States, anti-boycott laws and executive orders have passed in dozens of states and anti-boycott acts have been introduced federally (Palestine Legal 2020).

In a testament to BDS's impact, Israel apologists are deploying increasingly absurd attacks on the movement without engaging with its actual demands. This includes Prime Minister Trudeau, who, as Husseini discusses in Chapter 9, was among a number of provincial and federal politicians who have tried to malign BDS and IAW as having "no place on Canadian campuses" (Trudeau 2015). In a 2018 speech Trudeau went further to compare BDS to violent antisemitism:

> Jewish institutions and neighbourhoods are still being vandalized with swastikas. Jewish students still feel unwelcomed and uncomfortable on some of our college and university campuses because of BDS related intimidation. And out of our entire community of nations, it is Israel whose right to exist is most widely and wrongly questioned. Discrimination and violence against Jewish people in Canada and around the world continues at an alarming rate. Less than two weeks ago, not too far from here, a gunman opened fire on worshippers at the Tree of Life synagogue in Pittsburgh, killing 11 people and wounding six others. (*Global News* 2018)

The conflation of a nonviolent peoples' movement for liberation with the actions of a murderous white supremacist is almost too absurd to address. The BDS movement and IAW have always been clear — through a basis of unity, through official statements and through the work itself — that they are part of an anti-racist movement that challenges the violence of all forms of racism. But attacks like Trudeau's, which are empty of substance and rely on racist tropes of the "violent Arab," have forced Palestine advocates to dedicate a great deal of time to articulating a defence of a peaceful tactic. As Diana Ralph breaks down in Chapter 5, while Canadian politicians often claim their support for Israel is motivated by opposing antisemitism, the real reasons are related to politics, power and trade, including Canadian arms sales to Israel and a joint Canada-Israel security partnership. In the face of such attacks, I recall Toni Morrison's words of warning: "The function, the very serious function of racism is distraction. It keeps you from doing your work. It keeps you explaining, over and over again, your reason for being" (Portland State Library Special Collections 1975). IAW carves out a space for Palestinians, and those in solidarity with us, to move beyond reactionary responses. The week holds space for deeper conversations that uplift our collective understanding and allow us to undertake the difficult task of imagining a radically different future.

Growing Alongside Each Other: Shared Commitments and the Rhythm of Law

IAW has a centralized "basis of unity" that allows groups around the world to organize IAW events that are relevant to their local contexts while holding to a set of uncompromising principles. This basis of unity, which reiterates the mandate of IAW to raise awareness and support BDS, includes a commitment to anti-racism and anti-oppression:

> We understand Israeli apartheid as one element of a global system of economic and military domination. To this end, we stand in solidarity with all oppressed groups around the world, in particular, Indigenous communities suffering under settler colonialism, exploitation and displacement.
>
> We are against the racist ideology of Zionism, which is the impetus for Israeli colonialism, because it inherently discriminates against those who are not Jewish. We are against all forms of discrimination, and believe that there can never be justice without the restoration of full rights for everyone, regardless of religion, ethnicity, or nationality. (IAW International Coordinating Committee 2020)

In 2019, IAW events around the world were held under the theme "Stop Arming Colonialism," and in 2020 the IAW theme was "United Against Racism." Despite the decentralized nature of IAW, coordination between IAW organizers in different campuses and cities across Canada has allowed us to draw inspiration from one another, explore similar topics and share speakers. In 2014, for example, Yusuf Saloojee — who served as representative of the South African National Congress (ANC) in Canada during the anti-apartheid movement — was flown to Canada to present the keynote address at IAWs across Ontario, including London, Waterloo, Toronto and Ottawa. All these years later, what I recall most from his Ottawa presentation was his description of the harassment he faced from apartheid supporters in Canada at the height of his campaign. As a contingent of Zionist students at the back of the room interrupted the lecture with provocative comments, Saloojee urged us to remain resilient, reminding us that the South African anti-apartheid boycott movement was active for three decades before it became popular around the world. The coordinating of shared speakers across IAW events means that attendees across different cities heard this same message of critical hope and steadfastness.

At Carleton University in Ottawa, IAW is hosted every year by SAIA. By the time I became involved in organizing with them, there was a rhythm and routine that informed our annual efforts. We usually hosted one event each day of the week, combining workshops and guided discussions with panel lectures and film screenings, and we always wrapped up the week with an arts and music showcase. We planned our events thematically, trying to make sure we touched on a wide range of topics.

In Canada, IAW has made it a priority to draw attention to the similarities between settler-colonialism in Palestine and across Turtle Island. Like many other groups, SAIA opens every event with an Indigenous solidarity statement that urges us to take up opposition not only to Israeli apartheid but to apartheid policies in Canada as well. The statement reads:

> Many defenders of Israel argue that 'Canada's values are Israel's values,' and they're right: the dispossession and theft of Palestinian lands, and the creation of Palestinian open-air prisons and Bantustans,[1] mimic Canada's own policies. From its very foundations, Canada has been based on the theft of Indigenous lands, and the genocide and displacement of Indigenous Peoples

> ... Let us support both the resistance of Indigenous Palestinians, and the survival and struggles of [Indigenous Peoples across Canada]. From Palestine to Turtle Island: There is no justice on stolen land. (SAIA Carleton n.d.)

Carleton University sits on unceded Algonquin Anishinaabe land, and nearly every year since the launch of IAW at least one of the week's events has been dedicated to drawing links between settler-colonialism in Palestine and Turtle Island. These events have exposed similarities between the permit regime systems used by Canada and Israel, highlighted Indigenous women's leadership, celebrated creative and artistic resistance and nurtured reciprocal solidarity. In 2009, a lecture titled "Political Prisoners from Turtle Island to Palestine" featured both Robert Lovelace, retired Chief of the Ardoch Algonquin First Nation who was sentenced to prison as a result of his leadership role in resisting uranium exploration on Algonquin land, and Yafa Jarrar, a Palestinian activist and the daughter of parents who have both been political prisoners in Israeli jails (at the time of writing this chapter, her mother, Khalida Jarrar, is once again being held in Israeli prison without charge or trial). In his opening statement, Lovelace shared that he only began to learn about Palestine and "the bonds that connect us across the world — bonds of oppression, bonds of colonialism," after being invited to present at IAW 2006 in Toronto (SAIA Carleton 2010).

Other recurring themes explored at IAW include the "pinkwashing" or "greenwashing" of apartheid — referring to the practice of promoting 2SLGBTIQ or environmentalist narratives, respectively, in a way that whitewashes Israel's human rights abuses — and reflections on dismantling apartheid from South Africa to Palestine. IAW events have also drawn links between systemic racism and police and military violence. In 2015, an event featuring members of a recent "Dream Defenders" delegation of United States Black and Brown activists to Palestine spoke about systemic racism and police violence, asking the question: "What do Palestinian and Black liberation have in common?" The connections drawn between Black and Palestinian liberation did not emerge in a vacuum, but from a historically constituted revolutionary politics of anti-imperialism, anti-colonialism and anti-racism. Anti-Black racism in the United States and Canada was foundational to the establishment of both countries and their empires, in particular through the transatlantic slave trade. As Robyn Maynard (2017) argues, upon the abolishment of slavery in Canada two centuries ago, the disposability of Black life was reconsolidated into the criminal justice system — through law enforcement, jails and prisons, and courts (226–27). IAW events have explored the joint security training programs between Israeli and Canadian or US police, as well as the shared weapons industries profiting from Black and Palestinian repression. But moreover, when we say that "justice is indivisible" (the title of the 2020 keynote IAW lecture by Angela Davis that opened this chapter), we are not only saying that our liberation is linked as a matter of principled politics but also recognizing that the same empires that were established upon and maintained by Black oppression are those that enforce and uphold Israeli apartheid.

Another staple of IAW at Carleton University is the arts showcase "Verses vs Apartheid." Featuring many prominent Palestinian as well as other Black, Brown and Indigenous performers over the years, this annual evening of music, poetry and dance has been an opportunity for celebration and creative disruption. When a city-wide campaign in Ottawa launched in 2013 to support the call for a cultural boycott of Israel, dozens of local artists pledged their support on the spot — in great part because of the relationships that had been built through "Verses vs Apartheid."

All these events bolstered the BDS movement by directing members of our university community to support SAIA's divestment campaign. Launched in 2010, the campaign called on the Carleton University Pension Fund to divest from companies complicit in the violation of human rights in Palestine and beyond. In a comprehensive report, SAIA revealed that the pension fund had investments in military weapons and infrastructure companies like BAE Systems and Northrop-Grumman, calling for the university to adopt a binding socially responsible investment policy. Growing to include endorsements from students, alumni, faculty, staff and retirees across the Carleton community, the campaign won a major success when graduate students overwhelmingly voted in support of the motion to divest in 2012 (Abunimah 2012).

These years of organizing on campuses and beyond have allowed Palestine solidarity groups like SAIA Carleton to uplift and transform the political conversation on Palestine, to build coalitions with others fighting for justice and to grow its campaign for boycotts, divestments and sanctions. But these years have been met with significant opposition and even attempts at repression — from the Carleton University administration, from Zionist groups on campus and from external lobby groups. The attempts to undermine SAIA and IAW at Carleton fit into a pattern that we can see at universities across Canada — from the vocal condemnation of IAW and outright banning of IAW materials, to the refusal of SAIA funding or access to rooms, the imposition of campus security and the conflation of criticism of Israel with antisemitism.

From Its Foundations:
A Pattern of Repression and Censorship

From the onset, IAW and BDS have been subject to attacks from Israel and its advocates, who have attempted to dismiss it, minimize its impact or depict IAW as violent, dangerous or hateful. The very first IAW was organized by a group called the Arab Students' Collective at the University of Toronto in February 2005. Although the five days of lectures were filled to capacity and attracted global media attention, the Israeli Ambassador to Canada at the time called it "a cheap, misleading propaganda exercise detached from reality" (*Jewish Telegraph Agency* 2005). This sentiment was echoed a couple of years later when University of Toronto president David Naylor dismissed the importance of IAW, saying that "the future of Israel and its neighbours will not be decided by a small group of activists who talk mostly to themselves on a few North American university campuses" (CJPME 2010: 2).

Others have taken a more heavy-handed approach. In response to plans for the first IAW, B'nai Brith Canada launched a campaign demanding the University of Toronto cancel the event. They also alerted the Toronto Police Services Hate Crimes Unit and federal police and urged the university to step up its police presence. When the university allowed IAW to proceed, the vice-president of B'nai Brith told the *Globe and Mail*: "I guess they are just going to hope and pray that there is no violence" (Eisen 2005). The inaugural year of IAW would foreshadow so much of what was to come in the years ahead. Ironically, as in 2005, attempts to suppress IAW have often had the opposite effect, as they continuously thrust the event into the media and mobilized popular support.

In Ottawa in early February 2009, a month before IAW was set to begin, Carleton University banned the poster that SAIA was using to promote the week of events. Depicting a warplane marked "Israel" firing a missile at a child whose shadow spelled "Gaza," the poster was the official design of IAW and was being used that year in some forty cities around the world. The posters were torn down without notice, and only after inquiring were SAIA members informed that the poster had been banned by the administration on the grounds that it "could be seen to incite others to infringe rights protected in the Ontario Human Rights Code" (HRTO 2013: sec. 30). The University of Ottawa followed suit and also banned the IAW poster on their campus.

The ban came just two months after Operation Cast Lead, the deadly Israeli assault on Gaza that killed over 1,400 Palestinians and wounded 5,000 more (IMEU 2012). The animated poster, depicting a child being targeted by Israel, was a documentary depiction of the attack that had just left three hundred children in Gaza dead. For many Palestinian students and their supporters at Carleton who were still reeling from the horrific loss, the ban of the poster on the grounds that it "offended norms of civil discourse" was especially insulting.

Despite the harm caused by Carleton's stance, SAIA members were able to use the ban to mobilize mass support for the broader cause of Palestinian rights. With tape over their mouths and holding posters reading "Bombs and Walls Kill, Posters Don't" and "Lift the Ban: Stop Campus Repression," students, faculty and other members of the university community joined forces for a silent march to the president's office, where they read out a set of demands, including an immediate lift on the poster ban and a public apology. As these demands were refused by both Ottawa universities, a second march to the University of Ottawa president's office drew out even more supporters (SAIA Carleton 2009). The mobilization led to massive growth in SAIA's local and national networks, as supporters shocked by the university's actions were drawn to the group.

The poster ban at Carleton and the University of Ottawa was not an isolated incident. A year earlier at Hamilton's McMaster University, organizers of IAW 2008 were prevented from hanging a banner containing the words "Israeli Apartheid" by the administration's Human Rights and Equity Services office, who explained that "the university takes the position that this phrase is in violation of the university's efforts to ensure that all people will be treated with dignity and tolerance" (Hamdon and Harris 2010: 67).

Despite repeated requests for an explanation, Carleton University was never able to articulate how IAW or its poster encouraged the infringement of human rights, even when SAIA members filed an application against the university under the Human Rights Tribunal of Ontario (HRTO) a few years later. Although the Tribunal concluded that it was not the appropriate legal body to rule over the stifling of political expression by Carleton, it acknowledged that an infringement may have occurred: "To the extent the applicant argues that, as a human rights advocacy organization, it was denied a right of free political expression, as legitimate as that claim may be, it is outside the scope of the Tribunal's jurisdiction" (HRTO 2013: sec. 8). SAIA's challenge to the university was significant because it exposed the lack of substance behind their claims; the administrators who informed SAIA that the poster violated human rights standards could not explain their stance.

In Chapter 9, Husseini provides a history of anti-war, human rights and Palestine solidarity organizing on Ottawa campuses dating back to 1975, to show how sustained student activism has transformed the political possibilities for organizers today. Similarly, SAIA Carleton's efforts to resist the poster ban have had a positive effect by ensuring a future for Palestinian organizing on that campus. In January 2015, ahead of an event relaunching SAIA's divestment campaign (entitled "How Is Carleton Complicit?"), SAIA members became aware that the event's posters were being removed from the walls by a custodian, who when approached said he was told to remove them on the grounds that they depicted violence and implied Carleton's involvement. The poster depicted an Israeli war plane, which had the label: "Advanced Precision Kill weapon system manufactured by BAE systems: Carleton invests $150,269." A missile aimed at a baby carriage was labelled: "Hellfire Missiles manufactured by Lockheed Martin: Carleton invests $536,652." Like the 2009 poster, it was an image grounded in a stark reality, not provocative fiction. I immediately brought the issue to the director of Student Affairs, who at the HRTO two years earlier had attributed the 2009 poster ban to a fear that it would incite "young people to do stupid things" (HRTO 2013: sec. 48). The director immediately assured me that the university had not instructed the removal of the poster and that they would reimburse us for the cost of the posters lost. This vastly different response to a very similar poster is a testament to the work of earlier SAIA members to defend the right to freedom of expression. Moreover, it speaks to the reality that attempts to silence IAW or BDS that are grounded in empty claims will inevitably fail when challenged. Already, we have seen many United States anti-BDS laws blocked as unconstitutional by courts, including federal district courts in Texas, Arizona and Kansas (Ruane 2019).

The poster ban is just one example in a long history of the repression of discourse critical of Israel at Carleton University. The earliest case is as early as SAIA's first event in October 2008, when a panel providing a legal analysis of "Israeli Crimes, Canadian Complicity" was targeted by the pro-Israel Hillel Ottawa group. Freedom of information requests revealed an exchange between the group and Carleton senior management, who subsequently increased security and police presence at the lecture and issued a university-wide email distancing themselves from the event (Heaton 2014). On several occasions, SAIA Carleton faced harassment, vandalism, racism and assaults on campus that were not taken seriously by senior administration. Conversely, after Carleton professor Bill Skidmore brought in a Palestinian woman to speak at one of his lectures, Hillel was able to set up a meeting directly between a pro-Israel student who complained and the university provost. Correspondences show that an "alternative evaluation" of Skidmore was discussed, in violation of his collective agreement as a professor (Heaton 2014). This double standard is clear to anyone who has been vocal for Palestinian rights in classrooms and on campuses over the years. Perhaps one of the best-documented incidents in Canada was revealed after a freedom of information request by SAIA at York University: over 250 pages of emails revealed a mere week's worth of exchanges between senior administrators at York, University of Toronto and McMaster University conspiring on how best to deny SAIA's request for space for a 2008 conference entitled "Standing Against Apartheid: Building Cross-Campus Solidarity with Palestine" (Hamdon and Harris 2010: 68).

Conclusion

If the past sixteen years of Israeli Apartheid Week organizing have made one thing clear, it is that pro-Israel attempts at censorship and repression have only encouraged popular dissent and creative interventions in support of Palestine. When we urgently mobilize in the face of attacks, like the protests in response to Carleton's poster ban, this has the power to invigorate the movement and draw out the furies that propel us. However, what has proven to be invaluable about IAW is that it is not organized as a reaction, but it is set on the Palestine solidarity calendar. IAW sets aside space for organizers to explore the issues and connections that intrigue them and to empower their supporters. The Palestinian struggle is not a short one, and it can be difficult to maintain an impassioned movement in a political climate that only goes from hostile to more hostile. Each year, IAW renews our commitment to BDS and gives us a platform on which to connect with others who are working to dismantle systemic racism and defund the institutions that profit from state violence and colonialism. As a Palestinian-led and grassroots movement, IAW and BDS also serve as a model of internationalism. It is this space for imagining collectively that has the potential to break through the temporal limbo trapping Palestinians in a constant dismal present, denied a past and forbidden from the future. Returning to the words of Angela Davis, "It is in collectivities that we find reservoirs of hope and optimism" (2016: 49).

Note

1   "Bantustan" is a term from South Africa, referring to the "reserves" or "homelands" that were designated for Black South Africans during apartheid. These were isolated, mostly-rural territories that, much like "reservations" for Indigenous people on Turtle Island, offered little in the way of employment or education for residents, and were part of a system of restriction and impoverishment.

References

Abunimah, Ali. 2012. "In Canadian First, Carleton University Students Pass Israel Occupation Divestment Resolution by Large Margin." *Electronic Intifada,* March 23. <electronicintifada.net/blogs/ali-abunimah/canadian-first-carleton-university-students-pass-israel-occupation-divestment>.

ADC (American-Arab Anti-Discrimination Committee). 2020. "ADC Presents: Palestinian Solidarity with Black Communities with Noura Erakat, Ajamu Dillahunt, and Ahmad Abuznaid." June 4. <facebook.com/watch/live/?v=1644110072408320>.

Baroud, Ramzy, and Romana Rubeo. 2018. "Israel's $72m 'War Chest' to Fight BDS Arrives in Europe." *Al Jazeera,* November 14. <aljazeera.com/opinions/2018/11/14/israels-72m-war-chest-to-fight-bds-arrives-in-europe/?xif=Grassroots?gb=true>.

Bisharah, Marwan. 2002. *Palestine/Israel: Peace or Apartheid.* London: Zed Books.

CJPME (Canadians for Justice and Peace in the Middle East). 2010. "Factsheet: Israeli Apartheid Week." Factsheet Series no. 75, March. <d3n8a8pro7vhmx.cloudfront.net/cjpme/pages/1269/attachments/original/1437157400/75-En-Israeli-Apart­heid-Week-v3.pdf?1437157400>.

Davis, Angela. 2016. *Freedom Is a Constant Struggle.* Chicago: Haymarket Books.

Davis, Uri. 1987. *Israel: An Apartheid State.* London: Zed Books.

___. 2003. *Apartheid Israel: Possibilities for the Struggle Within.* London: Zed Books.

Dugard, John, and John Reynolds. 2013. "Apartheid, International Law, and the Occupied Palestinian Territory." *The European Journal of International Law* 24, 3.

Eisen, Hailey. 2005. "Arab Event at U of T Draws Controversy." *Globe and Mail,* January 31. <theglobeandmail.com/news/national/arab-event-at-u-of-t-draws-controver-

sy/article20419274/>.

Erakat, Noura. 2019. *Justice for Some: Law and the Question of Palestine.* Stanford: Stanford University Press.

Erakat, Noura, and Tareq Radi (eds.). 2016. *Gaza in Context: War and Settler Colonialism.* Virginia: Asi-Kp.

Falk, Richard, and Virginia Tilley. 2017. "Israeli Practices towards the Palestinian People and the Question of Apartheid." *Palestine — Israel Journal of Politics, Economics, and Culture* 22, 2/3.

Global News. 2018. "Justin Trudeau's Full Apology for Canadian Government Turning Away MS St Louis Refugees." November 7. <youtube.com/watch?v=WTQGr4OBEGE>.

Hamdon, Evelyn, and Scott Harris. 2010. "Dangerous Dissent? Critical Pedagogy and the Case of Israeli Apartheid Week." *Cultural and Pedagogical Inquiry* 2, 2.

Hawari, Yara, Sharri Plonski, and Elian Weizman (eds.). 2019. "Settlers and Citizens: A Critical View of Israeli Society." *Settler Colonial Studies* 9, 1.

Heaton, Sam. 2014. "Activists Refuse to 'Be Quiet': Speakers Expose Carleton Double Standard on Palestine." *The Leveller,* March 1. <leveller.ca/2014/03/activists-refuse-to-be-quiet/>.

HRTO (Human Rights Tribunal of Ontario). 2013. "SAIA v. Carleton University." January 22. <canlii.org/en/on/onhrt/doc/2013/2013hrto112/2013hrto112.pdf>.

HRW (Human Rights Watch). 2021. *A Threshold Crossed: Israeli Authorities and the Crimes of Apartheid and Persecution.* Report, April 27. <hrw.org/report/2021/04/27/threshold-crossed/israeli-authorities-and-crimes-apartheid-and-persecution>.

IAW (Israeli Apartheid Week) International Coordinating Committee. 2020. "Israeli Apartheid Week 2020 Information Pack: United Against Racism." <apartheidweek.org/resources/>.

IJV (Independent Jewish Voices) Canada. 2019. "Talking About Apartheid: IJV Factsheet." October 25. <ijvcanada.org/talking-about-apartheid-ijv-factsheet/>.

IMEU (Institute for Middle East Understanding). 2012. "Operation Cast Lead." January 4. <imeu.org/article/operation-cast-lead>.

Jewish Telegraph Agency. 2005. "Toronto's 'Israel Apartheid Week' Draws Few People, but Gets Headlines." February 9. <jta.org/2005/02/09/archive/torontos-israel-apartheid-week-draws-few-people-but-gets-headlines>.

Maynard, Robyn. 2017. *Policing Black Lives: State Violence in Canada from Slavery to the Present.* Black Point, NS: Fernwood Publishing.

Palestine Legal. 2020. "Ten Things to Know About Anti-Boycott Legislation." January 17. <palestinelegal.org/news/2016/6/3/what-to-know-about-anti-bds-legislation>.

Palestinian Civil Society. 2005. "Palestinian Civil Society Call for BDS." Open letter, July 9. <bdsmovement.net/call>.

Portland State Library Special Collections. 1975. "Black Studies Center Public Dialogue, Pt. 2." May 30. <soundcloud.com/portland-state-library/portland-state-black-studies-1?mc_cid=7a27cfd978&mc_eid=e2efbcffa9>.

Puar, Jasbir. 2011. "Citation and Censorship: The Politics of Talking About the Sexual Politics of Israel." *Feminist Legal Studies* 19.

Ruane, Kate. 2019. "Congress, Laws Suppressing Boycotts of Israel Are Unconstitutional. Sincerely, Three Federal Courts." *American Civil Liberties Union,* May 9. <aclu.org/blog/free-speech/congress-laws-suppressing-boycotts-israel-are-unconstitutional-sincerely-three>.

SAIA Carleton. n.d. Indigenous solidarity statement. Montreal version of statement.

(Posted Feb. 29 by Marcy Newman.) <usacbi.wordpress.com/2009/02/28/israeli-apartheid-week-montreal-indigenous-solidarity-statement/>.

___. 2009. "26 February 2009 Poster Ban Protest." YouTube, May 4. <youtube.com/watch?v=KS4IxlGmdNs>.

___. 2010. "Yafa Jarrar and Bob Lovelace — 2 March 2009 — Israeli Apartheid Week — University of Ottawa — Part 2." Vimeo, February 21. <vimeo.com/9631705>.

Shah, Samira. 1997. "On the Road to Apartheid: The Bypass Road Network in the West Bank." *Columbia Human Rights Law Review* 29, 1.

Shalhoub-Kevorkian, Nadera. 2014. "Human Suffering in Colonial Contexts: Reflections from Palestine." *Settler Colonial Studies* 4, 3.

Shear, David. 2013. "CIJA and UJA Call 'Israel Apartheid' a Massive Lie." *UJA Federation of Greater Toronto,* April 25. <https://web.archive.org/web/20200922175441/jewishtoronto.com/news-media/cija-and-uja-call-israel-apartheid-a-massive-lie>.

Tilley, V. (ed.). 2009. *Occupation, Colonialism, Apartheid? A Reassessment of Israel's Practices in the Occupied Palestinian Territories under International Law.* Cape Town: Middle East Project of the Democracy and Governance Programme, Human Sciences Research Council of South Africa. May. <repository.hsrc.ac.za/handle/20.500.11910/4619>.

Trudeau, Justin. 2015. Tweet. March 13. <twitter.com/justintrudeau/status/576465632884981760>.

Tuck, Eve, and K. Wayne Yang. 2012. "Decolonization Is Not a Metaphor." *Decolonization: Indigeneity, Education & Society* 1, 1.

UofT (University of Toronto) Divest. 2020. "Video Released of Angela Davis Keynote for Israeli Apartheid Week 2020: 'Justice Is Indivisible.'" June 25. <uoftdivest.com/angela-davis-2020.html>.

Chapter 5

Two Jews, Three Opinions

Jewish Canadians' Diverse Views on Israel-Palestine

Diana Ralph

Pro-Israel politicians in Canada often claim that their support for Israel is motivated by supporting Jews and opposing antisemitism. They portray Canadian Jews as wanting their government to show unquestioning loyalty to Israel against alleged threats posed by Palestinians and their supporters. And by doing so, they position themselves as heroic allies to Jews. But how many Jewish Canadians want this in reality? Until 2019, no one had asked that question. In this chapter, I analyze the results of two groundbreaking 2019 surveys of Jewish Canadian opinions about Israel/Palestine, Canadian government policies towards Israel and what they consider to be antisemitic. These survey findings reveal that many Jewish Canadians, like public opinion in general, are deeply critical of Israeli government policies and do not support Canada's condemnation of BDS supporters. They also show that almost half (48 percent) of Jewish Canadians believe that "accusations of antisemitism are often used to silence legitimate criticism of Israeli government policies." These findings undermine the legitimacy of the Canadian government's claims to be acting on behalf of Jews when it sides with Israel.

Are Canadian Jews as Loyal to Israel as the Canadian Government Is?

Since 2006, under both Prime Minister Stephen Harper's Conservatives and Prime Minister Justin Trudeau's Liberals, the Canadian government has been almost completely supportive of the Israeli government and fiercely opposed to those who support Palestinian rights (Macleod 2018; Seligman 2018). As Harper declared in a May 2008 speech, "Those who threaten Israel also threaten Canada" (Chase 2010). In many ways, the government under Trudeau has been even more loyal to Israel than it was under Harper (Yakabushi 2018). For example, Canada under Trudeau has voted against 87 percent of UN resolutions condemning Israel's treatment of Palestinians, compared to 61 percent under Harper, 19 percent under Martin and Mulroney and 3 percent under Chrétien (Housefather 2018).

This approach is deeply at odds with public opinion in Canada, which is far more critical of the Israeli government and supportive of Palestinian rights. Following Israel's 2014 assault on Gaza, a poll showed that 51 percent of Canadians disagreed with Stephen Harper's pro-Israel stance, compared to only 30 percent who agreed with it, and far more agreed (42 percent) than disagreed (25 percent) that Israel's reaction to Hamas rockets was "out of proportion" (Bozinoff 2014).

A 2017 national survey of people in Canada found that a majority disapproved of our government's policies on Israel and Palestine (Ralph et al. 2017a). Only about one in four (28 percent) Canadians expressed a positive opinion of the Israeli government, and almost half (46 percent) expressed a negative opinion of it (Ralph et al. 2017a: 7). Similarly, a 2020 poll found that three out of four Canadians wanted their government to oppose Israel's plans to annex parts of the West Bank, including 42 percent who wanted Canada to impose economic and/or diplomatic sanctions against Israel (Bueckert et al. 2020: 4).

Why is our government so out of step with the views of the people it is elected to represent, as well as the international consensus, which opposes Israel's occupation? The real reasons probably have to do with money, power and politics. Between 1997, when Canada signed the Canada-Israel Free Trade Agreement (CIFTA), and 2018, Canada's merchandise and services trade with Israel more than tripled, to more than $2 billion (Global Affairs Canada 2018; Government of Canada 2019). As Minister of International Trade Diversification Jim Carr wrote in 2019, "Canada and Israel are steadfast friends and allies, and we have an impressive number of cooperative activities taking place between our two countries. We expect this number to grow under the modernized CIFTA" (Global Affairs Canada 2019). Israel has also leveraged its expertise in intrusively monitoring, restricting, killing and imprisoning Palestinians to become the go-to source of weapons and tactics for controlling civil unrest worldwide, including in Canada (Halper 2015). Under the 2014 Canada-Israel Strategic Partnership, our military, prisons, police and border guards are trained and supported by Israel's weapons and spy industries, while the Canadian arms industry exports weapons to Israel (Global Affairs Canada 2014). Canada's support for Israel may also be explained in part as an attempt to pander to the evangelical vote (CBC Radio 2017) and to appease the United States, Israel's strongest ally.

Setting Up Jews as the Excuse to Justify Israeli Oppression of Palestinians

These pragmatic motives, however, are rarely acknowledged by Canada's political leaders. Instead, they repeatedly echo four popular arguments to justify their support for Israel. First, in the wake of the Holocaust and ongoing antisemitism, they say, Jews deserve and need a Jewish state for their security (that is, one in which Jews are in the majority and enjoy official superior status). Second, because Israel constitutes "the collective Jew" (Klug 2003), they consider most criticism of the Israeli state or even of specific Israeli policies to be antisemitic, constituting a "new antisemitism" (this idea is further discussed in Chapters 3 and 6 of this volume). Third, they claim that Palestinian demands for justice, especially the Boycott, Divestment and Sanctions (BDS) movement, are antisemitic because they are presumed to threaten the Jewish state, and therefore all Jews. And fourth, they treat all Jewish Canadians as one monolithic "community" and presume that Jews all agree with these claims.

These arguments have all but become Canadian policy under Harper and Trudeau. When he was elected prime minister in 2006, Harper: "immediately launched an unshakeable foreign policy in support of Israel, beginning that summer when the Jewish state launched a military ground offensive into Lebanon to combat Hezbollah" (Kennedy 2014). Years later, just a few months before Israel's brutal assault on Gaza in 2014, Harper gave a speech to the Israeli Knesset vowing loyalty to Israel and attacking the Palestine solidarity movement. While acknowledging the many commercial and military ties between Israel and Canada, Harper claimed that Canada's support for Israel was based on opposing the "new antisemitism" and vowed that "through fire and water, Canada will stand with you" (Harper 2014):

> People who would never say they hate and blame the Jews for their own failings or the problems of the world, instead declare their hatred of Israel and blame the only Jewish state for the problems of the Middle East…. But this is the face of the new

anti-Semitism. It targets the Jewish people by targeting Israel and attempts to make the old bigotry acceptable for a new generation. (Harper 2014)

Similarly, Trudeau has played the "antisemitism card" to justify his uncritical support of Israel. In November 2018, while apologizing for Canada's World War II refusal to admit Jewish refugees from the Holocaust, Trudeau repeated the unsubstantiated claim that

> Jewish students still feel unwelcome and uncomfortable on some of our college and university campuses because of BDS-related intimidation. And out of our entire community of nations, it is Israel whose right to exist is most widely — and wrongly — questioned. (Trudeau 2018)

In 2019, Trudeau again pledged uncritical support of Israel based on opposing antisemitism:

> We will continue to stand strongly against the singling out of Israel at the UN. Canada remains a steadfast supporter of Israel and Canada will always defend Israel's right to live in security. And we will always, always, speak up against anti-Semitism at home and abroad. You have my word. (Csillag 2019)

In the name of protecting Jews from "antisemitism," the Canadian government has both initiated and endorsed escalating attacks on Palestinian solidarity groups who criticize or protest Israeli policies toward Palestinians. In March 2009, the Harper government supported an ad hoc group of Canadian members of parliament to form the Canadian Parliamentary Coalition to Combat Antisemitism (CPCCA), which held hearings attempting to prove that rising support for Palestinian rights was antisemitic. The CPCCA generated widespread opposition, including among Jews. Even police chiefs and university administrators disagreed with the premise that Palestinian solidarity threatened Jews (Keefer 2010). Nevertheless, the CPCCA's final report in 2011 urged, among other things, that the Canadian government should train police to recognize Palestine solidarity as motivated by what it called "the new antisemitism" and that university administrators should ban Israeli Apartheid Week and other Palestine solidarity events (see Chapters 4 and 9 for a discussion of these debates on campus).

This approach has been officially adopted by the Canadian government in several ways. In September 2011, Canada became the first country to adopt the Ottawa Protocol, promoted by the CPCCA, which repeated the allegation that Palestine solidarity activities, and especially the BDS movement, are antisemitic (Government of Canada 2011). In 2016, Parliament passed a motion to reject BDS and to "call upon the government to condemn any and all attempts by Canadian organizations, groups or individuals to promote the BDS movement, both here at home and abroad" (Martin 2016). Finally in 2019, the Canadian government adopted the International Holocaust Remembrance Alliance (IHRA) working definition of antisemitism, which is widely understood to conflate criticism of Israel with antisemitism (see Chapters 3 and 8 for further discussion of IHRA) and allocated $45 million to promote the IHRA's acceptance and implementation by all three levels of government (CJN Staff 2019). Some pro-Israel groups even believe that those who criticize Israel should be criminalized as having committed an antisemitic hate crime (B'nai Brith Canada 2017).

Characterizing criticism of Israel as antisemitic erases the opinions of other communities who also have legitimate perspectives on the conflict. It privileges the presumed opinions of the 1 percent of the Canadian population who are Jewish over, for example, the views of the 3.2 percent of Canadians who are Muslim (World Population Review n.d.) or the 1.5 percent of Canadians who identify as Arabs (Statistics Canada n.d.). Politicians and media generally ignore the Palestinian experiences of Israeli state violence and anti-Arab racism, and they characterize Israel's violence as justified responses to "Hamas terrorism." For example, after IDF soldiers shot Palestinian Canadian Doctor Tarek Loubani, who was treating Gaza victims of Israeli snipers during the Great March of Return demonstrations, Canada's foreign affairs minister Chrystia Freeland opposed a UN Human Rights Council vote which would have established an investigation into Israel's killing of Palestinians during the protests along the Israeli-Gaza border. Instead, she called for an independent investigation "to ascertain how the actions of all parties concerned contributed to these events, including reported incitement by Hamas" (Fife 2018).

Equating Palestine solidarity with antisemitism also erases the opinions of Jews who stand in solidarity with Palestinians and/or who believe that it is legitimate to pressure Israel, like any other state, to comply with international and humanitarian law. Many Jewish Palestine solidarity activists argue that Israel's oppression of Palestinians in the name of Jews itself inflames antisemitic attacks. They believe that labelling their solidarity efforts as antisemitic is a cynical maneuver to discredit and silence legitimate criticism of Israel.

Of course, there are important elements within the Canadian Jewish community which do support these views. Most prominent is the Centre for Israel and Jewish Affairs (CIJA), which was first established in 2002 by several of Canada's Jewish corporate giants, notably Izzy Asper, Gerry Schwartz and Heather Reisman, in order to counter rising popular sympathy for Palestinians in response to the Second Intifada (Freeman-Maloy 2006; Ralph 2007). CIJA now claims to be "the only registered lobbyist for the Jewish Community" with a staff of over fifty people and a budget of over $11 million (CIJA 2021). CIJA treats virtually any criticism of Israel as an attack on all Jews and labels as antisemitic anyone (Gentile or Jew) who criticizes Israeli policy or Zionism. It uses its clout to demand that Canada maintain a steadfast pro-Israel and anti-Palestinian position and punishes politicians who deviate from that position with both public and private censure. As the sole voice of Canada's Jewish Federations, it exerts hegemonic pressure on synagogues, Jewish organizations and community institutions like the Canadian Jewish News to adopt its pro-Israel narrative.

CIJA often claims in its press releases to speak for "the Jewish Community," and it characterizes those Jews who openly criticize Israel — such as members of Independent Jewish Voices — as marginal. CIJA's claims that Jewish Canadians support its views are used to justify Canada's policies toward Israel and Palestine. But neither CIJA nor the Canadian government have ever published any evidence that Jewish Canadians actually support the assumptions outlined above.

The remainder of this chapter empirically answers the questions of how many Jewish Canadians believe that Canada's unconditional support for Israel is essential for their safety, and how many view criticism of Israel as antisemitic.

What Do Jewish Canadians Really Think?

In 2019, for the first time, two credible polls assessed the views of Jewish Canadians about the Israel/Palestine conflict and Canada's response to it. First, the Environics Institute for Survey Research conducted a comprehensive national survey of Jews in Canada (Brym, Neuman and

Lenton 2019), modeled closely on the Survey of American Jews conducted by the Pew Research Center in 2013 (Pew Research Center 2013). All its authors and sponsors are strongly supportive of Israel. This survey focused on "what it means to be Jewish in Canada today — specifically, patterns of Jewish practice, upbringing and intermarriage; perceptions of anti-Semitism; attitudes toward Israel; and personal and organizational connections that, taken together, constitute the community" (Brym, Neuman and Lenton 2019: 1).

Second, an EKOS survey (of which I was the principal investigator) was co-sponsored by Independent Jewish Voices Canada and the United Jewish Peoples Order (Ralph 2019). Both organizations are highly supportive of Palestinian rights and critical of many Israeli policies toward Palestinians. Given the political divide between the Jewish organizations who undertook the two studies, it is interesting to compare their findings.

The methodologies of the two surveys differed significantly. The Environics poll surveyed 2,335 Jews who live in the four Canadian cities, which together include more than 80 percent of the country's Jewish population. The survey employed several sampling strategies to maximize coverage, with quotas established for age and gender based on the most current population statistics from Statistics Canada. EKOS surveyed a representative sample of 359 respondents drawn from EKOS' broader pool of Canadian respondents who self-identified as "Jewish" religiously, ethnically or culturally. Respondents were sorted by their political party preferences and by three religious-practice categories; those who identified their religious affiliation as "Jewish," "other" or "none" (secular).

The Environics survey included several questions about respondents' views on Israel/Palestine issues and about whether they view criticism of Israel as antisemitic. The EKOS survey focused on the opinions of Jewish Canadians about the Israeli government and its policies affecting Palestinians and Canada's stances on the Israel/Palestine conflict. It also explored their views on whether criticism of Israel is antisemitic.

The respondents captured by the two surveys had remarkably similar demographic descriptors. Both samples of Jewish Canadians were far more highly educated than average Canadians (Brym, Neuman and Lenton 2018: 7; Ralph 2019: 15–16). In both samples, over 80 percent were of Ashkenazi (Eastern European) origin (Brym, Neuman and Lenton 2018: 12; Ralph 2019: 16). In the EKOS poll, only 29 percent belonged to a synagogue, and only 16 percent attended regularly (Ralph

2019: 18). By comparison, 60 percent of Environics respondents belonged to a synagogue, but only about the same proportion (15 percent) attended regularly (Brym, Neuman and Lenton 2018: 24). In both samples, most respondents were actively involved in Jewish organizations and activities (Brym, Neuman and Lenton 2018: 29; Ralph 2019: 18).

Understandably the two surveys asked very different questions related to Israel/Palestine. Taken together, they offer a rich and nuanced perspective of the diversity of opinion among Jewish Canadians, contrary to the image of a monolithic Jewish opinion as promoted by CIJA. The key finding of both surveys is that Jewish views differ dramatically and that a large proportion of them do *not* agree with either CIJA or the Canadian government's positions on Israel/Palestine. Below is a summary of the combined results of both surveys.[1]

Differences by Political Affiliation

According to the 2017 survey of public opinion mentioned above, political affiliation strongly predicted their views on Israel/Palestine. Those who supported the Conservative Party were by far most likely to support Israel and its policies. Liberal Party supporters were about evenly split on their view of Israel. And NDP and Green Party supporters were far more likely to be critical of Israel and its policies (Ralph et al. 2017a: 20). The EKOS survey of Jewish Canadians similarly found that the main predictor of Jewish views on Israel/Palestine was not their Jewishness but their political affiliation (Ralph 2019: 46). A far higher percentage of Jewish Conservative Party supporters, like most Conservative supporters, had a positive opinion of the Israeli government and its policies compared to supporters of any other party. Jewish Liberal Party supporters, like most Liberal Party supporters, tended to be somewhat less (and sometimes far less) supportive of Israel and its policies. Jewish NDP and Green Party supporters, like most NDP and Green Party supporters, were far more likely to hold a negative view of the Israeli government and its policies. The proportion of Jewish Liberal Party supporters who held negative views of the Israeli government was similar to the proportion of all Canadian Liberal Party supporters who held negative views of the Israeli government. Jewish NDP and Green Party supporters viewed the Israeli government even more negatively than all Canadian NDP and Green Party supporters (Ralph 2019: 20).

Differences between Religious versus Secular Jews

Across all variables, the EKOS survey also found a deep divide between religiously affiliated Jews on one hand, and secular Jews and those affiliated with other religions on the other hand. Canadian Jews who saw themselves as religiously Jewish tended to agree with the Israeli government and Canadian Israel/Palestine policies, while secular Jews and those affiliated with other religions tended to be far more critical of the Israeli government and of Canada's Israel/Palestine policies. But even among religiously affiliated Jews, the EKOS survey found that between 15 percent and 37 percent (depending on the issue) opposed Israeli policies toward Palestinians. Over half (52 percent) of religiously affiliated Jews agreed that criticism of an Israeli government policy is not necessarily antisemitic and 42 percent agreed that accusations of antisemitism are often used to silence legitimate criticism of Israel (Ralph 2019: 22, 41–42).

Attachment to Israel

The Environics survey found that Jewish Canadians had a high level of attachment to Israel, higher even than among Jewish Americans. Almost half (48 percent) felt very emotionally attached to Israel and 31 percent felt somewhat attached (Brym, Neuman and Lenton 2018: 57). However, "attachment" to Israel does not necessarily equate with "loyalty" to Israel. Even though Israel is important to many Jewish Canadians, many of those same individuals also felt deeply critical of Israeli policies, as I describe below.

Opinions of the Israeli Government

Both surveys found that many Jewish Canadians were critical of the Israeli government. The EKOS survey found that only half (50 percent) of respondents had a positive opinion of the Israeli government, and 37 percent viewed it negatively (Ralph 2019: 21). The Environics survey found that 44 percent believed that the current Israeli leadership is not making "a sincere effort to bring about a peace settlement," compared to only 35 percent who believed it was (Brym, Neuman and Lenton 2018: 59).

Jewish Claim to the Land

The Israeli government and many Zionists treat as a "sacrosanct title deed" (Masalha 2007: 15) God's alleged promise in Exodus 23:31 to give the ancient Israelites all the land "from the Sea of Reeds to the Sea of

Philistia, and from the wilderness to the Euphrates" (Jewish Publication Society 1985: 22; see also Nestel, Chapter 2). But the Environics poll found that 58 percent of Jewish Canadians either rejected or expressed no opinion on the belief that God had given the land of Israel to the Jews. Only 42 percent, most of them religious and especially Orthodox, believed this (Brym, Neuman and Lenton 2018: 61).

Canada's Support for Israel

The Environics survey found that most Jewish Canadians in 2018 (under Justin Trudeau's Liberals) believed that Canada's level of support for Israel was either "about right" (45 percent) or "not supportive enough" (36 percent). Only 6 percent believed it was too supportive (Brym, Neuman and Lenton 2018: 62). Given the high proportion who felt attached to Israel, it makes sense that they also would want Canada to support Israel. However, many also indicated that they disagreed with specific Israeli actions, as described below.

West Bank Settlements

The Environics survey found that only 43 percent of Jewish Canadians believed that the West Bank settlements are legal, and far more believed that the settlements are hurting (39 percent), rather than helping (14 percent) Israel's security (Brym, Neuman and Lenton 2018: 60).

The Blockade of Gaza

The EKOS poll found that almost one in three Jewish Canadians (31 percent) opposed Israel's blockade of Gaza and only 57 percent supported it. The rest did not express an opinion (Ralph 2019: 24).

Is Criticism of Israel Antisemitic?

Both surveys examined Jewish Canadians' experiences of and opinions about what constitutes antisemitism, and particularly, whether they consider criticism of Israel to be antisemitic. Many respondents to the Environics poll believed that discrimination against Jews in Canada occurs "often" (34 percent) or "sometimes" (80 percent), but even more thought that discrimination "often" occurs toward Indigenous Peoples (60 percent), Muslims (51 percent) and Black people (49 percent), and to gays and lesbians (38 percent). Thirty percent also think South Asians "often" experience discrimination (Brym, Neuman and Lenton 2018: 47). In other words, in contrast with Canadian government rhetoric,

Jewish Canadians do not tend to perceive antisemitism to be worse or more prevalent than other forms of racism.

The Environics survey also asked respondents about antisemitism they had personally experienced. Most (62 percent) did not report experiencing any antisemitism in the past five years. The forms of antisemitism the rest reported having endured were related to factors unrelated to Israel; their religion (21 percent), ethnicity or culture (18 percent), sex (16 percent) or language (12 percent) (Brym, Neuman and Lenton 2018: 49–50). This is about the same proportion that Muslim Canadians have reported personally experiencing, and far higher than proportions that other, mostly white, Canadians report experiencing (Brym, Neuman and Lenton 2018: 51; Environics Institute for Survey Research 2016; Statistics Canada 2013). Only 11 percent of Jewish Canadians report having been called offensive anti-Jewish names in the past year, and only 7 percent had felt socially snubbed because of being Jewish (Brym, Neuman and Lenton 2018: 51). None reported experiencing violence or other tangible abuses, such as police harassment, denial of housing or job discrimination, the common types of mistreatment that racialized people frequently experience.

The Environics survey found that about one in three Jewish Canadians said they had been criticized for either defending (34 percent) or criticizing (28 percent) policies or actions of the Israeli government in the past year (Brym, Neuman and Lenton 2018: 52). Of the former, 31 percent said this caused them to refrain from publicly expressing their support for Israeli policies and actions. Of the latter, 22 percent said that this caused them to not express their opposition to Israeli policies and actions in public (Brym, Neuman and Lenton 2018: 54). It is noteworthy that Jewish Canadians experienced "criticism" in similar proportions for both supporting and opposing Israeli policies.

What does "criticism" mean in this context? Does it simply mean disagreement? For example, if two Jews argue about Israel, they both might report having felt criticized. Or does it refer to an instance of antisemitism, for example, when a non-Jew aggressively holds a random Jew responsible for Israel's actions (much as racists accuse Muslims of being "terrorists")? The Environics survey did not ask whether these criticisms came from Jews or non-Jews, or from people in positions of authority, or whether the respondents had experienced these criticisms as antisemitism.

The EKOS survey took a different approach, which helps to make sense of what Jewish Canadians believe to be the relationship between anti-semitism and criticism of Israel. EKOS asked Jewish respondents whether they agreed with four statements. The first two equated criticism of Israel with antisemitism, using language drawn from the International Holocaust Remembrance Alliance (IHRA) and the Ottawa Protocol definition:

(1) Criticism of Israeli government policy which specifically singles out Israel is antisemitic.

(2) Those who criticize an Israeli government policy are being anti-semitic unless they also equally criticize other countries' human rights violations.

The second two statements, by contrast, differentiated criticism of Israel from antisemitism:

(3) Criticism of Israeli government policy is like criticism of any other countries' policies and is not necessarily antisemitic.

(4) Accusations of antisemitism are often used to silence legitimate criticism of Israeli government policies.

We discovered that using or not using emotionally loaded words had a major impact on what Jewish Canadians consider antisemitic. EKOS respondents were almost equally split (42 percent agreed, 38 percent disagreed) on the statement "Criticism of Israeli government policy which specifically singles out Israel is antisemitic." However, most agreed (63 percent agreed, 24 percent disagreed) with the statement, "Those who criticize an Israeli government policy are being antisemitic unless they also equally criticize other countries' human rights violations" (Ralph 2019: 26–39). In each of these two statements, which are commonly used by pro-Israel groups, the language evokes an image of someone unfairly targeting Israel, the Jewish state, and therefore, Jews in general. The first statement is often used to denounce critics of Israel who do not equally blame Hamas or the Palestinian Authority. However, it ignores the enormous power differentials between Israel and either of these Palestinian entities, as well as the question of who is oppressing whom. This argument is reminiscent of whites who claim "reverse discrimination." The second has been used to attack the United Nations and Palestine solidarity groups by claiming they are "singling out" Israel for blame, while not "equally" blaming other countries with as bad or worse human rights records (for example, see CIJA 2018; Love 2017; Lungen 2018; Sharansky 2005). In fact, the United Nations does regularly condemn human rights violations of other countries, such as China, India, Iran, Myanmar, the Philippines and the United States. The wording of these two statements deflects attention away from the content of the criticism and portrays Israel as the victim of unfair attacks.

The results were almost reversed, however, when the same Jewish Canadians assessed the second two statements, which differentiated between criticism of Israel and antisemitism. Most (58 percent agree to 30 percent disagree) agreed that "criticism of an Israeli government policy is like criticism of any other countries' policies and is not necessarily antisemitic." Similarly, more agreed than disagreed (48 percent agree to 39 percent disagree) that "accusations of antisemitism are often used to silence legitimate criticism of Israeli government policies" (Ralph 2019: 39–42).

Table 5-1 Jewish Canadians' Opinions on Different Definitions of Antisemitism (EKOS 2019)

Criticism of an Israeli government policy which specifically singles out Israel is antisemitic.	38% disagree
	42% agree
	20% neither agree nor disagree
Those who criticize an Israeli government policy are being antisemitic unless they also equally criticize other countries' human rights violations.	24% disagree
	63% agree
	12% neither agree nor disagree
Criticism of an Israeli government policy is like criticism of any other countries' policies and is not necessarily antisemitic.	58% agree
	32% disagree
	10% neither agree nor disagree
Accusations of antisemitism are often used to silence legitimate criticism of Israeli government policies	48% agree
	39% disagree
	13% neither agree nor disagree

It is noteworthy that almost one in three (30 percent) Jewish respondents believed that it would be reasonable for Canadians to boycott Israel, compared to 62 percent of Canadians in general (according to the 2017 survey: Ralph et al. 2017b). One in five (22 percent) agreed that it is reasonable for Canada to impose sanctions on Israel, and almost one in three (30 percent) thought it is reasonable to boycott Israeli prod-

Table 5-2 Summary of the 2017 EKOS Survey of Public Opinion in Canada and the 2018 Environics Survey of Jewish Canadians Compared to Canadian Government Policy Post-2006

Issues re: Israel-Palestine	Canadian government policy	Canadians' opinions	Jewish Canadians opinions
Opinion of Government of Israel	Loyally supports Israel	46% negative 28% positive 26% neither	37% negative 50% positive 13% neither
Opinion of blockade of Gaza	Supports Israeli blockade, condemns Hamas		31% opposes 57% supports 12% neither
Opinion of United States decision to recognize Jerusalem as Israel's capital	Abstained on United Nations vote, but issued a separate statement opposing this move		45% opposes 42% supports 13% neither
Is Palestinian boycott call reasonable?	Condemns boycott call	62% reasonable 21% not reasonable 17% neither	30% reasonable 53% not reasonable 17% do not know
Should people who support the Palestinian boycott call be condemned?	2016 Parliamentary vote to condemn supporters of the Palestinian boycott call; 7th November 2018 Prime Minister Trudeau criticizes BDS supporters.	53% no 26% yes 21% do not know	34% no 44% yes 22% do not know
Is it reasonable for Canada to impose sanctions on countries generally?	Sanctions against 20 countries	74% yes 8% no 14% do not know	82% yes 7% no 11% do not know
Is it reasonable for Canada to impose sanctions on Israel?	No Canadian sanctions of Israel	51% yes 27% no 22% do not know	22% yes 58% no 20% do not know

ucts. Finally, one in three (34 percent) of Jewish Canadians opposed Parliament's condemnation of BDS supporters (Ralph 2019: 27–33). These findings are somewhat surprising considering the years of intense anti-BDS campaigns by CIJA and other mainstream Jewish organizations, and in spite of the condemnation and hostility towards BDS as propagated by the Canadian government and mainstream media (see Chapters 4 and 7).

Conclusions

Both the Environics and the EKOS surveys of Jewish Canadians reveal that there is no monolithic "Jewish community," particularly on issues of Israel/Palestine. The EKOS survey shows that many Jewish Canadians reject the Israeli government's oppression of Palestinian people and its attempts to attack and muzzle principled critics, as do Canadians in general. Many also disagreed with the Canadian government's refusal to stand up against Israel's violations of international law. Almost half believed that accusations of antisemitism are "often" used to silence legitimate criticism of Israeli government policies.

Core Jewish values include justice, truth, loving-kindness and healing injustice. When Environics respondents were asked what they consider most essential to their Jewish identity, almost three-quarters (72 percent) said that "leading an ethical and moral life" is most essential to their Jewish identity and 52 percent felt that "working for justice/equality in society" was essential. Only 43 percent mentioned "caring about Israel" (Brym, Neuman and Lenton 2018: 18–19). Despite Holocaust-driven fears and heavy pro-Israel propaganda, a surprising proportion of Jewish Canadians supported justice for Palestinians and opposed Israeli policies which oppress them. Many felt deeply attached to Israel and considered caring about Israel a core element of being Jewish. But for many, caring about Israel also included holding it to a higher ethical standard than Israel currently plays.

These findings expose the groundlessness of the Canadian government's claims that "the Jewish community" supports Israel's oppression of Palestinians. Grassroots progressive Jewish groups, including Independent Jewish Voices Canada, If Not Now and the United Jewish Peoples Order, as well as progressive Jewish media like *Treyf*, are growing in size and influence, especially among a younger generation of Jews. Especially after the escalation of Israeli violence witnessed in May 2021, grassroots pressure to support justice for Palestinians appears to be rising within the ranks of the NDP, Green Party, Liberal Party and even the Conservative Party (Dyer 2021).

Neither public opinion in general nor a significant proportion of Jewish Canadians share our government's uncritical support for Israel. If Canada is indeed a democracy whose policies reflect the will of its citizens, human rights and international law, it has no legitimate excuse for continuing to condone Israeli oppression of Palestinians.

Note

1. Instances where results do not total 100% are explained by not reporting those who did not express an opinion.

References

B'nai Brith Canada. 2017. "A Guide to Fighting Antisemitism on Campus." <d3n8a8pro7vhmx.cloudfront.net/bnaibrithcanada/pages/2213/attachments/original/1504284577/English_BB_on_Campus_Guide.pdf?1504284577>.

Bozinoff, Lorne. 2014. "Support for Israel Trends Upwards." *Forum Research*, April 24. <poll.forumresearch.com/post/106/support-for-israel-trends-up-in-canada/>.

Brym, Robert, Keith Neuman and Rhonda Lenton. 2018. *2018 Survey of Jews in Canada: Final Report.* <environicsinstitute.org/docs/default-source/project-documents/2018-survey-of-jews-in-canada/2018-survey-of-jews-in-canada---final-report.pdf?sfvrsn=2994ef6_2>.

Bueckert, Michael. 2020. "Trudeau's Response to Annexation Is Already Failing." *Ricochet*, June 22. <ricochet.media/en/3193/trudeaus-response-to-israeli-annexation-is-already-failing>.

Bueckert, Michael, Thomas Woodley, Grafton Ross et al. 2020. "Out of Touch: Canada's Foreign Policy Disconnected from Canadians' Views." Part 1 of a national opinion survey of Canadians conducted June 5–10, 2020. Survey conducted by EKOS Research Associates, co-sponsored by Canadians for Justice and Peace in the Middle East, Independent Jewish Voices Canada, and United Network for Justice and Peace in Palestine-Israel. <www.cjpme.org/survey2020_r1>.

CBC Radio. 2017. "Christians Are Thrilled: American Evangelists Embrace Trump's Recognition of Jerusalem as Capital." *The Current*, December 11. <cbc.ca/radio/thecurrent/the-current-for-december-11-2017-1.4433520/christians-are-thrilled-american-evangelicals-embrace-trump-s-recognition-of-jerusalem-as-capital-1.4440096>.

Chase, Stephen. 2010. "An Attack on Israel Is an Attack on Canada, Kent Says." *Globe and Mail*, February 16. <theglobeandmail.com/news/politics/attack-on-israel-is-an-attack-on-canada-kent-says/article1365208/>.

CIJA (Centre for Israel and Jewish Affairs). 2018. "CIJA Criticizes Government Statement on Israel-Hamas Clashes." Press release, May 16. <cija.ca/press-release-cija-criticizes-government-statement-on-israel-hamas-clashes/>.

___. 2021. "CIJA: Frequently Asked Questions." <cija.ca/about-us/frequently-asked-questions/>.

CJN Staff. 2019. "Canadian Government Adopts IHRA Definition of Antisemitism." *Canadian Jewish News*, June 25. <cjnews.com/news/canada/canadian-government-adopts-ihra-definition-of-anti-semitism>.

Csillag, Ron. 2019. "Justin Trudeau Defends Anti-Israel UN Vote." *Canadian Jewish News*, December 10. <cjnews.com/news/canada/justin-trudeau-defends-anti-israel-un-vote>.

Dyer, Evan. 2021 "Violence in Gaza and Israel Has Left Behind a Changed Political Landscape in Canada." *CBC News*, May 29. <cbc.ca/news/politics/israel-palestinian-gaza-canada-1.6044837>.

Environics Institute for Survey Research. 2016. "Survey of Muslims in Canada 2016." April 30. Toronto. <environicsinstitute.org/projects/project-details/survey-of-muslims-in-canada-2016>.

Fife, Robert. 2018. "Canada Continues to Call for Independent Inquiry into Gaza Violence." *Globe and Mail*, May 22. <theglobeandmail.com/politics/article-canada-continues-to-call-for-independent-inquiry-into-gaza-violence/>

Freeman-Maloy, Daniel. 2006. "AIPAC North: 'Israel Advocacy' in Canada." *Zed Magazine*, June 26.

Global Affairs Canada. 2014. "Canada-Israel Strategic Partnership: Memorandum of Understanding." January 22. <international.gc.ca/name-anmo/canada_israel_MOU-prot_ent_canada_israel.aspx?lang=eng>.

___. 2018. "Minister Champagne Welcomes Modernized Canada–Israel Free Trade Agreement." News release, May 28. <canada.ca/en/global-affairs/news/2018/05/minister-champagne-welcomes-modernized-canada-israel-free-trade-agreement.html>.

___. 2019. "Statement by Minister Carr on Modernized Canada–Israel Free Trade Agreement Now in Force." September 1. <canada.ca/en/global-affairs/news/2019/08/statement-by-minister-carr-on-modernized-canada-israel-free-trade-agreement-now-in-force.html>.

Government of Canada. 2011. "Canada Becomes First Country to Sign the Ottawa Protocol." News release, September 19. <canada.ca/en/news/archive/2011/09/canada-becomes-first-country-sign-ottawa-protocol.html>.

___. 2019 [modified May 2021]. "Country Profile: Israel." September 12. <international.gc.ca/trade-commerce/trade-agreements-accords-commerciaux/agr-acc/israel/country_profile-israel-profil_pays.aspx?lang=eng>.

Halper, Jeff. 2015. *War Against the People*. London: Pluto Press.

Harper, Stephen. 2014. "Read the Full Text of Harper's Historic Speech to Israel's Knesset." *Globe and Mail*, January 20. <theglobeandmail.com/news/politics/read-the-full-text-of-harpers-historic-speech-to-israels-knesset/article16406371/>.

Housefather, Anthony. 2018. "Liberal MP Defends His Party's Record on Israel and Jewish Community." *Canadian Jewish News*, August 28. <cjnews.com/perspectives/opinions/liberal-mp-defends-his-partys-record-on-israel-and-jewish-community>.

Jewish Publication Society (ed.). 1985. *Tanakh: A New Translation of The Holy Scriptures According to the Traditional Hebrew Text*.

Keefer, Michael (ed.). 2010. *Antisemitism Real and Imagined: Responses to the Canadian Parliamentary Coalition to Combat Antisemitism*. Toronto: Canadian Charger.

Kennedy, Mark. 2014. "The Harper Doctrine: Why Canada's Prime Minister Supports Israel" *Ottawa Citizen*, August 3. <ottawacitizen.com/news/national/the-harper-doctrine-why-canadas-prime-minister-supports-israel>.

Klug, Brian. 2003. "The Collective Jew: Israel and the New Antisemitism." *Patterns of Prejudice* 37, 2.

Love, Myron. 2017. "Irwin Cotler Tackles the Rise of Modern Anti-Semitism." *Canadian Jewish News*, May 4. <cjnews.com/news/canada/cotler-tackles-rise-modern-anti-semitism>.

Lungen, Paul. 2018. "Elizabeth May, Jagmeet Singh Slammed by Jewish Groups over Gaza Comments." *Canadian Jewish News*, April 13. <cjnews.com/news/canada/elizabeth-may-jagmeet-singh-slammed-by-jewish-groups-over-gaza-comments>.

Macleod, Jennifer Tzivia. 2018. "Canada's Support for Israel is 'Ironclad,' Foreign Minister Says." *Canadian Jewish News*, November 2. <cjnews.com/news/canada/canadas-support-for-israel-is-ironclad-foreign-minister-says>.

Martin, Patrick. 2016. "Parliament Votes to Reject Israel Boycott Campaign." *Globe and*

Mail, February 23. <theglobeandmail.com/news/world/parliament-votes-to-reject-campaign-to-boycott-israel/article28863810/>.

Masalha, Nur. 2007. *The Bible and Zionism: Invented Traditions, Archaeology and Post-Colonialism in Israel-Palestine.* London: Zed.

Pew Research Center. 2013. *A Portrait of Jewish Americans.* Oct. 1. <pewforum.org/2013/10/01/jewish-american-beliefs-attitudes-culture-survey/>.

Ralph, Diana. 2007. "Fortress CJC: The CIJA Takeover." *Outlook: Canada's Progressive Jewish Magazine*, Aug. 9.

___. 2019. "Two Jews, Three Opinions: Jewish Canadians' Diverse Views on Israel-Palestine." Results of a national opinion poll of Jewish Canadians conducted June 25 and September, 2018. Issued by Independent Jewish Voices. January. <ijvcanada.org/wp-content/uploads/2019/02/report.Finpdf.pdf>.

Ralph, Diana, Murray Dobbin, Dimitri Lascaris and Thomas Woodley. 2017a. *Disconnect: Canadians' Views of the Israeli Government vs. Canadian Government Policy toward Israel and Palestine.* A report on a Canadian national opinion survey conducted January 25 to February 2, 2017, by EKOS Research Associates. Issued by Independent Jewish Voices Canada, Canadians for Justice and Peace in the Middle East, Murray Dobbin, and Dimitri Lascaris. February 16. <d3n8a8pro7vhmx.cloudfront.net/cjpme/pages/2537/attachments/original/1488331789/EKOS_Poll_Results_Report_-_2017-02-16-Final-v3.pdf?1488331789>.

___. 2017b. *A Survey on Canadians' Views Toward Israel/Palestine: Most Canadians Say Sanctions and Boycott Are Reasonable Measures to Defend Palestinian Rights.* Report on Part 2 of a Canadian national opinion survey conducted January 25 to February 2, 2017, by EKOS Research Associates. Issued by Independent Jewish Voices Canada, Canadians for Justice and Peace in the Middle East, Murray Dobbin, and Dimitri Lascaris. March 2. <d3n8a8pro7vhmx.cloudfront.net/cjpme/pages/2537/attachments/original/1488423127/EKOS_Poll_Results_Report_R2_-_2017-03-02-Final-v1.pdf?1488423127>.

Seligman, Stephen. 2018. "How Far Apart Are Trudeau and Harper?" *Canadian Jewish News*, June 13. <cjnews.com/news/canada/how-far-apart-are-trudeau-and-harper>.

Sharansky, Natan. 2005. "Antisemitism in 3-D." *The Forward*, January 21. <forward.com/opinion/4184/antisemitism-in-3-d/>.

Statistics Canada. n.d. "Immigration and Ethnocultural Diversity Statistics." Last updated November 22, 2021. <statcan.gc.ca/en/subjects-start/immigration_and_ethnocultural_diversity>.

___. 2013. "General Social Survey." <www23.statcan.gc.ca/imdb-bmdi/instrument/5024_Q1_V3-eng.htm>.

Trudeau, Justin. 2018. "Prime Minister Delivers Apology Regarding the Fate of Passengers of the MS St. Louis." November 7. <pm.gc.ca/en/news/news-releases/2018/11/07/prime-minister-delivers-apology-regarding-fate-passengers-ms-st-louis>.

World Population Review. n.d. "Canada Population 2021." <worldpopulationreview.com/countries/canada-population>.

Yakabuski, Konrad. 2018. "On Israel, Trudeau Is Harper's Pupil." *Globe and Mail*, May 11. <theglobeandmail.com/opinion/article-on-israel-trudeau-is-harpers-pupil/>.

Chapter 6

Knowing and Not Knowing

Canada, Indigenous Peoples, Israel and Palestine

Michael Keefer

On November 7, 2018, the eightieth anniversary of Kristallnacht, Prime Minister Justin Trudeau offered an apology in the House of Commons for an event that occurred in June 1939, seven months after that Nazi massacre — Canada's refusal of landing rights to Jewish refugees aboard the MS *St. Louis*, some 250 of whom subsequently died in the Shoah — and for the antisemitism that had prompted that refusal.[1]

Trudeau spoke also of present-day antisemitism:

> Holocaust deniers still exist…. Jewish institutions and neighbourhoods are still being vandalized with swastikas. Jewish students still feel unwelcome and uncomfortable on some of our college and university campuses because of BDS-related intimidation. And out of our entire community of nations, it is Israel whose right to exist is most widely — and wrongly — questioned. (CJN Staff 2018)

He then made an extended reference to the murder by a white supremacist of eleven Jewish worshippers in the Tree of Life synagogue in Pittsburgh less than two weeks prior.

Responses to this apology included an open letter of January 15 signed by 236 Canadian academics (of whom I was one). Thanking Mr. Trudeau for acknowledging Canada's complicity in the deaths of Jewish refugees murdered in the Holocaust, the letter emphasized the need to recognize Canada's history of bigotry and "recommit to preventing such tragedies from ever happening again." It therefore expressed disappointment with Trudeau's condemnation of the Boycott, Divestment and Sanctions movement (BDS) and conflation of BDS with violent hate crimes: "This … does nothing to stop anti-Semitism, but instead only targets and misrepresents peaceful advocacy for Palestinian human rights … and help[s] to perpetuate a chilling, anti-democratic climate on campuses." The letter also echoed Independent Jewish Voices Canada (IJV) in noting the government's recent announcement "of plans to substantially increase deportation of migrants by 25–35%" (Ghabrial and Razlgova 2018).

The open letter thus exposed a two-fold hypocrisy. Trudeau's apology for a heartless plunging of refugees back into Nazi persecution was undercut by his government's willingness to act in a similar manner toward present-day migrants who would be seriously endangered if returned to their strife-torn homelands. Noting that the crime and tragedy of turning away the MS *St. Louis* "was committed — let us be frank — by white settler Canadians," the letter called it "shameful" to displace guilt "for white Canada's complicity in the Holocaust onto the peaceful, grassroots work of students, faculty and community members active in the BDS movement today" (Ghabrial and Razlgova 2018).

Asked whether this letter had altered his thinking, Mr. Trudeau reiterated his condemnation of BDS. Antisemitism, he said, motivates hate crimes and "a new condemnation or antisemitism against the very state of Israel" which "my friend Irwin Cotler" (a former minister of justice and attorney general) defines in terms of "demonization of Israel, a double standard around Israel, and a delegitimization of the state of Israel." Stating that BDS propagates these forms of "new" antisemitism, and makes Jewish students "fearful," Trudeau declared it unacceptable — "not because of foreign policy concerns, but because of Canadian values" (YouTube 2019; see also Kestler-D'Amours 2019).

This prompted a wave of responses on Twitter. The Centre for Israel and Jewish Affairs (CIJA) thanked Trudeau "for standing with the Jewish community against the divisive BDS campaign" — while IJV said Trudeau "isn't 'standing with us.' He's using our identities as Jews to go after support for Palestinian human rights." Rabbi David Mivasair wrote: "Other Jews and I support BDS 100% and oppose antisemitism 100%. BDS is about freedom, justice and equality for Palestinians. Justin Trudeau doesn't know what he's talking about." (RT Online 2019).

But Trudeau's repeated smearing of BDS may have been less a matter of ignorance than of what Hannah Arendt, in a classic essay on "Lying in Politics," termed image-making, defactualization and ideologizing (1972: 44). His apology for the *St. Louis* affair sandwiched a claim of

"BDS-related intimidation" between references to neo-Nazi propaganda and to the Pittsburgh mass murder — thereby dumping anti-racist supporters of the rights of Palestinian refugees and victims of occupation into the same category as vicious racists and a mass-murderer who identified himself in online postings as violently opposed to refugees and Jews — especially those, like the Tree of Life Congregation, who aid refugees (Silverstein 2018). And the words in which Trudeau insisted that "all Canadians must stand up against xenophobic and antisemitic attitudes" and "guard our communities and institutions against the kinds of evils that took hold in the hearts of so many, more than 70 years ago," resonated with the imagery of our national anthem: "O Canada … we stand on guard for thee."

This statement conflated Canadian activists (many of them Jewish) who are working for the rights of refugees with a man who murdered Jews and was enabled by a pervasive defactualization. Trudeau occulted the actuality of the BDS movement, and likewise the fact that the BDS campaign's demands — an end to Israel's occupation and colonization of Arab lands and dismantling of the Wall, recognition of the rights of Arab-Palestinian citizens of Israel to full equality, and respecting, protecting and promoting the right of Palestinian refugees to return to their homes and properties as stipulated in UN General Assembly Resolution 194 — conform "100% with Canada's official policy on Israel, Palestine, and human rights" (Independent Jewish Voices Canada 2016). Moreover, Trudeau's claims about intimidation of Jewish students on Canadian campuses have no basis in fact, although they have been a mainstay of pro-Israel *hasbara*.[2]

During the "political correctness" debates of the 1990s, polemicists sought to create a mood of moral panic by regailing narratives — most of them wildly exaggerated, if not pure fiction — of the victimization of conservative students and faculty by politically correct radicals (Keefer 1996). The same pattern has re-emerged among pro-Israel polemicists (Keefer 2010c; Keefer 2016; Barrows-Friedman 2015; Blumenthal and Carmel 2015; and Abunimah 2019). In 2010 public hearings were conducted by a group of Canadian MPs calling themselves the Canadian Parliamentary Coalition to Combat Antisemitism (CPCCA), whose principal organizer was Irwin Cotler. They were annoyed to be told by university administrators that Canadian campuses "are not hotbeds of anti-Semitism or racism of any kind" (Palestine Freedom of Expression

Campaign 2010: 9).[3] As Robert Steiner, assistant vice-president of the University of Toronto, declared: "There is no evidence of generalized anti-Semitism" or "of Jewish students being systematically harassed and intimidated on our campuses. There is no evidence that it is dangerous to be a pro-Israel student, faculty member, or staff member on our campuses — in fact, quite the opposite" (quoted by Briemberg and Campbell 2010). The CPCCA's final report smeared the administrators as having "little knowledge" of relevant facts and "failing in their duties" (*Report* 2011: 60).

The ideological system shaping Justin Trudeau's image-making and defactualization was identified when he acknowledged Irwin Cotler as the source of his understanding of a "new antisemitism." Antony Lerman, the founding editor of *Antisemitism World Report,* has described Cotler as "one of the key figures" in disseminating this ideology (Lerman 2017: 8) — a fact which does not contribute to Cotler's credit (see Keefer 2010a; Keefer 2010c; Engler 2019; and Beeley 2019).

The "new antisemitism," as Norman G. Finkelstein has written, is "neither new nor about antisemitism." He notes that the term was first deployed by leaders of the US Anti-Defamation League, "not to fight anti-Semitism but rather to exploit the historical suffering of Jews in order to immunize Israel against criticism" and to resist pressures on Israel after the October 1973 war "to withdraw from the Egyptian Sinai and to reach a diplomatic settlement with the Palestinians" (2005: 21, 22, 24). More recent iterations of this ideology have worked to stir up "a calculated hysteria" designed "to deflect criticism of an unprecedented assault on international law" (Finkelstein 2005: 45).[4]

The "new antisemitism" can be defined as a rhetorical gambit which involves claiming that the tropes of antisemitism, which sought to justify excluding Jews from full citizenship in whatever country they inhabit, are now being turned against the "collective Jew," as embodied in the State of Israel — with the purpose this time of excluding Jews as a national collective from enjoying full rights of participation in the family of nations (see Cotler 2009).[5] This rhetorical turn defends Israeli policies and actions by proposing that critics only pretend to be impelled by principles of justice and equity: they are actually antisemites redirecting their hatred of Jews against the Jewish nation-state.

If criticisms of Israel are simply antisemitic tropes, then Israelis accused of war crimes or crimes against humanity become victims of hate crimes. Thus, a well-substantiated account of the filth and squalor to which Israel has condemned Palestinians in the West Bank and Gaza by denying them adequate sewage facilities and fuel to run pumping stations has been attacked as reviving antisemitic tropes of Jewish impurity and contamination, and authoritative accusations of Israeli atrocities against Palestinian civilians have been dismissed as renewals of the blood libel (Keefer 2010b, Keefer 2010c).

The "new antisemitism" aims then to dispose of the facts and the evidence supporting criticisms of the Israeli state's oppressions and crimes and to discover in their place libellous slurs against Israel that resonate with the shameful tropes of European antisemitism.

Political Lying, "Différends," Genocide

To expose the fraudulent ideology at work in Justin Trudeau's condemnation of BDS is not the same thing as understanding the causalities involved. A similarly uncritical support for the State of Israel is widespread among Canada's political elite — the people who control our country's major media outlets as well as the major political parties. Let us consider why.

The open letter of January 15 signalled the indecency of linking the official antisemitism that prevailed eighty years ago within Canada's highly racialized settler-colony culture with the explicitly anti-racist civic activism of present-day Canadians who support the Palestinians' struggle against colonization by another highly racialized state with which Canada is closely allied. In December 2018, Hamid Dabashi drew a link between Trudeau's "incoherent" and "vacuous" apology-plus-BDS-condemnation and his treatment of Indigenous Peoples in Canada. Dabashi saw the hypocrisy of Trudeau's position on antisemitism reappearing in his decision to push ahead with the Kinder Morgan pipeline from the Alberta tar sands through First Nations territories to the tidewater of British Columbia — which contradicted his professed respect for climate science, overrode the strenuous objections of First Nations leaders and exposed the emptiness of his proclamations that reconciliation with Indigenous Peoples was one of his top priorities. For Dabashi, this showed that his "electioneering song and dance about being truly apologetic for the terror white European settler colonialists had unleashed upon the First Nations, similar to the one Trudeau's favourite Zionists have practised upon Palestinians," was a deception — but one that his condemnation of BDS has helped to expose: "His lies about his commitment to the rights of the First Nations ... become transparent by his racist position against the Palestinians" (Dabashi 2018).

Justin Trudeau's condemnations of BDS in January 2019 coincided with the moment at which a long-simmering dispute over a proposed fracked-gas pipeline through the ancestral territories of the Wet'suwet'en people of northern British Columbia came to the boil (and has continued since), the demolition of Indigenous blockades by heavily armed RCMP units making parallels between Canada and Israel as settler-colony states all the more obvious. Many recent conflicts between First Nations and the Canadian state, among them the resistance of the Elsipogtog Mi'kmaq to fracking exploration in 2013 (see Howe 2015), have been prompted by resource exploitation issues. It is hard not to see resonances between such episodes and Israel's behaviour in relation to Palestinian water and gas resources (Hass 2014; Antreasyan 2013), and it seems relevant that in December 2018 Canada was one of a handful of countries that voted against a UN General Assembly resolution affirming the right of the Palestinian people to sovereignty over their natural resources (Palestinian Information Center 2018).

As a basis of comparison between Canada and Israel as settler-colonies, in both cases the same structural principle underlies the relations between settler-colonists and Indigenous Peoples. That principle is what the philosopher Jean-François Lyotard called "*le différend.*" A *différend* can be described, in Lyotard's terms, as arising out of the intersection of heterogeneous, incommensurable or mutually exclusive regimens of discourse within a domain characterized by a significant differential in power. Lyotard offers a judicial example to illustrate his meaning:

> A plaintiff is someone who has incurred damages, and who disposes of the means to prove it. One becomes a victim if one loses these means. One loses them, for example, if the author of the damages turns out directly or indirectly to be one's judge....
> A case of différend between two parties takes place when the "regulation" of the conflict that opposes them is done in the idiom of one of the parties while the wrong suffered by the other is not signified in that idiom. (1988: 8–9)

In Israel, the Zionist slogan, "a land without people for a people without land," implies a particularly brutal form of *différend*, because in the lived reality of Palestine (as opposed to the discredited pseudo-scholarship of ideologues like Joan Peters and Alan Dershowitz[6]) it could only be actualized through an implicitly genocidal project of emptying the land of its inhabitants in order to produce the requisite vacancy. This *différend* might take present-day forms such as these:

1) A descendant of refugees, you present yourself as a plaintiff, holding the door key of the Jaffa house from which your grandparents were expelled during the Nakba. Your case will be adjudicated by the expropriators' heirs, and under the settler-colonists' law you are a non-person and your case a nullity.

2) Expelled in 1967 from your home in Imwas, a village in the West Bank, what recompense can you seek? No such village exists, because Imwas was bulldozed when all its inhabitants were violently displaced.

In this second instance, the "disappeared" village of Imwas is probably Emmaus, the site of the most extended of the *New Testament*'s post-resurrection narratives. Jesus, who had effectively been "disappeared" three days before in the most agonizing and humiliating way that Roman imperial power could devise, reappeared to two of his disciples on the road from Jerusalem to Emmaus and "interpreted to them in all the scriptures the things concerning himself" (*Luke* 24: 27). In the village's inn they were suddenly able to recognize him when he broke and blessed the bread they were to eat. But the road to Emmaus now leads to a forested recreation area known as Canada Park — constructed with tax-deductible donations from Canadians to the JNF, which has contributed to projects of ethnic cleansing throughout Israel and the West Bank by erasing the physical evidence of Palestinian lives and culture (Cook 2009).[7]

Here, then, is the material form of a discursive *différend*: through a deliberate disappearing act, the millennia of a people's dwelling on the site of Emmaus/Imwas have been made to vanish. However, counter-memory has been asserting itself: "Canada Park," a place of idyllic beauty, has become the signifier of a crime against humanity and of Canada's complicity in a program of cultural genocide.

But the Israel-Palestine *différend* goes deeper: the genocide involved is not merely cultural. The fact that Israel has imposed a system of apartheid upon its Palestinian subjects has been definitively established (see Tilley 2009; Corrigan 2016). Yet as Eva Illouz, one of Israel's most distinguished sociologists, wrote in 2014, Israel has subjected the Palestinians in the occupied territories to something worse than apartheid: "a condition of slavery." Citing leading experts on slavery, she says its defining feature is not that people are bought and sold as property, but rather that they live in a condition of permanent, violent and complete subjugation. In occupied Palestine, this "matrix of domination" includes subjection to arbitrary arrest, incarceration and torture; the imposition of a Kafkaesque legal system; military attacks, as well as violence and property destruction inflicted with impunity by settlers; severe restrictions on movement, marriage and property ownership; and the imposition of "a permanent sense of dishonor" on people who "live in fear of Jewish terror and of the violence of the Israeli military power, and are afraid to have no work, shelter, or family" (Illouz 2014).

A searching analysis by Kent McNeil of Indigenous and Crown sovereignty can expose the workings of a parallel *différend* in Canadian settlement history. *De facto* sovereignty, McNeil observes, is an empirical matter of who inhabits, controls and exercises authority over a territory. Legal or *de jure* sovereignty, in contrast, "depends on the application of a particular body of law." The question is, whose? In North America, European nation states deployed legal fictions resting on the idea that the continent, though visibly populated, was *terra nullius*,[8] to support assertions of *de jure* sovereignty: these included claims based upon a supposed right of discovery, "symbolic acts of possession" and royal charters "purporting to grant huge expanses of territory to individuals and companies" (McNeil 2018: 297). At the same time, Indigenous Peoples possessed *de facto* sovereignty over their territories and systems of domestic and inter-nation Indigenous law. Although the European law of nations gave little if any recognition to Indigenous sovereignty, France, Britain and the Netherlands all at different times made formal treaties with Indigenous Peoples, thereby producing a body of inter-societal law that implied a relationship between sovereign powers.

Canada's historical inheritance thus pulls in two directions: on one hand, toward a situation in which the relationship between the settler-state and Indigenous Peoples is an unmitigated *différend*, with the dominant social discourses refusing validation of Indigenous rights; and on the other hand, toward a situation in which — once issues of redress, restoration and restitution have been engaged with — a dialogical process leading toward reconciliation might become possible.

The current state of Canadian law, as defined by the Supreme Court in 2014, is that "the doctrine of *terra nullius* (that no one owned the land prior to European assertion of sovereignty) never applied in Canada, as confirmed by the *Royal Proclamation* (1763), R.S.C. 1985, App. II, No. 1." The court's definition of the relationship between settler-state and Indigenous land claims (in this case, in British Columbia) gives ambiguous weight to Aboriginal title:

> At the time of assertion of European sovereignty, the Crown acquired radical or underlying title to all the land in the province. This Crown title, however, was burdened by the pre-existing legal rights of Aboriginal people who occupied and used the land prior to European arrival.... The Aboriginal interest in land that burdens the Crown's underlying title is an independent legal interest, which gives rise to a fiduciary duty on the part of the Crown. (*Tsilqot'in Nation v. British Columbia* 2014 SCC 44, quoted by Harrington 2014)

Canada is also burdened, however, by a history in which — during a period that Shin Imai has described as "a century-long Dark Ages in [Canada's] relations with Indigenous peoples" (2017: 372) — government policies were shaped by racist ideologies of nationalism and imperialism and by a determination (still active) to exploit land and resources under private and corporate property ownership. As John Milloy has written, "The centrality given to the [*Royal Proclamation* of 1763] in the 1982 Constitution, and its respect for Aboriginal rights, is only a relatively recent feature of Canada's history. For most of that history, from 1869 forward, the Proclamation's principles were … ignored [and] violated" (2008: 1–2). Post-Confederation treaties between Canada and Indigenous Peoples have also been systematically violated.

Canadian Confederation in 1867 was followed by actions that attempted to lock Indigenous Peoples into a condition of unmitigated *differénd*. An 1869 *Act for the Gradual Enfranchisement of Indians* abolished Indigenous forms of government, substituting cultural forms of leadership with elected councils with municipal-level responsibilities and controlled by Indian agents with federal jurisdiction. In 1876 the *Indian Act* attempted to reduce Indigenous Peoples to a state of impotence so complete that even the question of who belonged to Indigenous communities was determined by the Department of Indian Affairs

(Milloy 2008: 4–11). These effects have been compounded by under-funding, bureaucratic inertia and incompetence, so that, as Dr. Michael Dan observes, "All the social determinants of health that are governed by the Indian Act … have been allowed to fail" (Dan n.d.).

The violence involved in moving Indigenous Peoples into reserves consisting of a small fraction of their traditional lands and confining them there with a pass system unsanctioned by Canadian law (Barron 1988)[9] has been erased from the historical consciousness of Canadians. (This massive act of disappearance and forgetting might appropriately be described as "Canada Park writ large.") But one major episode, studied by James Daschuk in his book *Clearing the Plains* (2013), stands out as an exception. The situation inherited by the Canadian government when it acquired *de jure* sovereignty over the former territories of Rupert's Land and North-West Territories in December 1869 included the impending collapse of an economy based on buffalo hunting. But the government failed to fulfil the obligations it took on in treaty negotiations with the Plains Cree in 1876 with respect to food, medicines, education and support in moving into an agricultural economy.

The results included mass starvation and epidemics of smallpox and tuberculosis. Sir John A. Macdonald was directly responsible, with government agents acting on his orders to minimize expenditures on relief. "We cannot allow them to die for want of food," he said. But at the same time, "We are doing all we can, by refusing food until the Indians are on the verge of starvation, to reduce the expense" (Lux 2001: 69–70, quoted by Daschuk 2013: 235 n.209). Macdonald's most notorious action, "the forced removal of communities from their chosen reserves in the Cypress Hills after the decision to build the Canadian Pacific Railway along the southern prairies," was carried out in 1882. This was attempted ethnic cleansing: the rations of some 5,000 already starving people were withheld until they capitulated (Daschuk 2013: 123).

The results of these genocidal policies were striking. In 1955 Dr. R.G. Ferguson, an authority on tuberculosis, estimated, on the basis of mortality data from annuity lists, that "the death rate on the Qu'Appelle reserves rose from 40 per 1,000 in 1881 to 127 per 1,000 in 1886, an increase of 87 per 1,000 in only five years." Daschuk remarks that "a European population would not experience a comparable rate until 1942 — among the Jewish population of the Warsaw ghetto" (Daschuk 2013: 177, citing Ferguson 1955: 4–8).

Another more notorious genocidal policy was the system of residential schools, with the first school opened in 1883 and the last one closed down in 1996. I have written elsewhere on this subject (Keefer 2021: 104–11); here I restrict myself to comments on a figure who was responsible for the system for a quarter century: Duncan Campbell Scott, a highly regarded writer and culturally central figure.[10]

A 1907 inspection of residential schools in the prairie provinces by Dr. Peter Bryce, chief medical officer of the Indian Department, produced shocking revelations: after fifteen years of operation, "24 per cent of all the pupils which had been in the schools were known to be dead," and fully three-quarters of the pupils who had attended one school "were dead [of tuberculosis] at the end of the 16 years since the school opened" (Bryce 1922: 4, see Sproule-Jones 1996). Bryce's report leaked out to the press, causing a scandal, but Scott, the department's superintendent of schools, blocked Bryce's recommendations for radical changes. Scott wrote in 1910, "It is readily acknowledged that Indian children lose their natural resistance to illness by habituating so closely in the residential schools, and that they die at a much higher rate than in their villages. But this alone does not justify a change in the policy of this Department, which is geared towards a final solution of our Indian problem" (Letter to BC Indian Agent Gen. Major D. MacKay, 12 April 1910, *Department of Indian Affairs Archives,* RG 10 series, quoted by Spear 2010). Indigenous author Thomas King has remarked: "Final solution. An unfortunate choice of words. Of course, no one is suggesting that Adolf Hitler was quoting Scott when Hitler talked about the final solution of the 'Jewish problem' in 1942. That would be tactless and unseemly. And just so we're perfectly clear, Scott was advocating assimilation, not extermination. Sometimes people get the two mixed up" (2012: 114).

In an essay titled "Indian Affairs, 1867–1912," published in 1914, Scott ascribed high death rates in the schools to faults in building design and "the well-known predisposition of Indians to tuberculosis"; he wrote complacently, "It is quite within the mark to say that fifty per cent of the children who passed through these schools did not live to benefit from the education which they had received therein" (2000: 204–05). Any population that is malnourished, ill clothed, inadequately housed, brutalized, denied adequate medical services and exposed to sources of infection will show a "predisposition to tuberculosis." But Scott was willing to accept a murderous death rate among helpless children as a short-cut to his goal of a Canada with no unassimilated Indians, and hence no "Indian problem."

Epidemic disease remained among Indigenous Peoples after Scott's retirement in 1932. In February 1940, a Dr. J.D. Galbraith wrote to British Columbia's provincial secretary from the Nuxalk community of Bella Coola, urging action to address the fact that "the Canadian Indian is the only person in Canada who is excluded entirely from the nation-wide organization to cope with the disease of tuberculosis" (Rutty and Sullivan 2010: Ch. 5, 5.7). According to the Canadian Public Health Association, malnutrition and "the confinement of First Nations people on crowded reserves" were encouraging a continuing spread of tuberculosis: "Death rates in the 1930s and 1940s were in excess of 700 deaths per 100,000 persons, among the highest ever reported in a human population. Tragically, TB death rates among children in residential schools were even worse — as high as 8,000 deaths per 100,000 children" (Change to Canadian Public Health Association n.d.).[11] A comparison with the countries now most afflicted by tuberculosis is revealing. In Mozambique, the Congo and Angola (countries ravaged by proxy and civil wars), the annual death rates from tuberculosis are, respectively, 75, 67 and 64 per 100,000 population (see Statista 2021).

In June 2008, then-Prime Minister Stephen Harper issued a formal apology for the residential school system. Indigenous responses were guarded. Kevin McKay, chair of the Nisga'a Lisims Government, said that its acceptability "is very much a personal decision of residential school survivors" and that the Nisga'a would assess its sincerity "on the basis of the policies and actions of the government in the days and years to come" (Hanson, Games and Manuel 2020). The question of Harper's sincerity was answered by his declaration in September 2009 at the Pittsburgh G20 Summit that Canada has "no history of colonialism" (Ljunggren 2009). That assertion, Derrick O'Keefe wrote, exposed "the pervasive racism-fuelled historical amnesia and denial in Canadian society" and showed what the apology "was really worth" (O'Keefe 2009).

Canada Faced with Palestinian and Indigenous Resistance

One cannot expect an adequate understanding of the refusal of Canada's political elites to engage decently with the issue of Palestine to emerge from a discussion as brief as this. But a consideration of salient differences between Israel and Canada as settler colonies may help bring the issue into focus.

The non-Jewish population of that "Greater Israel" toward which the policies of Benjamin Netanyahu have been moving — people subjected to petty apartheid within Israel's pre-1967 borders, and to a condition of slavery in the occupied territories — constitute over half the population of that territory as a whole.[12] As Gideon Levy, Jonathan Cook, Lia Tarachansky and others have explained, Israel faces an aporetic situation exposing the incoherence of its self-definition as a democracy and a Jewish state. Given the prominence of racist, indeed genocidal discourse within present-day Israel (see Hider 2008, and Blumenthal 2013: 252–54, 303–12, 321–24, 342–47), further hardening of the Israel-Palestine *différend* could lead to a possible repetition of the Nakba. An unravelling of that *différend*, making Israel/Palestine the state of all its citizens, would require a concession of *liberté, fraternité* and *égalité* on the part of the Jewish population to Palestine — or as Jewish liberation theologians like Marc Ellis declare, a return to the tradition of prophetic Judaism, with its commitment to a universalized equity and justice, as adumbrated in the writings of the biblical prophets (Ellis 2010). This means a turn away from Israel's founding project toward the binational state advocated in the 1930s and 1940s by Judah Magnes (see Stuart 2015).

In Canada, where Indigenous Peoples make up about 5.5 percent of the population, violence tends more often to be structural and systemic rather than overtly military — though as Indigenous resistance has become increasingly well-organized and sophisticated, a "security state" mentality has found expression in forms of surveillance and militarized intervention that, as Andrew Crosby and Jeffrey Monaghan write, constitute a "staggering affront to activities protected by the *Canadian Charter of Rights and Freedoms*" (Crosby and Monaghan 2018: 2). But wouldn't an elimination of structural and militarized violence, and an undoing of the *différend* between Indigenous Peoples and the Canadian state, fulfil rather than undo the nation's formally stated constitutive principles?

Why then is this *différend* not immediately resolved? Journalist Nora Loreto is largely correct in recognizing deep linkages between the Israeli and Canadian forms of *différend*: "Justin Trudeau is so strongly opposed to BDS because he says it opposes Canadian values. Which is accurate, because genocide, land dispossession, white supremacy and violence are all at the centre of our so-called values. Settler states stick together" ("Twitter up in arms").

Our country's *enacted* values are indeed for the most part those of the corporate and security-state interests that have guided public policy. But it may be short-sighted to ignore the fact that many Canadians oppose those interests and espouse the egalitarian values that have been expressed by writers like Naomi Klein, Linda McQuaig, Michael Harris and John Ralston Saul. Moreover, Supreme Court decisions, such as the Tsilhqot'in decision, have been moving, if still fumblingly, toward formulating a way out of the *différend* between Indigenous and settler-state understandings of territorial rights and sovereignty. Most importantly, as with the international struggle for Palestinian rights — which has been energized by Palestinian artists, writers, filmmakers and scholars (the latter including, in the wake of Edward Said, figures like Ali Abunimah, Omar Barghouti, Ramzy Baroud, Marwan Bishara, Saree Makdisi, Basem Ra'ad and Steven Salaita) — crucial forms of self-representation, as well as ethical guidance for settler-colonial Canadians, have been provided by Indigenous artists working in many mediums, as well as by scholars who have been rising to well-earned prominence in Canadian universities and governance systems — among them Taiaiake Alfred, Àpihtawikosisân (Chelsea Vowel), John Borrows, Glen Coulthard, Mizanay Gheezhik (Murray Sinclair), Pamela Palmater and Tamara Starblanket.

Yet systemic repetitions are glaringly obvious. Prime ministers make disingenuous apologies over past actions by the Canadian state that they themselves promptly compound. The RCMP's militarized assault on Wet'suwet'en rights in British Columbia in 2019 and in the years following reproduces the pattern of its 2013 assault on Mi'kmaw rights in New Brunswick (likewise in support of gas-fracking interests), and of its 1922 and 1924 assaults on Six Nations rights in Ontario (see Cox 2020; Howe 2015: 144–78; Windle 2016; Elliott 2015; Smith n.d.). This pattern persists in the struggle over the logging of Fairy Creek, one of the last surviving pockets of old-growth rainforest on Vancouver Island, where since the summer of 2020 Indigenous people and non-Indigenous activists have maintained rotating blockades of logging roads.

Arno Kopecky (2021) sums up his experience of covering the Fairy Creek struggle in these words:

This clock was wound up 150 years ago. The colonial experiment was the thing that set the stage, wrote the script, built the machine.... If you come to Fairy Creek you can't *not* see the way its parts all whir and click and spin in perfect harmony.

They wanted the land. In order to take it, they had to remove the people who lived on it. The same forces of destruction were unleashed on First Nations and forests alike.

What of the consciousness of most Canadians? "All these generations later," Kopecky writes,

> Settlers are still carrying out a mission so ingrained we don't even perceive it.... It doesn't seem strange that the provincial capital's daily paper is called the *Times Colonist*. Until it does, the colonial machine will grind on ... at two parallel time scales: a glacial pace in matters of justice and reform, fast as a buzzsaw in all matters of plunder.

Of overlapping news reports of the ground-penetrating radar discovery of an unmarked mass grave containing the bodies of 215 Indigenous children at the site of a Kamloops, BC, residential school, Kopecky writes: "There is no distance between that story and this one" (Kopecky 2021).

Those unmarked graves, and the thousands identified since across Turtle Island, David Climenhaga says, are "irrefutable evidence of a crime against humanity.... As for the details and intent of the crime, if it marches like genocide, and talks like genocide, it is genocide." And now, "whether we like it or not we are going to be asked to face our national reality and do something about it" (Climenhaga 2021).[13]

In a manner that matches their violations of Indigenous Rights, Canadian leaders have been consistent in their responses to crimes against humanity committed by the State of Israel against the Palestinian people. In 2008–09, 2012 and 2014, Canada supported Israel's violent attacks upon the civilian population of Gaza, and when the weekly repetitions of the Great March of Return began in Gaza on March 30, 2018, the Trudeau government refused to condemn the massacre by Israeli snipers "of Palestinian children, women and men ... defending their dignity, sovereignty and humanity during peaceful demonstrations on Palestinian soil" (Mitrovica 2018).

This pattern was repeated in May 2021, when accelerated ethnic

cleansing in East Jerusalem and the tear-gassing and beating of worshippers inside the Al Aqsa Mosque, as well as aerial attacks on Gaza, provoked a rocket-fire response from Gaza, which the Israeli government
used as a pretext for radically intensifying its bombardments. By the
time on May 21 a negotiated ceasefire came into effect, 256 Palestinians,
including sixty-six children, had been killed, along with thirteen Israelis,
two of them children.

The Canadian government issued a statement on May 16, a week
after the intensified conflict began. While defining Israel's "continued
expansion of settlements, demolitions, and evictions" as "a violation
of international law," it made no mention of Israel's role in provoking
the violence, of what major human rights organizations have belatedly
recognized as the apartheid nature of Israel's structures of governance,
of the hugely disproportionate suffering and deaths inflicted upon the
population of Gaza or even of the basic fact that Israel's armed forces
were actually bombarding Gaza. This statement condemned the "continued indiscriminate barrage of rocket attacks fired by Hamas and
Palestinian Islamic Jihad into Israel against civilians," while supporting
"Israel's right to live in peace with its neighbours" and "Israel's right to
assure its own security" (Global Affairs Canada 2021) — thus making it
appear that Israel was a passive victim of Palestinian aggression. Given
this impudent falsification by subtractive politicizing,[14] the text's expressions of concern over the "devastating" and "heartbreaking" loss of life
can be dismissed as hypocritical virtue-signalling.

Would it be unfair to set this statement about the slaughter in Gaza
alongside official responses to the discovery of unmarked graves in
Kamloops? Minister of Indigenous Services Marc Miller called the latter news "absolutely heartbreaking"; Prime Minister Trudeau declared
that "The news … breaks my heart" (Paperny 2021).[15] Perhaps not, since
Trudeau's words involve, once again, a pretence of not knowing something that he knows very well.

Shelagh Rogers, journalist and chancellor of the University of Victoria,
responded to Trudeau's statement with indignation:

> May I start with "The news"? I don't understand how could this
> be news when a whole volume of the TRC report (V. 4, 266 pages)
> is dedicated to … *Canada's Residential Schools: Missing Children
> and Unmarked Burials*. Have you read it, Prime Minister?…

I was there in December of 2015 when the full 6 volume TRC report was presented to you, Prime Minister.... You saw the two empty chairs on the platform which symbolized the children who never came home from residential school. After making a territorial acknowledgement ... those two chairs were the first things [TRC Chair] Murray Sinclair addressed....

And you heard Dr. Marie Wilson share these devastating facts.... She said that in 1/3 of these deaths, the government and the schools did not record the name of the student who died; in 1/4 of these deaths the government and the schools did not record the gender of the student who died; that in 1/2 of these deaths, the government and the schools did not record the cause of death.... You were in the presence of ... Survivor Advisor, Eugene Arcand, when he said, "No one can say, unless you live under a rock or in a cave that you don't know about this any more." (2021)

Rogers ended her text with a series of demands:

I remember you, Prime Minister, saying that day in December 2015.... "Our goal ... is to lift this burden from your shoulders, from those of your families and communities. It is to fully accept our responsibilities and our failing as a government and as a country."

Let's lift the burden. Stop going to court when Indigenous people want documents pertaining to their lives. Stop fighting them. Set the truth free. Let it see sunlight. Answer the Calls to Action. Live up to past promises.

Conclusion

Given that the government of Canada has continued to abuse and obstruct those who uphold Palestinian as well as Indigenous Rights and continues to "stand on guard" in support of the violators of those rights, it seems appropriate to conclude with a second, parallel set of demands. Let us lift the burden of occupation, colonization, apartheid and effective enslavement from Palestinians in Israel and the occupied territories. Stop obstructing the movement pressing for a peaceful exertion of economic pressures on the State of Israel. Drop the pretence that principled opposition to that state's ongoing violations of human rights and international law can only be motivated by antisemitism. Live up to Canada's obligations as a signatory of the Geneva Conventions. Let the light of truth shine through.

Notes

1. An early draft of this chapter was posted in April 2019 at <www.michaelkeefer. com/blog/2019/4/25/knowing-and-not-knowing-canada-indigenous-people-israel-and-palestine>.
2. *Hasbara* (the Hebrew word means "explanation," or "propaganda") is the full-time occupation of Israel's Ministry of Public Diplomacy.
3. Carefully selected witnesses from the United Kingdom, United States, Germany and Israel had previously "buttress[ed] the contention that Canada and the West are in the throes of a wave of antisemitism of a new kind and that Canadian campuses were breeding grounds for this new form of race hatred" (*Silencing* 9).
4. This and the next two paragraphs of my text condense my analysis in Keefer 2010c: 207 ff.
5. Cotler's coinage "Judenstaatsrein" in this essay asserts a continuity between present-day critiques of Israel and the Nazi project of making Europe "Judenrein."
6. Peters claimed in *From Time Immemorial* that Arabs expelled during the Nakba were mostly immigrants drawn by employment created by Jewish settlements in what had been largely empty territory. Her scholarship was fraudulent; despite this, Dershowitz plagiarized from her book in *The Case for Israel*. See Finkelstein 2005: 229–254.
7. Jonathan Cook writes that "86 Palestinian villages lie buried underneath JNF parks," and another 400 destroyed villages in Israel and the West Bank "had their lands passed on to exclusively Jewish communities" (2009).
8. This Latin term, meaning "land belonging to no-one," dates from the late nineteenth century. But the concept is implicit in the behaviour of European colonizers.
9. By way of comparison, see Abu-Zahra and Kay, *Unfree in Palestine*.
10. For a brief account of Scott's career with the Department of Indian Affairs from 1879 to 1932, and his parallel career as a literary figure who between 1899 and 1939 received every major honour Canada could bestow, see Keefer 2021.
11. The total number of Indigenous children taken into the residential schools during the more than one hundred years of their operation is estimated at about 150,000. The peak figure of a mortality rate of 8,000 deaths per 100,000 children implies that out of every 5,000 children inducted into the residential schools during the 1930s and 1940s, up to 400 would have died of TB. Death rates from TB appear to have been highest during the pre-World War I years referred to by Dr. Peter Bryce and Duncan Campbell Scott, and were significantly lowered once penicillin became available during the late 1940s.
12. In Israel, the West Bank and Gaza there are currently just over 7 million Palestinians, 6.56 million Jews, and 400,000 people defined by the Israeli state as "other" (people of Jewish ancestry deemed non-Jewish by religious law, Christian and Muslim non-Arabs, and residents with no religious/ethnic affiliation). See *World Population Review* 2019 and *Wikipedia* 2019.
13. The Canadian media have treated the discoveries of residential school gravesites

as an appalling surprise. But Bryce's revelations and Scott's acknowledgment of their truth have been public for over a century; Milloy's exposure of the residential school system was published in 1999 and reprinted in 2017; detailed accounts by Indigenous people of that system were published by the Truth and Reconciliation Commission in 2015 (Mizanay Gheezhik 2015a, b, c) and numbers 71 to 76 of the Commission's Calls to Action (Mizanay Gheezik 2015d) demanded investigation of the deaths of the thousands of children who perished in the residential schools.

14. For a definition and application of this term see Keefer 1996: 86–96.

15. The brief responses of Trudeau and Miller can also instructively be compared with that of Mizanay Gheezhik (Murray Sinclair), the chair of the Truth and Reconciliation Commission (for video and transcription, see Blum 2021).

References

Abu-Zahra, Nadia, and Adah Kay. 2012. *Unfree in Palestine: Registration, Documentation and Movement Restriction*. London: Pluto Press.

Abunimah, Ali. 2019. "How Israel Lobby Fakes Campus Anti-Semitism." *Electronic Intifada*, February 3. <electronicintifada.net/blogs/ali-abunimah/how-israel-lobby-fakes-campus-anti-semitism>.

Antreasyan, Anaïs. 2013. "Gas Finds in the Eastern Mediterranean: Gaza, Israel, and Other Conflicts." *Journal of Palestine Studies* 42, 3 (Spring). <oldwebsite.palestine-studies.org/jps/fulltext/162608>.

Arendt, Hannah. 1972. "Lying in Politics: Reflections on the Pentagon Papers." In *Crises of the Republic*. New York: Harcourt Brace Jovanovich.

Barron, F. Laurie. 1988. "The Pass System in the Canadian West, 1882–1935." *Prairie Forum* 13, 1: 25–42.

Barrows-Friedman, Nora. 2015. "False Claims of Anti-Semitism Climb on US Campuses: New Report." *Electronic Intifada*, May 19. <electronicintifada.net/blogs/nora-barrows-friedman/false-claims-anti-semitism-climb-us-campuses-new-report>.

Beeley, Vanessa. 2019. "Faux Humanitarian Irwin Cotler, the White Helmets, and the Whitewashing of an Appalling Agenda." *Mint Press News*, August 1. <mintpressnews.com/irwin-cotler-white-helmets-israel-whitewashing/261073/>.

Blum, Benjamin. 2021. "Canadians Should Be Prepared for More Discoveries Like Kamloops, Murray Sinclair [Mizanay Gheezhik] Says." cbc *News*, June 1. <cbc.ca/news/canada/sinclair-kamloops-residential-remains-1.6049525>.

Blumenthal, Max. 2013. *Goliath: Life and Loathing in Greater Israel*. New York: Nation Books.

Blumenthal, Max, and Julia Carmel. 2015. "Exposed: Pro-Israel Modern Day McCarthyites Going to Extremes to Slime Human Rights Activists." *AlterNet*, September 30. <alternet.org/2015/09/modern-day-mccarthyists-are-going-extremes-slime-activists-fighting-israels/>.

Briemberg, Mordecai, and Brian Campbell. 2010. "Anti-Semitism and Free Speech: In Parliament This Weekend." *Rabble.ca*, November 4. <rabble.ca/news/2010/11/anti-semitism-and-free-speech-parliament-weekend>.

Bryce, Peter H. 1922. *The Story of a National Crime: An Appeal for Justice to the Indians of Canada*. Ottawa: James Hope & Sons.

Canadian Public Health Association. n.d. "TB and Aboriginal People." *History of Public Health*. <cpha.ca/tb-and-aboriginal-people>.

cjn Staff. 2018. "Full Text of Justin Trudeau's St. Louis Apology." *Canadian Jewish News*, November 7. <cjnews.com/news/canada/full-text-of-justin-trudeaus-st-louis-apology>.

Climenhaga, David. 2021. "The Appalling Discovery in Kamloops Is Irrefutable Evidence of a Crime Against Humanity." *Rabble.ca*, May 30. <rabble.ca/blogs/bloggers/alberta-diary/2021/05/appalling-discovery-kamloops-irrefutable-evidence-crime-against>.

Cook, Jonathan. 2009. "Canada Park and Israeli 'Memoricide.'" *Electronic Intifada*, March 10. <electronicintifada.net/content/canada-park-and-israeli-memoricide/8126>.

Corrigan, Edward C. 2016. "Israel and Apartheid: A Framework for Legal Analysis." In *Apartheid in Palestine: Hard Laws and Harder Experiences*, edited by Ghada Ageel. Edmonton: University of Alberta Press.

Cotler, Irwin. 2009. "Making the World 'Judenstaatsrein': New Anti-Semitism Discriminates Against the Jewish People's Right to Live as an Equal Nation." *Jerusalem Post*, February 22. <https://www.jpost.com/opinion/op-ed-contributors/making-the-world-judenstaatrein>.

Cox, Sarah. 2020. "'What Cost Are Human Rights Worth?' UN Calls for Immediate RCMP Withdrawal in Wet'suwet'en Standoff." *The Narwhal*, January 9. <thenarwhal.ca/what-cost-are-human-rights-worth-un-calls-for-immediate-rcmp-withdrawal-in-wetsuweten-standoff/>.

Crosby, Andrew, and Jeffrey Monaghan. 2018. *Policing Indigenous Movements: Dissent and the Security State*. Halifax and Winnipeg: Fernwood Publishing.

Dabashi, Hamid. 2018. "The Discreet Sham of Justin Trudeau." *Al Jazeera*, December 5. <aljazeera.com/opinions/2018/12/5/the-discreet-sham-of-justin-trudeau>.

Dan, Michael. n.d. "The Impact of Colonization on the Health of Indigenous People in Canada." <https://www.med.mun.ca/getattachment/ca784440-194d-4972-b070-e336f6db224c/Impact-of-colonization-on-the-health-of-Indigenous-people-in-Canada-(for-Memorial-U).pdf.aspx>.

Daschuk, James. 2013. *Clearing the Plains: Disease, Politics of Starvation, and the Loss of Aboriginal Life*. Regina: University of Regina Press.

Elliott, Alicia. 2015. "The Meaning of Elections for Six Nations." *Briarpatch Magazine*, May 21. <briarpatchmagazine.com/articles/view/the-meaning-of-elections-for-six-nations>.

Ellis, Marc H. 2010. "The Ongoing Nakba and the Jewish Conscience." *Palestine Center*, May. 27 <thejerusalemfund.org/ht/d/ContentDetails/i/12975/pid/897>.

Engler, Yves. 2019. "'Canada's Dershowitz,' Apologist for Israeli War Crimes, Nominated for Peace Prize." *Palestine Chronicle*, March 10. <palestinechronicle.com/canadas-dershowitz-apologist-for-israeli-war-crimes-nominated-for-peace-prize/>.

Ferguson, R.G. 1955. *Studies in Tuberculosis*. Toronto: University of Toronto Press.

Finkelstein, Norman G. 2005. *Beyond Chutzpah: On the Misuse of Anti-Semitism and the Abuse of History*. Berkeley: University of California Press.

Ghabrial, Sarah, and Elena Razlgova. 2018. "Justin Trudeau Conflating BDS with Anti-Semitism Is Dangerous." *Huffington Post*, November 15. <huffpost.com/archive/ca/entry/bds-anti-semitism-trudeau-holocaust_a_23590519>.

Global Affairs Canada. 2021. "Statement by Canada Following UN Security Council Session on the Devastating Violence in Israel, the West Bank, and Gaza." May 16. <canada.ca/en/global-affairs/news/2021/05/statement-by-canada-following-un-security-council-session-on-the-devastating-violence-in-israel-the-west-bank-and-gaza.html>.

Hanson, Eric, Daniel P. Games, and Alexa Manuel. 2020. "The Residential School System." *Indigenous Foundations*. September. <indigenousfoundations.web.arts.ubc.

ca/residential-school-system-2020/>.

Harrington, Joanna. 2014. "Canada Was Never Terra Nullius." *Currie, Forcese, Oosterveld, Harrington: International Law: Doctrine, Practice and Theory*, June 30. <craig-forcese.com/blog/2014/6/30/canada-was-never-terra-nullius.html>.

Hass, Amira. 2014. "The Israeli 'Watergate' Scandal: The Facts about Palestinian water." *Haaretz*, February 16. <haaretz.com/news/mddle-east/1.574554>.

Hider, James. 2008. "Israel Threatens to Unleash 'Holocaust' in Gaza." *Times Online*, March 1. <timesonline.co.uk/tol/news/middle_east/article3459144.ece>.

Howe, Miles. 2015. *Debriefing Elsipogtog: The Anatomy of a Struggle*. Halifax and Winnipeg: Fernwood Publishing.

Illouz, Eva. 2014. "47 Years a Slave: A New Perspective on the Occupation." *Haaretz*, February 7. <haaretz.com/news/features/.premium-1.572880>.

Imai, Shin. 2017. "Consult, Consent, and Veto: International Norms and Canadian Treaties." In *The Right Relationship: Reimagining the Implementation of Historical Treaties*, edited by John Borrows and Michael Coyle. Toronto: University of Toronto Press.

Independent Jewish Voices Canada. 2016. "BDS Demands Are as Canadian as Maple Syrup." <https://socialistproject.ca/2019/07/bds-in-the-face-of-israeli-apartheid/>.

Keefer, Michael. 1996. *Lunar Perspectives: Field Notes from the Culture Wars*. Toronto: Anansi.

____ (ed.). 2010a. "Introduction." *Antisemitism Real and Imagined: Responses to the Canadian Parliamentary Coalition to Combat Antisemitism*. Waterloo, ON: Canadian Charger. <michaelkeefer.com/blog/2015/9/15/antisemitism-real-and-imagined-introduction>.

____. 2010b. "Data and Deception: Quantitative Evidence of Antisemitism." *Antisemitism Real and Imagined: Responses to the Canadian Parliamentary Coalition to Combat Antisemitism*. Waterloo, ON: Canadian Charger. <michaelkeefer.com/blog/2015/9/15/data-and-deception-quantitative-evidence-of-antisemitism>.

____. 2010c. "Desperate Imaginings: Rhetoric and Ideology of the 'New Antisemitism.'" *Antisemitism Real and Imagined: Responses to the Canadian Parliamentary Coalition to Combat Antisemitism*. Waterloo, ON: Canadian Charger. <michaelkeefer.com/blog/2015/9/15/desperate-imaginings-rhetoric-and-ideology-of-the-new-antisemitism>.

____. 2016. "Resisting McCarthyism: From the 'PC Wars' to 'New Antisemitism.'" *Trans-Canadiana: Polish Journal of Canadian Studies* 8: 226–258. Issue on *Canadian Sites of Resistance*, edited by Weronika Suchacka and Hartmut Lutz. <michaelkeefer.com/blog/2016/10/21/9jno16s94cjfxh84gr7w7nzt5bcbdu>.

____. 2021. "Indigenous Human Rights in Canada." In *Gender and Rights. Key Concepts in Indigenous Studies, Vol. 2*, edited by G.N. Devy and Geoffrey W. Davis. London and New York: Routledge.

Kestler-D'Amours, Jillian. 2019. "Asked to Reverse Anti-BDS Stand, Justin Trudeau Doubles Down." *Middle East Eye*, January 17. <middleeasteye.net/news/asked-reverse-anti-bds-stance-justin-trudeau-doubles-down>.

King, Thomas. 2012. *The Inconvenient Indian: A Curious Account of Native People in North America*. Toronto: Anchor Canada.

Kopecky, Arno. 2021. "Three Days in the Theatre of Fairy Creek." *The Tyee*, June 1. <thetyee.ca/Analysis/2021/06/01/Three-Days-Fairy-Creek-Theatre/?utm_source=dailyandutm_medium=emailandutm_campaign=010621>.

Lerman, Antony. 2017. "Antisemitism Redefined: Israel's Imagined National Narrative of

Endless External Threat." In *On Antisemitism: Solidarity and the Struggle for Justice*, edited by Rebecca Vilkomerson and Jewish Voice for Peace. Chicago: Haymarket Books.

Ljunggren, David. 2009. "Every G20 Nation Wants to Be Canada, Insists PM." *Reuters*, September 25. <reuters.com/article/columns-us-g20-canada-advantages-idUS-TRE58P05Z20090926>.

Lux, Maureen. 2001. *Medicine That Walks: Disease, Medicine, and Canadian Plains Native People, 1880–1940*. Toronto: University of Toronto Press.

Lyotard, Jean-François. 1988. *The Differend: Phrases in Dispute*, translated by Georges Van Den Abeele. Manchester: Manchester University Press.

McNeil, Kent. 2018. "Indigenous and Crown Sovereignty in Canada." In *Resurgence and Reconciliation: Indigenous-Settler Relations and Earth Teachings*, edited by Michael Asch, John Borrows, and James Tully. Toronto: University of Toronto Press.

Milloy, John S. 2008. "Indian Act Colonialism: A Century of Dishonour, 1869–1969." *National Centre for First Nations Governance/Centre National pour la Gouvernance des premières Nations*. May. <fngovernance.org/ncfng_research/milloy.pdf>.

____. 2017 [1999]. *A National Crime: The Canadian Government and the Residential School System, 1879 to 1976*. Winnipeg: University of Manitoba Press.

Mitrovica, Andrew. 2018. "Canada's Silence on Israel's Crimes Isn't Surprising." *Al Jazeera*, May 8. <aljazeera.com/opinions/2018/5/8/canadas-silence-on-israels-crimes-isnt-surprising>.

Mizanay Gheezhik (Murray Sinclair), Chair, Truth and Reconciliation Commission of Canada. 2015a. *Canada's Residential Schools. The History, Part 1: Origins to 1939. The Final Report of the Truth and Reconciliation Commission of Canada, Volume 1*. Montréal and Kingston: McGill-Queen's University Press.

____. 2015b. *Canada's Residential Schools. The History, Part 2: 1939 to 2000. The Final Report of the Truth and Reconciliation Commission of Canada, Volume 1*. Montréal and Kingston: McGill-Queen's University Press.

____. 2015c. *Canada's Residential Schools: Missing Children and Unmarked Burials. The Final Report of the Truth and Reconciliation Commission of Canada, Volume 4*. Montréal and Kingston: McGill-Queen's University Press.

____ 2015d. *Truth and Reconciliation Commission of Canada: Calls to Action*. Winnipeg, Manitoba: Truth and Reconciliation Commission of Canada. <gov.bc.ca/assets/gov/british-columbians-our-governments/indigenous-people/aboriginal-peoples-documents/calls_to_action_english2.pdf>.

O'Keefe, Derrick. 2009. "Harper in Denial at G20: Canada Has 'No History of Colonialism'." *Rabble.ca*, September 28. <rabble.ca/blogs/bloggers/derrick/2009/09/harper-denial-g20-canada-has-no-history-colonialism>.

Palestine Freedom of Expression Campaign. 2010. *Silencing Criticism of Israeli Apartheid*. <http://www.aurdip.org/pfex_colour_report_on_CPCCA_for_web.pdf>.

Palestinian Information Center. 2018. "UN Adopts Resolution on Palestinian Sovereignty over Natural Resources." December 22. <english.palinfo.com/news/2018/12/22/un-adopts-resolution-on-palestinian-sovereignty-over-natural-resources>.

Paperny, Anna Mehler. 2021. "Remains of 2015 Children Found at Former Indigenous School Site in Canada." *Reuters*, May 30. <reuters.com/world/americas/remains-215-children-found-former-indigenous-school-site-canada-2021-05-28/>.

Report of the Inquiry Panel, Canadian Parliamentary Coalition to Combat Antisemitism. 2011. *Jewish Virtual Library*. July. <jewishvirtuallibrary.org/jsource/anti-semitism/canadareport2011.pdf>.

Rogers, Shelagh. 2021. "Shelagh Rogers." *Facebook.com*, June 6. <https://www.facebook. com/sutherland.rogers/posts/1778893715616038>.

RT Online. 2019. "Twitter Up in Arms after Trudeau Says He'll 'Continue to Condemn BDS." January 17. <rt.com/news/449037-trudeau-bds-antisemitic-town-hall/>.

Rutty, Christopher, and Sue C. Sullivan. 2010. *This Is Public Health: A Canadian History.* Canadian Public Health Association. <cpha.ca/sites/default/files/assets/history/book/history-book-print_all_e.pdf>.

Scott, Duncan Campbell. 2000. "Indian Affairs, 1867–1912." In *Duncan Campbell Scott: Addresses, Essays, and Reviews,* edited by Leslie Richie. University of Western Ontario: Canadian Poetry Press.

Silverstein, Jason. 2018. "Robert Bowers, Pittsburgh Shooting Suspect, Was Avid Poster of Anti-Semitic Content on Gab." *CBS News Online,* October 29. <cbsnews.com/news/robert-bowers-gab-pittsburgh-shooting-suspect-today-live-updates-2018-10-27/>.

Smith, Donald B. n.d. "Deskaheh (Levi General)." *Dictionary of Canadian Biography,* vol. 15. <biographi.ca/en/bio/deskaheh_15E.html>.

Spear, Wayne K. 2010. "Indian Residential Schools Were 'Really Detrimental to the Development of the Human Being." *Wayne K. Spear.com.* March 10. <waynekspear.com/2010/03/10/indian-residential-schools-2/>.

Sproule-Jones, M. 1996. "Crusading for the Forgotten: Dr. Peter Bryce, Public Health, and Prairie Native Residential Schools." *Canadian Bulletin of Medical History* 13, 2.

Stuart, Jack. 2015. "The Lost Legacy of Judah L. Magnes." *Jewish Currents,* July 3. <jewishcurrents.org/the-lost-legacy-of-judah-l-magnes>.

Tilley, V. (ed.). 2009. *Occupation, Colonialism, Apartheid? A Reassessment of Israel's Practices in the Occupied Palestinian Territories under International Law.* Cape Town: Middle East Project of the Democracy and Governance Programme, Human Sciences Research Council of South Africa. May. <repository.hsrc.ac.za/handle/20.500.11910/4619>.

Statista. 2021. "Tuberculosis Death Rate in High-Burden Countries Worldwide in 2016." <statista.com/statistics/509760/rate-of-tuberculosis-mortality-in-high-burden-countries/>.

Wikipedia. 2019. "Demographics of Israel." <wikipedia.org/wiki/Demographics_of_Israel>.

Windle, Jim. 2016. "December 1922: The First Raid on Six Nations." *Two Row Times,* December 28. <tworowtimes.com/historical/december-1922-first-raid-six-nations/>.

World Population Review. 2019. "Palestinian Population 2019." <worldpopulationreview.com/countries/palestine-population/>.

YouTube. 2019. "Justin Trudeau on BDS — January 15, 2019." January 15. <youtube.com/watch?v=rtFT9cD8L5I>.

Part III

Close-Ups — Media, Non-Profits, Campuses

Chapter 7

Canadian Media and Pro-Israel Bias

An Insider's Perspective

Davide Mastracci

A year before writing this chapter, I almost quit journalism. A major reason for this desire to quit was that my perspective on the industry evolved. My first journalism experience was at the *McGill Daily* as an undergraduate student in Montreal. The *Daily* was explicitly leftist, so my understanding of journalism was built from a progressive perspective. As such, I had an antagonistic relationship to corporate media. One of the problems I recognized in corporate media was its pro-Israel and anti-Palestine bias. Regardless, when I decided to pursue journalism as a career, I still thought that I could carve out a niche for the sort of work that inspired me and that in my work I could actively combat the kinds of bias I saw in the industry. Yet after moving to Toronto for a master's program in journalism at Ryerson, I started to see things differently. I realized that you cannot be part of a system which perpetuates harm and not be complicit in it.

In this chapter, I explore pro-Israel bias in Canadian media, detailing my own experiences with writing on Israel's oppression of Palestinians and how I have come to understand the ways in which bias functions in the industry.[1] This bias is pervasive and it is upheld by journalists, corporate owners and lobby groups, among other actors. I demonstrate how these journalistic failures impact the information that readers get on Israel and Palestine, therefore posing an obstacle to the ability of solidarity movements to grow and helping to ensure that Israel is rarely held to account for its actions.

Experiencing Pro-Israel Bias

To date, I have never had anything more than an entry-level position in corporate media. I have had roles at eight different publications, and I have done freelancing for dozens of others. This experience has shown me how pro-Israel bias works at a low level. A few years ago, I pitched a relatively uncontroversial article regarding Prime Minister Justin Trudeau's comments on the location of Canada's embassy in Israel to a publication with which I had little prior experience. It was accepted, edited by a junior staff member, published and well-received. A day later, I was informed by a senior editor that the junior editor should have run the article by them before sending it to publication. I was not made aware of this procedure beforehand and did not understand why I, as a new writer, was being reprimanded. The editor casually added that their publication was not sure of their editorial stance on "Israel/Palestine," so it would be especially important to consult with them on this topic. I realized the issue was not primarily about chain of command but that the article was critical of Israel. This sent me an implicit message: do not tackle this subject again if I want to continue working with this publication.

Another time, an article I wrote about Canadian media's pro-Israel bias was pushed out on social media late on a weekend night — a traffic graveyard — despite being published earlier. This seemed like an attempt to bury the story. I mentioned it to someone in that newsroom, and they told me that the person responsible for the scheduling had interfered with other journalists' critical work relating to Israel in the past, so the scheduling was likely intentional.

On another occasion a few years back, I was invited onto a radio show to discuss an issue regarding Israel's oppression of Palestinians. At the time, I was required to get approval from my employer to do any outside writing or appearances, so I asked. These appearances were typically quickly approved and celebrated because it meant people cared about our work. This time around, however, I had to follow up with my employer before being called into a meeting with a few people. I was told that I could appear on the radio show but that I could not give my opinion and that I could only describe the events from an "objective" perspective. They explained that this was because the brand was not sure about their stance on the "complicated" issue. It did not matter to them that I would not be speaking on behalf of the company or that I had previously made other outside appearances offering views that higher-ups likely disagreed with. Something about this topic was special.

Finally, a few years back I tweeted a mild criticism of an Israeli official. It did not get any retweets and just a couple of likes — hardly noteworthy. A few days later, I got a phone call from a higher-up asking me to remove the tweet because someone had complained. They would not tell me who or even if it came from within the company. They did not even seem to understand the alleged problem with the tweet. Regardless, they wanted it taken down. I was also asked to remove any mention of the company from my Twitter bio. While they claimed that this was standard procedure, the timing made the real issue clear, especially since others in my position had not been asked to do the same.

I have written on many "controversial" issues over the years, and this is the only topic where I have faced this sort of interference. Other journalists have had more egregious experiences. I know from speaking with Arab journalists that many either avoid the subject entirely or received so much hate when they did speak out — and faced a lack of support or even condemnation from higher-ups — that they would not approach it again.

Personal Views of Mid- to Senior-Level Journalists

The personal views of mid- to senior-level journalists can have a major impact on what gets published. One way this happens is that critical pitches on Israel's treatment of Palestinians may be rejected regardless of quality, which, if done often enough, tells journalists not to bother. Stories in progress might get killed or edited beyond recognition. If even just a couple of individuals hostile to publishing content critical of Israel are in the right positions, they can make a difference in upholding pro-Israel bias at the publication.

The editorial pages of major newspapers in Canada are instructive in this regard. They are not representative of all journalists, but they do mark the publication's official view. In 2018, I looked at the editorial stances that the *Toronto Star, Globe and Mail* and *National Post* had taken on the Israeli military's bombardment of Palestinians in Gaza (Mastracci 2018). In the next few paragraphs, I quote heavily from my findings. While these are just a few examples, focusing on one aspect of Israel's oppression of Palestinians over just six years, they are indicative of how Canada's major outlets are willing to cheer on military efforts that cause mass civilian deaths.

In 2009, Israel launched a ground invasion into Gaza, killing more than 760 Palestinian civilians, including 345 minors. Israel violated international law and used white phosphorus, an aerosol that burns everything and cannot be extinguished until it is deprived of oxygen, in civilian areas. Despite this, the *Globe* wrote that the invasion of Gaza, which they referred to as "Hamas's 'statelet,'" was "well justified," with no mention of the destruction it caused (Globe and Mail Editorial Board 2011). In a June 2010 editorial, they simply referred to the invasion as a "regrettable incident" but claimed that the more important issue was the need to turn Gaza into a territory that would not pose a threat to Israel (Globe and Mail Editorial Board 2010).

In 2012, Israel rained missiles on Gaza, killing more than a hundred Palestinians, including four children playing soccer on a beach. The *Post* published a pair of editorials in support of these strikes, writing "Our view is that [Israeli Prime Minister Benjamin Netanyahu] waged this mini-war in exactly the right way" and that "Israel had no choice but to strike at Gaza" (National Post Editorial Board 2021a). They claimed that Israel is a "civilized and humane nation" in contrast to Gaza and argued that Israel had been careful to limit rocket fire to "terrorists" (National Post Editorial Board 2012b). The *Star* applauded the bombardment, claiming that Netanyahu could not be "faulted" for his supposedly justified actions (Toronto Star Editorial Board 2012). No Palestinian civilian casualties were mentioned, and while they claimed that the "scope" of the airstrikes "raised a few eyebrows," they concluded Netanyahu could not seem soft on security in the upcoming elections.

In 2014, Israel launched its most destructive attack on Gaza yet, killing more than 1,460 Palestinian civilians, while suffering just six Israeli civilian deaths. The *Globe* wrote, "It cannot be wrong for Israel to defend itself," referring to this invasion as the "latest round of grass-mowing" in Gaza, where Israel supposedly "cut back the military capabilities of their enemies" (Globe and Mail Editorial Board 2014). The *Post* described Israel's attack on Gaza as a "fight between a Canadian ally and a vicious terrorist group," failing to mention civilian casualties (National Post Editorial Board 2014).

This record demonstrates that Canadian editorial boards have been willing to publicly offer widespread and consistent support for Israel even in light of some of its worst atrocities. This pro-Israel bias has likely had a major influence on journalists at lower levels within these publications.

Corporate Interference

While the views of journalists at the editorial level clearly make a difference in upholding pro-Israel bias, upper-management and ownership can be more important, especially as the media becomes increasingly monopolized and centralized (Winseck 2020). Before proceeding with this discussion of media ownership and pro-Israel bias, it is important to note that we are staying far away from the field of conspiracy theories. Clearly, any suggestion that the media is owned by a secret Jewish cabal, as many antisemites believe, is wrong and should be vigorously opposed. On the contrary, not all Jews are Zionists, and most newspaper chains are not owned by Jewish people. Moreover, not every owner of a paper interferes to the extent you will notice, and when they do so, it is not always or exclusively about Israel, and interference often occurs in relation to other issues as well. Support for Israel just so happens to be a uniting factor of a wide range of right-wingers, from Hindutva extremists to American evangelicals, and liberal Zionism is a typical editorial position at more progressive corporate publications such as the *Toronto Star.*

Owners of news chains do, however, have a record of using them to advocate for their own financial interests and ideological beliefs, including, in some cases, support for Israel. The CanWest news chain — whose properties now belong to Postmedia — offers an illuminating case study of the pro-Israel bias because of how openly and proudly it was carried out with countless employees testifying to its existence.

CanWest Global Communications was founded in 1974 by Israel Asper, a Winnipeg lawyer and self-identified Zionist who declared his "unshakeable commitment" to Israel, which he saw as a "symbol and teacher of excellence for all of humankind" (Asper 2002; CBC News 2000a). In July 2000, CanWest announced its $3.2 billion purchase of media properties from Hollinger Inc., a media company established by *National Post* founder Conrad Black (CBC News 2000b). CBC News noted the significance of the deal for Canada's media landscape: "CanWest picks up 136 daily and weekly newspapers, including half of the *National Post*, thirteen large big-city dailies, eighty-five trade publications and directories … [and] all of the Hollinger and Southam Internet properties" (CBC News 2000b).

In an October 2002 speech to the Israel Bonds Gala, which the *Post* published, Asper described his disgust with Canadian media for supposedly "destroying the world's favourable disposition toward" Israel.

Asper claimed that this is because journalists, including his own, are "lazy, or sloppy, or stupid" or "biased, or anti-Semitic." Asper concluded the speech by stating that all Canadians should "stand tall ... for the right of Israel to exist and to take whatever actions it needs to battle its savage attackers, and to demand that our media and our politicians act with honour in this quest" (Asper 2002). Asper's newspaper chain had already become a battleground for this war, with, as detailed below, many journalists being censured or fired for being anything less than completely supportive of Israel.

In September 2001, Michael Goldbloom, the publisher of then-CanWest property the *Montreal Gazette*, quit his job citing differences with the company. The *Globe and Mail* reported that this was due in part to "senior editors at the paper [being] told in August to run a strongly worded, pro-Israel editorial on a Saturday op-ed page" (Marotte and Peritz 2001). In December 2001, Bill Marsden, an investigative reporter at the *Gazette*, went on the CBC's *As It Happens* to discuss how reporters were pulling their bylines from the publication after CanWest imposed a policy requiring all its local papers to run editorials written by the chain's editor-in-chief, Murdoch Davis (Parry and King 2001). Marsden noted that this had resulted in those papers adopting a strong pro-Israel perspective. Marsden told CBC:

> They do not want to see any criticism of Israel. We do not run in our newspaper op-ed pieces that express criticism of Israel and what it is doing in the Middle East etcetera. We do not have that free-wheeling debate that there should be about all these issues. We even had an incident where a fellow, a professor at ... the University of Waterloo, wrote an op-ed piece for us in which he was criticizing the anti-terrorism law and criticizing elements of civil rights etcetera. Now that professor happens to be a Muslim and happens to have an Arab name. We got a call from head-quarters demanding to know why we had printed this. Now this kind of questioning goes on all the time. (Quoted in Parry and King 2001)

The CBC also interviewed Davis, asking him: If a chain in the paper wanted to write an editorial about Israel that was "absolutely contrary to the editorial written from your office, would they be able to write that?" Davis replied, "No. It is clearly the intent that the newspapers will speak with one voice on certain issues of overarching national or international importance" (Parry and King 2001).

In November 2001, Peggy Curran, a TV critic at the *Montreal Gazette*, wrote a column on a CBC documentary, *In the Line of Fire,* which criticized Israel for its treatment of Palestinian journalists (Kimber n.d.). The column was initially held by editors, and Curran had to file a union grievance and make a major change to the column for it to be published. Curran quit her job soon thereafter in protest. In April 2002, Curran told the *Washington Report on Middle East Affairs*: "Usually criticism is criticism and you're allowed to say what you want. I can't think of another occasion when this has happened to me." Curran added, "Whether you know it or not, you start censoring yourself" (Khan 2002).

In January 2002, Doug Cuthand, a First Nations columnist for CanWest's *Regina Leader-Post* and *Saskatoon Star Phoenix,* wrote a column sympathizing with the Palestinians. According to a *Toronto Star* article published that month, Cuthand wrote: "Their loss of land, placement in camps and control by a more powerful force, made them similar to Canada's [*sic*] aboriginal peoples" (Schiller 2002). The article was killed by editors, the first time that this had happened to Cuthand in ten years of writing for the publications. Cuthand said that some in the newsroom told him the column was too anti-Israel for CanWest, telling Reuters: "Of course I'm going to carry on and continue writing. But it will never be the same.... I'll always be looking over my shoulder" (*Reuters* 2002). In August 2002, shortly after *Halifax Daily News* was sold by CanWest, columnist David Swick wrote about the pro-Israel bias under their ownership:

> Following the Sept. 11 terrorist attacks, I wrote a few columns about that event. I was soon informed I was no longer allowed to write anything to do with the Middle East. The reason: I was not perceived to be adamantly pro-Israel. The Aspers are adamantly pro-Israel, and their papers must reflect this sentiment.

Peter March, another *Daily News* columnist, said he was dropped from his position of ten years because of a column he wrote criticizing Israel (Kimber n.d.). Describing this period, Charles Shannon, a copy editor at the *Montreal Gazette,* told *The Nation* in 2007: "One definite edict that came down was that there should be no criticism of Israel. And by that, I mean not even a mild rapping of the wrist" (Hendler 2007).

This corporate-enforced bias was not limited to editorials or opinion writing but has also influenced reported news. In 2006, the Near East Cultural and Educational Foundation of Canada released a study looking at the *National Post*'s depiction of Palestinians in 2004. As described by a 2008 *Georgia Straight* article, the report found that the "*National Post* was 83.3 times more likely to report an Israeli child's death than a Palestinian child's death in its news articles' headlines or first paragraphs," which "made it appear that Israeli kids were killed at a rate four times higher than Palestinian children during 2004 when, in fact, twenty-two Palestinian children were killed for every Israeli child that year" (Murray and Moiseiwitsch 2008). That same year, the chain's bias became so blatant that Reuters asked CanWest to remove the names of Reuters' reporters from wire stories before using them or to not include any connection with Reuters at all (Austen 2004). The request came after CanWest implemented a policy to use the word "terrorist" more liberally, for example swapping out "rebel" in Reuters articles with "terrorist." CanWest was also forced to issue multiple corrections after doing the same thing with Associated Press, including calling six Palestinians killed by Israeli troops "terrorists," when the original referred to them as "fugitives" (Austen 2004; Adams 2004). Asper died in 2003 and his children took over, but the bias lived on. In 2010, the chain was sold and became the Postmedia Network, and yet, much has remained the same.

In 2008, CanWest appointed Paul Godfrey, then on the company's board of directors, to the position of *National Post* president and CEO (Canwest 2008). Godfrey was the one to assemble the ownership group that purchased the CanWest media properties, becoming the CEO and president of the new Postmedia Network, a position he remained in until 2019 (Olive 2015). As of the time of writing, he is still the company's executive chairperson (Canadian Press 2019). In 2015, Godfrey ordered every major Postmedia publication to write an endorsement of then-Prime Minister Stephen Harper for the upcoming election (Honderich 2015). The endorsement claimed that Conservatives "kept Canada firmly on the right side of history in Ukraine, the Middle East and in North Africa" (National Post Editorial Board 2015). Moreover, according to a 2019 *Canadaland* article, "Postmedia has given a directive for all of its papers to shift to the political right, in an unprecedented, centralized fashion," which employees fear "will eradicate the local perspectives and political independence of some of Canada's oldest and most important newspapers" (Craig 2019).

While it may be tempting to write this off as the work of one newspaper chain, Postmedia is the largest in the country, controlling nearly 30 percent of the Canadian newspaper market as of 2019 (Winseck 2020). It would be very dangerous if the newspaper chain's rightward drift furthers the continued maintenance of uncritical support for Israel. Journalists scoff at the idea that higher-ups tell them what to do, but the record proves that it happens often. To make matters worse, the sort of groups that used to call out corporate interference have become part of the problem.

Journalist Advocacy Groups

When the Asper family was pushing a pro-Israel line in their newspapers, journalism watch groups in Canada and abroad took notice and fought back. According to the *Washington Report on Middle East Affairs*: "The [Canadian Association of Journalists], the Quebec Federation of Professional Journalists (FPJQ), the Campaign for Press and Broadcasting Freedom, the Newspaper Guild of Canada, the international writers' freedom of expression group PEN Canada and the US National Conference of Editorial Writers all have condemned CanWest's editorial policy and the chill it causes in newsrooms by forcing journalists to self-censor" (Khan 2002). The Canadian Association of Journalists (CAJ) and the FPJQ, for example, wrote to members of parliament and senators regarding the issue and mentioned "repeated instances of censorship in CanWest-owned newspapers across the country" (Khan 2002). Some journalism groups have, however, worked to effectively maintain a pro-Israel bias. A particularly galling example happened in April 2018 with the Canadian Journalists for Free Expression (CJFE), ostensibly a group that "defends and promotes free expression and access to information in Canada and internationally" (CJFE n.d.). This incident, more than almost any other, was what most damaged my faith in the profession.

On March 30, 2018, Palestinians in Gaza took part in the first of a series of protests calling for the right of return to their land. Israel killed at least seventeen Palestinians and injured more than fourteen hundred that day, including ten journalists (Committee to Protect Journalists 2018). On April 2, CJFE's promotions and communications coordinator Kevin Metcalf put out a statement calling on the government to "condemn the one-sided use of military force against civilian demonstrators and media in Gaza" (Metcalf 2018). Despite the organization's mission of protecting journalists, the clear violation of press freedom and international law by Israel and the fact that CJFE had put out similar statements about other countries, this statement was publicly condemned by a range of journalists (Brown 2018). On April 8, two days after Israel killed a Palestinian journalist wearing a blue PRESS vest, the statement was removed from the website. That same day, Metcalf wrote: "I have learned that in the last week, a half-dozen resignations have been tendered on [CJFE]'s executive committee and Gala committee, including the resignation of the acting Executive Director and President of the Board." He added: "CBC employees who were powerful contributing members of the Gala fundraising committee resigned after they or their handlers at CBC disapproved of the statement." Metcalf, who would be fired a week later, also wrote:

> It is troubling that pressure exerted by public employees at the state broadcaster has led to the censorship of a protest letter by an advocacy organization. It is my opinion that this illustrates an attempt by public employees to exert undue influence over a civil society group, ostensibly on behalf of a foreign government. (Quoted in Metcalf 2018)

One of the CBC employees who resigned from CJFE was "As It Happens" host Carol Off, who told another CBC journalist: "I think Israel's excesses should be treated differently than those of Saudi Arabia. Israel has democratic institutions, a free press and a claim to transparency. Saudi Arabia does not. And so I think the language is different, as it would be for the United States" (Macdonald 2018). The CJFE also released a statement, noting:

> This recent event at CJFE has made it clear that the Board needs to review its governance processes, but most importantly, it needs to focus its efforts on its core mandate and on securing adequate funding to carry on its work. ... We will take the next few months to review, refocus, and ensure CJFE is an organization that continues long into the future. (Tunley 2018)

This statement, and the testimonies of other CJFE employees, made it clear that the mass resignations and donation withdrawals following the Israel statement effectively forced the organization to pause its work.

Over the next few months, Israel killed more than 180 Palestinians in these protests, wounding more than 9,200. This included two journalists killed and at least thirty-nine injured with live ammunition. A United Nations Human Rights Council commission report on the protests found "reasonable grounds to believe that Israeli snipers shot journalists intentionally, despite seeing that they were clearly marked as such" (Human Rights Council 2019). The pro-Israel bias had become so entrenched in Canadian media that a journalism advocacy organization could not stomach mild criticism of a government that likely intentionally killed journalists.

Pro-Israel Lobby Groups

On the occasion that any language or analysis remotely critical of Israel manages to slip into publication, lobby groups spring into action. To be clear, lobby groups exist for all sorts of causes. Yet those working on behalf of Israel are particularly well-funded and effective, as outlined in Al Jazeera's series on the lobby in the United Kingdom and the United States, the latter of which was censored and is only available because it was leaked (*Electronic Intifada* 2018). Many of these groups exist in Canada, but here I am going to focus on one in particular because its sole purpose is to "defend" Israel in the media.

HonestReporting Canada (HRC), founded in 2003, describes itself as an "independent grassroots organization promoting fairness and accuracy in Canadian media coverage of Israel and the Middle East" (HonestReporting Canada n.d.c). The group's Endorsements page includes glowing praise from a former Israeli ambassador to Canada, the former consul general of Israel in Montreal and former CanWest president and CEO, Leonard Asper, son of Israel Asper. The HRC's website boasts of having more than 45,000 subscribers and of having "prompted hundreds of apologies, retractions, and revisions from news outlets," efforts which they claim are "changing the face of the media and reporting of Israel throughout the world" (HonestReporting Canada n.d.b). The way the HRC functions is that its employees and subscribers scan Canadian media for content critical of Israel that they do not like. HRC staff then work to get corrections, retractions or apologies or seek to have favourable rebuttals published, using their email list to flood targets with complaints or lean on relationships with compliant journalists.

A 2004 incident involving the *British Medical Journal* (BMJ) provides an insightful example, although it involves HRC's United Kingdom affiliate "HonestReporting." In October 2004, the BMJ published an article by senior lecturer Derek Summerfield critiquing "what he saw as systematic violations of the fourth Geneva Convention by the Israeli army in Gaza" (Summerfield 2004: 924). Afterwards, as recounted by Karl Sabbagh, the journal and its editor were flooded with criticism, much of which he claims "resulted from a request from HonestReporting" for readers to send emails to the journal and its editor (Sabbagh 2009: 509). More than 970 emails came in, including death threats against the editor, claims of bias because of his "mid-eastern name" and violent Islamophobia. Unlike the "average heated but civilised debate one expects to find in a scientific or medical journal" (510), Sabbagh writes that these campaigns focus on getting articles retracted and editors fired. Crucially, Sabbagh also wrote:

> For that suppression to take place it has to be directed at people who are unfamiliar with the issues and who might be persuaded that they have somehow got it wrong. Reading through the emails sent to the BMJ, editors, and the people who manage and fund their publications, might well believe that a ghastly editorial mistake had been made. And creating that belief is, of course, the intention. If straying into the Israel-Palestinian conflict provokes such a large and hostile reaction, not to mention strident allegations that important details are wrong, then the temptation is quietly to avoid the topic in future. (2009: 511)

In 2002, the United States branch of HonestReporting quoted the *Jerusalem Post* to boast: "HonestReporting.com readers sent up to six thousand e-mails a day to CNN executives, effectively paralyzing their internal e-mail system" (HonestReporting 2002). As an editor, I have been the recipient of these sorts of emails before, although nowhere near the extent of the BMJ or CNN. The HRC website lists more than seventy-five Canadian publications they have successfully taken action against, providing details on each one (HonestReporting Canada n.d.a). Some of the corrections on the list are simple errors, such as an article getting a date wrong. However, many of their other "corrections," or their attempts to get them, are not responding to errors at all, but are efforts to push HRC's own political positions. For example, a June 5, 2020, "Media Alert" focused on Andray Domise, a contributing writer for *Maclean's,* who had tweeted: "Shout out to the Palestinian freedom fighters holding space in your hearts for Black folks in our shared struggle." The HRC took issue with the tweet, writing: "So much for objectivity and political neutrality in Canadian media. HonestReporting Canada has alerted Maclean's editors of this matter" (Fegelman 2020e). Domise is not being accused of a crime or ethical lapse here. He simply dared to express solidarity between Black people in North America and the Palestinian people.

While many journalists resist this pressure, the HRC is occasionally able to bully unwilling journalists into submission to their demands. Two examples come to mind that give a sense of the toxic effect of the group's actions on Canadian media. The first hits particularly close to home.

As I mentioned in the introduction to this chapter, my first journalism experience was at the *McGill Daily* in Montreal. The way I look at journalism was informed by the newspaper's leftist outlook. So, it was with disgust in November 2019 that I learned the university administration was forcing the independent student publication to print a pro-Zionist letter. The *Daily*'s Letter Policy states that they have the right to reject any submitted letter "whose content displays racial, ethnic, sexual, and socioeconomic prejudice" (*McGill Daily* n.d.). The paper includes pro-Zionist letters within this category, noting in a 2016 editorial: "The *Daily* maintains an editorial line of not publishing pieces which promote a Zionist worldview, or any other ideology which we consider to be oppressive" (*McGill Daily* 2016). The *Daily* also notes that it will not publish letters of more than five hundred words. As such, a long, pro-Zionist letter submitted to the *Daily* on September 10, 2019, by two McGill law students was ignored (*McGill Daily* 2019). Eventually, the students met with Deputy Provost (Student Life and Learning) Fabrice Labeau, asking him to force the paper to publish their letter. Labeau agreed and threatened the paper with a "nuclear option" of entering into arbitration to terminate the funding agreement between them. A *Daily* article describing this ordeal noted: "This process would ultimately require time and money which the *Daily* does not have, but which the administration does. If the *Daily* were to lose in arbitration, it would mean our funding would be withheld, as would funding for *Le Délit français,* thereby jeopardizing the existence of both papers" (Shapiro and Aarenau 2019). As such, the paper caved in and published the law students' letter in full, along with an accompanying article explaining that they had done so against their will (Shapiro and Aarenau 2019).

The *Daily* had become a frequent target of HRC, who published many articles mentioning the *Daily* between the time the law students submitted their letter and the time it was published, including one attacking the paper for writing about a Jewish anti-Zionist Holocaust survivor (Fegelman 2020b). The HRC published at least five more articles on the *Daily* by the end of 2019. In one of these articles, the HRC claims: "HRC has requested a meeting with McGill University administrators and has filed a grievance asking the administration to conduct a formal investigation and to take immediate action to ensure that the *Daily* ceases its anti-Israel animus and avowed discriminatory policies" (Fegelman 2019). This was published the same day the *Daily* caved to the administration's demands, which was not enough for the HRC. Since then, the HRC has confirmed that the meeting took place and has pointed out that the *Daily* has been forced to publish other pro-Zionist articles, effectively meaning that its statement of principles has been rewritten and hijacked by outside forces (McGill et al. 2019; Fegelman 2020a). As the *Daily* noted in a disclaimer above a pro-Zionist article in November 2019,

> Our letters policy contains a clause that allows the editorial board to reject letters "whose content displays racial, ethnic, sexual, and socioeconomic prejudice." The definition of these terms is subject to interpretation by McGill, as per our Memorandum of Agreement. The Daily's editorial board feels that the letter below contains the prejudice outlined in its letters policy, but the McGill administration disagrees, which is why it is appearing in the paper, and why others with similar content may appear in the future. (McGill et al. 2019)

The HRC was not solely or primarily responsible for this outcome, but this event illustrates how these groups can help pressure independent organizations into violating their own editorial standards.

Another example took place at Radio-Canada. On April 24, 2020, Radio-Canada published an article by reporter Kamel Bouzeboudjen about how Israel has exacerbated the dangers Palestinians in Gaza face from COVID-19, featuring interviews with Gazans themselves (Bouzeboudjen 2020). Four days later, the HRC sent a complaint to Radio-Canada ombudsman Guy Gendron about the article, claiming it was "replete with errors" (Fegelman 2020c). As *Canadaland* host Jesse Brown noted: "In fact, this list of 'ten errors' was not a list of ten errors. It was a counterargument. Nine of the points were simply saying, 'It's not, in fact, Israel to blame. It's Hamas" (Brown 2020). Despite this, on May 12, Gendron replied to the HRC, letting them know that "we decided … to withdraw this article from our platforms" and that "follow-up was done with Mr. Bouzeboudjen and the team to make them aware of this situation" (Fegelman 2020d). The article was then removed from the website, with a retraction notice published at another URL. As Brown pointed out, CBC and Radio-Canada's editorial policies make this decision an incredible oddity (CBC/Radio-Canada n.d.). According to CBC/ Radio-Canada's "Journalistic Standards and Practices" on article deletion:

> Our published content is a matter of public record. To change the content of previously published material alters that record. Altering the record could undermine our credibility and the public's trust in our journalism. There can be exceptions to this position — where there are legal or personal safety considerations to the person named. (CBC/Radio-Canada n.d.)

These exceptions clearly do not apply to this story.

In sum, the HRC was able to get Radio-Canada to violate their own standards to censor an article and scold a reporter because he dared to speak to Gazans, who are rarely heard in the media. This is just one example, but there are hundreds of listed corrections on the HRC's website. As you can imagine, these add up to a restricted media, squashing much of the critical reporting on Israel that manages to evade other filters.

Conclusion: Calling Out the Bias

Enforcement of pro-Israel bias in Canadian media, whether by editors, owners or lobby groups, undermines the core journalistic function of informing the public. All coverage of Israel's oppression of Palestinians is influenced by these pressures, and the outcome is an understanding of the issue among the public that is marred by propaganda. This is a failure.

Yet the unwillingness of journalists to address power imbalances through coverage is even worse. Israel is a settler-colonial state built on the murder and dispossession of Palestinians, who are subjected to an apartheid system. Israel is in flagrant violation of international law at many levels. When the media works to enforce a pro-Israel bias today, it is the equivalent of defending South Africa in the apartheid era. This certainly did happen, as Michael Bueckert demonstrates in Chapter 3, but it was far less common than the widespread editorial support Israel enjoys. Crucially, the Canadian government remains one of Israel's major supporters on the international level. This means that journalists are failing to do justice by the oppressed, but they also effectively fall in line with their government's foreign policy stance, leading to an abdication of responsibility internationally and at home.

This coverage also plays a role in dissuading the public from working to hold Israel to account. In Chapter 9, Hassan Husseini notes that the strength and energy of the Palestine solidarity movement in Canada is "organically tied to the changing conditions and events on the ground in Palestine and the region." As such, the quality of media coverage in Canada may play a role in enhancing or constraining the solidarity movement. For example, coverage that ignores or minimizes Israeli atrocities in Palestine, and/or demonizes Palestinian resistance to them, may suppress sympathies with Palestine and prevent the movement from growing, while coverage that accurately reports on Israeli actions may motivate people to join the fight, giving a boost to the movement. Meanwhile, social media has allowed Palestinians to bypass traditional media gatekeepers and bring the realities of occupation to the world, and this is often cited as a reason for the growing solidarity with Palestine among young people (Yee and El-Naggar 2021).

While Palestinian Canadians are occasionally successful in publishing an opinion article in a newspaper, it is more common to hear stories of writers denied access (Ayyash 2021). Independent and progressive media, as well as international sources, therefore, play a critical role in publishing the sort of critical analysis that mainstream media in Canada avoids. While these spaces are important, it will be more difficult for solidarity activists to win over a broader public if they are shut out of mainstream, national publications. As such, pro-Israel bias in the media must be addressed to build a general movement against apartheid.

I hope that this chapter proves useful in contextualizing the state of Canadian media coverage of Israeli colonialism and gives readers the tools to combat the pro-Israel bias wherever they see it. I have been silenced by these pressures before. That will not happen again.

Note

1. This chapter builds upon an article published by the author: Davide Mastracci, "Uncovering Canadian Media's Devastating Pro-Israel Bias," *Passage*, 23 June, 2020 <readpassage.com/uncovering-canadian-medias-devastating-pro-israel-bias/>.

References

Adams, James. 2004. "CanWest, Reuters at Odds over Use of 'Terrorist,'" *Globe and Mail,* September 21. <theglobeandmail.com/news/national/canwest-reuters-at-odds-over-use-of-terrorist/article18273711/>.

Asper, Israel. 2002. "We Must End Media Bias Against Israel." *National Post*, October 31.

Austen, Ian. 2004. "Reuters Asks a Chain to Remove Its Bylines." *New York Times*, September 20. <nytimes.com/2004/09/20/business/media/reuters-asks-a-chain-to-remove-its-bylines.html>.

Ayyash, Mark Muhannad. 2021. "Urgently Needed — A 'Palestinian-Montrealer'!" *Al Jazeera*, May 25. <aljazeera.com/opinions/2021/5/25/urgently-needed-a-palestinian>.

Bouzeboudjen, Kamel. 2020. "Gaza, le Double Confinement." *Radio-Canada*, April 24. <https://ici.radio-canada.ca/nouvelle/1702224/retrait-covid-gaza-double-confinement>.

Brown, Jesse. 2018. "What's Going on with cjfe." *Canadaland*, April 10. <canadalandshow.com/whats-going-on-with-cjfe/>.

___. 2020. "A Case for Bad Art." *Canadaland*, May 21. <canadalandshow.com/podcast/263-a-case-for-bad-art/>.

Canadian Press. 2019. "Paul Godfrey Steps Down as Postmedia ceo as Company Announces $1.4M Loss." cbc, January 10. <cbc.ca/news/canada/toronto/paul-godfrey-steps-down-as-postmedia-ceo-as-company-announces-1-4m-loss-1.4974050>.

Canwest. 2008. "Paul Godfrey Named President and ceo, National Post." Canwest Global, December 1. <web.archive.org/web/20100519061559/http://www.canwestglobal.com/media/viewNews.asp?NewsroomID=904>.

cbc News. 2000a. "The Rapid Expansion of CanWest Global." July 31. <cbc.ca/news/canada/the-rapid-expansion-of-canwest-global-1.235852>.

___. 2000b. "What's in It for Hollinger and CanWest?" July 31. <cbc.ca/news/business/what-s-in-it-for-hollinger-and-canwest-1.210338>.

cbc/Radio-Canada. n.d. "Journalistic Standards and Practices." <cbc.radio-canada.ca/en/vision/governance/journalistic-standards-and-practices>.

cjfe (Canadian Journalists for Free Expression). n.d. "Advocacy." <cjfe.org/advocacy>.

Committee to Protect Journalists. 2018. "Palestinian Journalists Injured Covering Mass Protest in Gaza Strip." April 2. <cpj.org/2018/04/palestinian-journalists-injured-covering-mass-prot/>.

Craig, Sean. 2019. "You Must Be This Conservative to Ride: The Inside Story of Postmedia's Right Turn." *Canadaland*, August 12. <canadalandshow.com/the-conservative-transformation-of-postmedia/>.

Electronic Intifada. 2018. "Watch the Film the Israel Lobby Didn't Want You to See." November 2. <electronicintifada.net/content/watch-film-israel-lobby-didnt-want-you-see/25876>.

Fegelman, Mike. 2019. "hrc Disturbed by *McGill Daily*'s Reaffirming Its Discriminatory Anti-Zionist Policy." HonestReporting Canada, November 5. <honestreporting.ca/hrc-disturbed-by-mcgill-dailys-reaffirming-its-discriminatory-anti-zionist-policy/>.

___. 2020a. "McGill Daily Publishes Another Pro-Zionism Letter After Outcry." January 20. <honestreporting.ca/mcgill-daily-publishes-another-pro-zionism-letter-after-outcry/>.

___. 2020b. "*McGill Daily* Back to Its Old Anti-Israel Tricks." HonestReporting Canada, March 30. <honestreporting.ca/mcgill-daily-back-to-its-old-anti-israel-tricks/>.

___. 2020c. "Radio-Canada Blames Israel for Gaza's Plight in Fighting Coronavirus." HonestReporting Canada, April 28. <honestreporting.ca/radio-canada-blames-israel-for-gazas-plight-in-fighting-coronavirus/>.

___. 2020d. "Success! Radio-Canada Deletes Article Blaming Israel for Gaza's Plight in Fighting Coronavirus." HonestReporting Canada, May 13. <honestreporting.ca/success-radio-canada-deletes-article-blaming-israel-for-gazas-plight-in-fighting-coronavirus/>.

___. 2020e. "*Macleans* Editor Praises Palestinian 'Freedom Fighters.'" HonestReporting Canada, June 5. <https://honestreporting.ca/23182-2/>.

___. n.d.a. "Corrections, Clarifications and Retractions." <honestreporting.ca/corrections-clarifications/>.

___. n.d.b. "Endorsements." <honestreporting.ca/who-we-are/endorsement/>.

___. n.d.c. "Who We Are." <honestreporting.ca/who-we-are/>.

___. 2002. "When CNN Is the Story." June 30. <honestreporting.com/when-cnn-is-the-story/>.

Globe and Mail Editorial Board. 2010. "Disproportionate Force Feeds Propaganda Against Israel." *Globe and Mail*, June 1. <theglobeandmail.com/opinion/editorials/disproportionate-force-feeds-propaganda-against-israel/article1371738/>.

___. 2011. "How to Reconstruct the Peace Process." *Globe and Mail*, May 25. <theglobeandmail.com/opinion/editorials/how-to-reconstruct-the-peace-process/article580974/>.

___. 2014. "Peace Talks Must Resume Soon Between Israel, Palestinians." *Globe and Mail*, August 1. <theglobeandmail.com/opinion/editorials/israel-gaza-and-how-to-plan-for-peace-while-fighting-a-war/article19893825/>.

Hendler, Clint. 2007. "TNR's New Owners." *The Nation*, March 6. <thenation.com/article/archive/tnrs-new-owners/>.

Honderich, John. 2015. "Postmedia Let Down Readers by Dictating Election Endorsements." *Toronto Star*, November 9. <thestar.com/opinion/commentary/2015/11/09/postmedia-let-down-readers-by-dictating-election-endorsements-honderich.html>.

Human Rights Council. 2019. *Report of the Independent International Commission of Inquiry on the Protests in the Occupied Palestinian Territory*. February 25. <ohchr.org/Documents/HRBodies/HRCouncil/CoIOPT/A_HRC_40_74.pdf>.

Khan, Saleem. 2002. "'Unapologetically Pro-Israel' CanWest Imposes National Editorials on Local Papers." *Washington Report on Middle East Affairs*, April. <wrmea.org/002-april/anada-calling-unapologetically-pro-israel-canwest-imposes-national-editorials-on-local-papers.html>.

Kimber, Stephen. n.d. "The Wonderful World of Iz… Is 1984 All Over Again." <stephenkimber.com/bio/journalism/from-silenced/>.

Macdonald, Neil. 2018. "Call Me Radical, but Journalists Should Be Able to Pledge Support for Palestinian Journalists." CBC, April 15. <cbc.ca/news/opinion/cfje-statement-1.4620246>.

Marotte, Bertrand, and Ingrid Peritz. 2001. "Gazette Publisher Steps Down." *Globe and Mail*, September 1.

Mastracci, Davide. 2018. "Canadian Media: Cheerleading War on Palestine." April 3. <medium.com/@DavideMastracci/canadian-media-cheerleading-war-on-palestine-6dc2aff395e8>.

McGill, Am, Chabad at McGill, Hillel McGill, and Israel on Campus at McGill. 2019. "Letter to the Editorial Board." November 25. <mcgilldaily.com/2019/11/letter-to-the-editorial-board-november-25/>.

McGill Daily. n.d. "Policies." <mcgilldaily.com/policies/>.

___. 2016. "In Response to a SSMU Equity Complaint About anti-Semitism, Mentioning the *Daily*." November 7. <mcgilldaily.com/2016/11/in-response-to-a-ssmu-equity-complaint-about-anti-semitism-mentioning-the-daily/>.

___. 2019. "Our Response." November 4. <mcgilldaily.com/2019/11/our-response/>.

Metcalf, Kevin. 2018. "Full Statement and Termination Notice." Facebook post. April 8. <facebook.com/photo.php?fbid=10156053030311211>.

Murray, Gordon, and Carel Moiseiwitsch. 2008. "CanWest Huffs and Puffs While Free Speech Burns." *Georgia Straight*, July 16. <straight.com/article-153833/canwest-huffs-and-puffs-free-speech-burns>.

National Post Editorial Board. 2012a. "Netanyahu Rightly Picked Least Bad Option." November 24. <nationalpost.com/opinion/national-post-editorial-board-netanyahu-rightly-picked-least-bad-option/>.

___. 2012b. "Dealing with an Empowered Abbas." November 30. <nationalpost.com/opinion/national-post-editorial-board-dealing-with-an-empowered-abbas/>.

___. 2014. "Elizabeth May's 'Engaged Neutrality' on Hamas Is Just Another Brand of Moral Relativism." July 30. <nationalpost.com/opinion/national-post-editorial-board-elizabeth-mays-engaged-neutrality-on-hamas-is-just-another-brand-of-moral-relativism/>.

___. 2015. "Our Choice for Government." October 17. <nationalpost.com/opinion/national-post-view-our-choice-for-government>.

Olive, David. 2015. "Postmedia and the Heavy Price it Pays to Survive." *Toronto Star*, January 23. <thestar.com/business/2015/01/23/postmedia-and-the-heavy-price-it-pays-to-survive-olive.html>.

Parry, Nigel, and Laurie King. 2001. "The CanWest Chill." *Electronic Intifada*, December 11. <electronicintifada.net/content/canwest-chill-we-do-not-run-our-newspaper-op-ed-pieces-express-criticism-israel/4240>.

Reuters. 2002. "Canadian Newspaper Bias Against Palestinians." January 25. <archive.vn/9OGVG>.

Sabbagh, Karl. 2009. "Perils of Criticising Israel." *British Medical Journal* 338.

Schiller, Bill. 2002. "Axing of Column Sparks Controversy." *Toronto Star*, January 12.

Shapiro, Josh, and Michael Aarenau. 2019. "Response to *McGill Daily* on Zionism." *McGill Daily*, November 3. <mcgilldaily.com/2019/11/our-response/response-to-mcgill-daily-on-zionism/>.

Summerfield, Derek. 2004. "Palestine: The Assault on Health and Other War Crimes." *British Medical Journal* 329.

Swick, David. 2002. "From Thrilled to the Truth: Many Weren't Happy with Newspaper Owner's Policies." *Halifax Daily News*, August 14.

Toronto Star Editorial Board. 2012. "Gaza Crisis Highlights the Risk of a Go-Nowhere Peace Process." *Toronto Star*, November 15. <thestar.com/opinion/editorials/2012/11/15/gaza_crisis_highlights_the_risk_of_a_gonowhere_peace_process.html>.

Tunley, Philip. 2018. "Statement from the CJFE Board of Directors." April 11. <cjfe.org/

statement_from_the_cjfe_board_of_directors>.

Winseck, Dwayne. 2020. "Media and Internet Concentration in Canada, 1984–2019." *Canadian Media Concentration Research Project.* <cmcrp.org/media-and-internet-concentration-in-canada-1984-2019/>.

Yee, Vivian, and Mona El-Naggar. 2021. "'Social Media Is the Mass Protest': Solidarity with Palestinians Grows Online." *New York Times,* May 18. <nytimes.com/2021/05/18/world/middleeast/palestinians-social-media.html>.

Chapter 8

Palestinian Solidarity Work in Canada

Strengths, Weaknesses, Opportunities, Threats

Thomas Woodley

Canadians for Justice and Peace in the Middle East (CJPME) was founded in Montreal in 2004 to invigorate the public discussion in Canada around Palestinian human rights and ultimately to make the Canadian public more sympathetic to the grievances of the Palestinian people. In its early years, CJPME's leaders often struggled to get the ear of policymakers and to penetrate the mainstream Canadian media. In its advocacy work, especially, they looked at other successful organizations — including pro-Israel organizations — to see whether strategic concepts could be easily transplanted into CJPME's organizational framework or if successful advocacy might result from the proper application of lobbying "formulas."

The leadership quickly found that many such organizations differed in such fundamental ways that "replicating" their strategies would be impossible, impracticable and sometimes even counterproductive. What is more, the approaches of such organizations often ignored opportunities that CJPME could capitalize on with very little effort.

To explore these fundamental differences between organizations, CJPME's founders conducted a SWOT analysis. Short for "Strengths, Weaknesses, Opportunities and Threat," SWOT is an analytical tool which has been used widely in the business world since the 1960s (Friesner 2008) and is traditionally used to improve corporate planning and enable better decision-making. It has also been successfully leveraged in a broad number of other contexts, including by non-governmental organizations (NGOs) (Grant 2020). Ideally, a SWOT analysis should guide the user toward strategies that are likely to be most effective — those that are more aligned with the user's strengths and context. Conversely, a SWOT analysis is likely to reveal strategic dead ends and potential risk areas. A SWOT matrix (Figure 8-1) helps to identify these factors.

What CJPME's own SWOT analysis made clear is that it has many strengths inherent to its mandate and its constituency which are not enjoyed by the other groups, while its weaknesses, opportunities and threats were also distinct. This was true even of groups

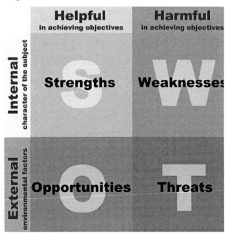

Figure 8-1 SWOT Matrix

that shared CJPME's advocacy space — including and especially some of the most influential pro-Israel groups. This analysis confirmed what CJPME's leaders had intuitively concluded: a strategy which sought to copy the approach of other groups would be a poor use of resources. It makes far more sense to adopt a strategy which leveraged CJPME's unique strengths and opportunities, while circumventing its particular weaknesses and avoiding its threats.

Every movement and organization has its own SWOT, and it can be a useful task to take the time to identify and contemplate them at the organizational and "movement" levels. When CJPME first performed its SWOT analysis, it focused the analysis at the organizational level: what were the conditions specific to the CJPME and its defined mandate? A SWOT analysis of the broader Palestine solidarity movement can serve to give the movement new ideas and greater confidence in some strategic areas, as well as more realistic attitudes and wariness in other strategic directions.

What/Who Is the Palestine Solidarity Movement in Canada?

There is no common accepted definition of the Palestine solidarity movement (PSM); membership tends to be self-defined, and perceptions can vary drastically depending on who is discussing the movement. CJPME has defined its mandate primarily around Palestinian human rights, but there are many other justifications for supporting Palestinians and valid ways to support their aspirations which have little relationship with "human rights" per se. For example, an organization which seeks to nurture Palestinian culture or art could just as easily claim a place in the PSM as CJPME. CJPME has chosen a human rights focus because we believe it is an effective vehicle to reach beyond a core of ethnic Palestinians (and even beyond a core of sympathetic Middle Eastern immigrants to Canada). Successful solidarity movements must attract and involve people of all backgrounds. The movement must engage deeply held convictions to coax such individuals to stand in solidarity with the Palestinians, potentially at a political cost. In our experience, premising the Palestinian solidarity movement on universally valued principles of life and liberty — human rights — has often proved an effective way of building solidarity quickly across the broader Canada public.

To ensure this SWOT exercise is focused enough to be useful, in this chapter I focus on people who live in Canada who seek political change in support of the human rights of Palestinians and their advocates. The insight derived from this SWOT analysis will be most useful to the organizations which have mandates like that of CJPME. Other PSM organizations with much different mandates — ones which concentrate on Palestinian arts or culture, or ones that emphasize Palestinian nationalism — should apply a different focus, given their differing strategies. As a result of our focus in this analysis, our approach highlights, for example, strengths related to potential electoral power and the ability to sway federal elections, rather than tactics using the arts to shift public discourse, even though each of these forms has been used successfully for social change in other contexts. Similarly, this analysis discusses law and legal institutions as an asset, whereas other members of the PSM may have valid reasons to perceive the law and legal institutions as threats. The analysis described below reflects a specific viewpoint and should not be seen as a one-size-fits-all proposal or framework.

Strengths of the Palestine Solidarity Movement in Canada

The point of listing strengths of the PSM is to identify and exploit potential resources available to the movement. Taking the first listed strength — a large number of communities and movements which may be open to solidarity — as an example, the PSM must find ways to create or build upon existing connections to generate and mobilize their solidarity.

A Large Number of Communities and Movements
That May Be Open to Supporting Palestine Solidarity

Although many PSM activists complain that too few people take an interest in their cause, compared to many other social causes, they should actually be grateful. There are in fact a large number of communities and movements here in Canada that may be easily won over to support Palestinian human rights. In some cases, the common cultural bonds and lived experiences within certain constituencies can predispose vast numbers in such groups (e.g., Muslim Canadians) to be sympathetic to Palestinian aspirations. In other cases, decades of solidarity work have slowly changed perceptions across certain sectors of society (e.g., much of Canada's labour movement) and paved the way for members to become allies in the work.

For instance, while not all Arab Canadians take Palestinian rights to heart, many do. According to Canada's 2016 census, 948,330 Canadians claimed Arab ancestry (Statistics Canada 2017). This number is up significantly from the 2011 census, in which 661,750 Canadians claimed Arab ancestry (Statistics Canada 2019). Many Arab and Muslim Canadians are highly concerned for the human rights of the Palestinians. Jerusalem is meanwhile the third holiest city for Muslims, who share a broad concern for the right of Muslims to worship in the city's Al-Aqsa Mosque. Jerusalem is also considered the future capital and national symbol of self-determination for Palestinians of all faiths and, in turn, a site of concern for their allies. According to Statistics Canada's 2011 National Household Survey, there were 1,053,945 Muslims in Canada, constituting well over 3 percent of Canada's total population (Statistics Canada 2016). Given the type of migration to Canada since 2011, the numbers of Muslims and Arabs have very likely grown substantially since 2011 and 2016 respectively.

For better or worse, the Palestine human rights issue is to some degree a bellwether for a portion of the progressive political spectrum. In the summer of 2020, twenty-two of the twenty-four New Democratic Party (NDP) MPs in Parliament supported CJPME's pledge to oppose Israeli annexation (CJPME n.d.). EKOS Survey results from both 2017 (Ralph et al. 2017) and 2020 (Bueckert et al. 2020) make clear that a strong majority of NDP supporters — as well as large numbers of Green Party and Liberal Party supporters — feel that Israel's human rights abuses against Palestinians should be addressed. The Labour movement in Canada is also very sympathetic to Palestinian rights: large and important labour unions consistently endorse statements of support for Palestinian rights. Finally, certain churches and church organizations have also taken positions publicly in support of Palestinian human rights.

Many separatists in Quebec identify closely with the call for Palestinian self-determination. As such, separatist Quebec parties and their supporters are consistently supportive of Palestinian rights. For instance, in May of 2017, the Bloc Québécois announced a motion inviting the House of Commons to express support for Palestine as an independent state (CJPME 2017). More recently, in July 2020, the entire Bloc caucus in Parliament supported CJPME's MP Pledge to oppose Israeli annexation (CJPME n.d.: "Pledge Endorsements").

To leverage this strength, the PSM must make a special effort to reach out to these communities and movements which may be open to greater solidarity with Palestinians, showing a special sensitivity to the specific concerns of each segment of these constituencies.

A Highly Motivated Constituency

Not only are each of the constituencies above quite large, but they are also relatively highly motivated, even beyond a generalized ethical support for Palestinians. Many devout Muslim Canadians, for example, feel a religious conviction to ensure that the Al-Aqsa Mosque in Jerusalem is administered by Muslims. Many Arab Canadians support Palestinian human rights because they yearn for greater political stability and accountability in the Middle East. Separatist Quebeckers have a political stake in supporting independence movements around the world. While most Canadians are not single-issue voters, Palestinian rights are clearly a priority for many members of the above constituencies.

In addition to the motivational influences mentioned above — religious convictions, separatist convictions, etc. — one's personal exposure to an issue can also be highly influential. Palestinian, Lebanese, Jordanian, Syrian, Egyptian and Iraqi Canadians may have had experiences, such as personally suffering human rights abuses, experiencing Israeli invasion or bombing, or personal contact with Palestinian refugees in their countries of origin, which may help shape their motivation to support Palestinians. Some Jewish Canadians have also been exposed to the rights abuses that Israel inflicts on Palestinians and they too are personally affected by what they have witnessed.

Because immigrants to Canada often have this first-hand exposure to the regional impacts of the Palestine/Israel conflict, when they arrive in Canada they share their experiences with their children, neighbours, co-workers, friends and Canadian-born spouses. Many of these people are personally moved by the stories of upheaval and dispossession experienced by the Palestinians. Many of the leaders within the PSM emerged from such groups. Ultimately, all of them are highly motivated by the way the issue has touched them directly or indirectly.

The "personally touched" phenomenon is certainly not unique to the PSM. Obvious analogues are cancer-cure advocacy groups, groups like Mothers Against Drunk Driving and similar groups where victims band together in common purpose. Like these other groups, the PSM is sustained and galvanized by people who have first-hand or second-hand exposure to the human rights issues. To be sure, personal experience alone is not always sufficient to galvanize one to action. In fact, in some cases, personal experience can be so traumatizing that victims may be prevented from engaging politically. Nevertheless, with the appropriate discursive or political catalyst, such personal experiences often compel individuals to become involved with the PSM.

A Cause That Is Broadly Supported by International Law and International Organizations

International law supports the Palestinian legal position at virtually every turn. Article 1 of the United Nations Charter upholds the right to self-determination. The Hague Regulations and the Fourth Geneva Convention make clear that Israel is a military occupier of Palestinian territory and has myriad obligations as occupier. Key international bodies, such as the High Contracting Parties to the Fourth Geneva Convention, the International Court of Justice (ICJ) and the Chief Prosecutor of the International Criminal Court (ICC) have repeatedly upheld Palestinian rights and the applicability of international law.

Given the tragic history of the Palestinian people and given that international law is so supportive of the Palestinian case, it is not surprising that there is very strong international support for Palestinian rights. The United Nations General Assembly (UNGA) annually condemns Israel's human rights violations against the Palestinians, usually passing 15 to 16 symbolic resolutions by huge margins. In 2012, for example, 138 nations voted in support of upgrading Palestine to non-member observer state status in the UNGA (although Canada voted against the resolution) (UN News 2012). Independently, countries also indicate their willingness to recognize a Palestinian state. As of July 2019, 138 of the UN's 193 member states recognize Palestine (World Population Review n.d.).

The United Nations also has several mechanisms for collecting and disseminating data on Palestine, such as the United Nations Information System on the Question of Palestine (UNISPAL), an online collection of all historic United Nations and international publications relating to Palestine/Israel. The United Nations also appoints the Special Rapporteur on the situation of human rights in the Palestinian Territory, who enjoys access to and the cooperation of many players on the ground in the Palestinian territories (although Israel itself is highly uncooperative). Typically possessing a strong legal background, the Rapporteur regularly issues useful statements and reports on Palestinian rights and the impact of ongoing developments. In addition, UNRWA, the United Nations aid agency for Palestinian refugees; OCHA, the United Nations Office for the Coordination of Humanitarian Affairs; the ICRC, the International Committee of the Red Cross; and other United Nations and aid and human rights agencies produce copious documentation in support of Palestinian human rights issues.

Beyond the support of international organizations, the Palestinian cause also benefits from the work of international human rights organizations. Amnesty International, Human Rights Watch and other organizations regularly issue reports documenting and critiquing Israel's human rights abuses against Palestinians. As third party observers of the Palestine/Israel conflict, these organizations and their reports bring strong legitimacy to the human rights grievances of the Palestinians.

While international political obstacles have prevented Palestinians from obtaining justice on many fronts, the international legal framework still fully supports their cause. As such, Palestinians and their advocates would be wise to leverage all possible legal avenues available to them. In addition, since many of the small grassroots organizations that constitute the PSM have trouble performing primary research on Palestinian human rights, they should lean on the published reports made available by international bodies. The PSM has many powerful opponents, so the advantage of international law and international support is certainly not a "slam dunk." Practically speaking, both in Palestine and elsewhere, international law has often failed to produce tangible benefits for the victims of oppression. Nevertheless, by pursuing its aspirations through international law (e.g., through the International Criminal Court) the PSM has a very defensible and "inexpensive" path by which to pursue its goals.

A Cause That Resonates with a Natural Sense of Justice

It is difficult to precisely qualify what exactly resonates with people's natural sense of justice, but there are several factors which garner sympathy for the justice of the Palestinian cause. Outside observers can often empathize with peoples dispossessed of their land and with the refugees that creates. This further engenders sympathies to resistance movements and criticisms of an occupying force, all of which are the case for Palestinians. The disparity in casualty numbers when armed violence occurs between Palestinians and Israelis — where frequently Palestinian casualty numbers are one or two orders of magnitude greater than Israeli casualties — and the disparity in the standard of living and lifestyles between Palestinians and Israelis seems unjust to many, as does Israel's use of disproportionate force, failure to distinguish between civilian and combatants, and the arrest and imprisonment of children (Azarova 2017). In general, this hearkens to the biblical tale of David and Goliath, and a natural inclination many, if not most, people have to support the underdog. Palestinians share a natural, similar constituency with other Indigenous Peoples displaced and erased by settler-colonialism, like the Indigenous Nations on Turtle Island or Australia and New Zealand.

However, mainstream media coverage regularly fails to provide the context to enable readers to understand the power imbalance between Israel and the Palestinians. Made aware of factors like the above, most people will sympathize with the plight of the Palestinians. As such, it is incumbent on the PSM to get such facts into the public conversation around Israel and the Palestinians.

A Cause That Resembles Other Historic Human Rights Causes

Aspects of the Palestinian struggle bring to mind stirring and historic struggles of the recent past. For instance, travel permit systems for Palestinians and forced displacement of Palestinian Bedouins and other non-Jewish communities are reminiscent of similar policies in South Africa under apartheid. Israel's incentives to discourage teaching Palestinian narratives in Palestinian schools are similar to the many efforts made in North America to destroy Indigenous cultural preservation. The desecration of historic Muslim cemeteries by Israel in the West Bank is very similar to the desecration of sacred Native American sites by federal, state and local authorities in the United States. Israel's separation wall, bypass roads, Jewish-only settlements and other infrastructure in the West Bank bear strong resemblance to the segregationist laws and practices of the Jim Crow era in the American South. The oppressive conditions faced by Palestinian political detainees in Israeli jails hold many parallels to the conditions faced by Irish nationalists in British jails during the Troubles in Northern Ireland, and the arbitrary and indefinite detainment of Palestinian political prisoners by Israel is reminiscent of many oppressive Eastern European countries during the Cold War. Israel's frequent choice to shoot unarmed Palestinian protesters, such as took place in Gaza in 2018–20 during the Great March of Return resulting in 214 Palestinians killed and 36,100 injured (United Nations 2020) can be compared to many brutal colonial episodes of the past, like the 1919 Jallianwala Bagh (Amritsar) Massacre a century earlier, where British colonial forces fired upon unarmed Indian protesters, killing at least 379 and wounding at least 1,200 (Pletcher n.d.).

For human rights advocates, the historic parallels between what is happening to the Palestinians and what happened to other oppressed groups of the past sometimes makes it easier to highlight the injustices. Many Canadians remain unfamiliar with Israel's abuses against the Palestinians and their historical analogues. CJPME has worked to leverage these historical parallels as an educational tool, and other PSM organizations may find it valuable to do the same.

Weaknesses of the Palestine Solidarity Movement in Canada

By identifying the weaknesses of the PSM, the movement can try to mitigate, compensate or circumvent the resulting challenges. These weaknesses are inherent; they cannot be avoided or ignored. But by understanding them, the PSM can manage expectations, plan realistically and avoid pitfalls.

A Constituency That Is Still Establishing Itself Civically and Economically

At public protests and demonstrations for Palestinian human rights, it is typical to see people of all different backgrounds. However, as racialized communities made up largely of first- and second-generation immi-grants, Arab, Muslim and South Asian communities are still establishing themselves economically (Baldassare et al. 2018), which means young people may be encouraged to pursue professional careers, rather than working in activist or charity work, as the latter may be perceived as risk-ier or less financially lucrative. These racialized communities also face barriers in establishing a political voice which is taken seriously by those in power. Even those communities with a long-established presence in Canada may continue to be dismissed as "immigrants," rather than ac-cepted as "average Canadians," due to the role of race and whiteness in building Canadian identity, and this can negatively limit their ability to be heard and have their concerns addressed. Becoming "Canadian" is a complex process intertwined with race, historical European imperialism and identity which, in the case of Palestinians, has been interwoven with a socially accepted Islamophobia that is wielded against them politi-cally in the War on Terror era. Those who have more recently arrived in Canada may also be less comfortable discussing their issues publicly, meeting with politicians, writing to the media, commenting in social media and participating in other ways. Many come from countries where expressing oneself politically could lead to intimidation, impris-onment or even death; and they are cognizant of socially oppressive Islamophobia that threatens their well-being in Canada. Even when they come to Canada, individuals who have grown up in such societies may still be reluctant to engage politically out of a vague fear of retribution. Establishing community organizations and representation takes years, and in the meantime these communities are often easily ignored by poli-ticians and the media.

However, the 2015 election saw an encouraging increase of Muslims and South Asians in Parliament. Similarly, academia, professional asso-ciations, the media and other institutions see increasing representation from racialized and newcomer communities. The communities which most consistently demonstrate support for the PSM must be encouraged and trained to exercise their political rights — without caving into vague fears. These communities are large, and as they increasingly find their voice, they will increasingly have a political impact.

A Constituency That Faces Other Important Challenges

While Arab, Muslim and South Asian communities may have a concern for Palestinian rights, it is not their sole concern, and it is rarely their most pressing concern. All three groups continue to face deep issues of racial and religious discrimination in Canada. This affects their financial and social well-being as they face barriers to employment and acceptance in many other spheres. Their struggle to organize to fight Islamophobia in Canada, for example, distracts from their ability to be active for Palestinian rights. In addition, many people who are sympathetic to the Palestinian cause come from countries which have their own concerns. For instance, between 2010 and 2020, all of the following Middle Eastern countries dealt with serious social or political issues: Tunisia, Algeria, Libya, Sudan, Egypt, Lebanon, Syria, Qatar, Yemen, Iraq and Turkey. There are also other beleaguered non-state groups being oppressed by regional states, like the Kurdish and Sahrawi peoples, with their own unique concerns. Immigrants from these countries may find themselves organizing around these issues, not Palestine.

The above examples are reflective of the intersectional nature of various social causes. The PSM must recognize and accept these challenges and use the opportunity to build intersectional bridges with other social causes.

A Constituency That Is Sometimes Divided within Itself

No community is monolithic, and this is certainly true of the diverse community of people who support Palestinian human rights in Canada. The divisions within the community are not static but can change and evolve over time. Nevertheless, there are situations where different communities and movements which support the PSM have trouble working alongside each other. For instance, conflict between Syria and Lebanon or Iran and Iraq, or conflicts among Lebanese, Syrians, Iraqis or others, can make it harder for those communities to work together. In addition, these communities can have deep cultural differences. When Muslims or Arabs who hold conservative positions on gender, for instance, work with left-wing activists (Arab or non-Arab) who have strong beliefs about women's and 2SLGBTIQ rights, there can be conflict and disagreement, and it can be hard to build common cause. Such differences can make collaboration tentative, uneasy and short-lived.

To some degree, the PSM must "roll with the punches" as these tensions rise and subside, pushing for maximum collaboration, support and broader coalitions whenever possible.

A Cause That Has Not Been Able to Establish Strong Institutions

The PSM has struggled to create long-term institutions to serve as a foundation for advocacy efforts. Established institutions are better able to train skilled advocacy staff, develop leaders, nurture long-standing political and media relationships and accrue institutional knowledge that can be shared across the community. What is more, politicians and the media find it easier to work with communities which have institutions they can deal directly with — representative, hierarchical organizations being the easiest.

While in 2020, there *are* a handful of organizations in the PSM which are starting to establish "institutional" strength, none of them have existed for more than twenty years. They are also still small and fragile as compared to the institutions serving other communities. Whereas the pro-Israel Centre for Israel and Jewish Affairs (CIJA) has fifty to sixty employees with offices across Canada (Centre for Israel and Jewish Affairs n.d.), no Canadian PSM organization has more than two full-time paid employees, and fewer still have an office.

Opportunities for the Palestine Solidarity Movement in Canada

When speaking of opportunities, the focus is on untapped possibilities available to the PSM. Nevertheless, in most cases, it will require time, valuable and dedicated skills and resources (including funding) to exploit the available opportunities. As such, it is less a question of, "We never thought of that," and more a question of, "This is going to take some work!"

An Increasing Interest in Cooperation among PSM Actors

As of 2020, there is some exciting collaboration taking place within the PSM — collaboration that had not been present in the preceding decades. Both the Palestine Advocacy Network (PAN) and the Coalition of Canadian-Palestinian Organizations (CCPO) were founded in 2018, bringing together, in the case of the former, organizations with an interest in political advocacy for Palestinian human rights and, in the case of the latter, representatives of the many Palestinian-Canadian organizations across the country. Both coalitions provide opportunities to share resources, speak out as one and create new advocacy opportunities. In addition, the 2019 Canada-Palestine Symposium in Ottawa was an example of collaboration among Canadian academics with the intent of elevating academic research on Canada-Palestine relations and the related human rights issues. Finally, there are several groupings of organizations — including the Canadian BDS Coalition and the Quebec BDS Coalition — which meet informally and collaborate on an ad hoc basis around the international Boycott, Divestment and Sanctions (BDS) campaign.

The opportunity for the PSM is to nurture and grow this collaboration and parlay these efforts into concrete wins for the PSM. Such collaboration can compensate somewhat for the lack of paid personnel and resources staffing the PSM. The information sharing among such groups can also improve the strategic initiatives undertaken by the movement overall.

A Growing Interest in Intersectional Politics in Canada

Intersectionality expresses the idea that different forms of oppression or prejudice have the same root, based in the prevailing societal power structures (Carbado et al. 2013). Thus, for example, the systems of oppression faced by Indigenous Peoples have common roots with the systems of oppression faced by Palestinians. Intersectionality also suggests that choosing to oppose only one form of oppression requires an improper selectivity or favouritism, elevating the importance of one type of oppression over another (Carbado et al. 2013). So, for example, intersectionality suggests it would be incongruous to support Indigenous rights while opposing Palestinian rights.

There are a number of different ways to understand intersectionality for the purposes of the PSM. For example, Palestinians and their cause in Canada may find their cause dismissed because of racism against Arabs. They may also face prejudice in Canada because of religious discrimination — like Islamophobia. Palestinian women may be dismissed by their peers because of sexism. Yet racism, religious discrimination and sexism are all forces which underlie the challenges faced by other disadvantaged groups in Canada. Recognizing this, disparate groups are starting to talk more intentionally about how to join forces to address these overarching forces. Collaboration between PSM groups and Indigenous groups, groups representing racialized minorities and Muslim groups combatting Islamophobia or representing their community, is starting to be more common.

In another example, the opportunity for the PSM provided by intersectionality can be seen in the competing ideas of Zionism and equality. Dating from the colonial era, Zionism suggests that a Jewish state is the only way that Jews will enjoy security. In deep contrast, from the intersectionality playbook, equality suggests that the security of Jews is tied to the security of all other minority groups (Munayyer 2019). The adoption of intersectional thinking will inevitably lead to the reorientation of priorities and alliances among social causes. This reorientation has the real possibility of bringing PSM out of the shadows and into the mainstream of progressive social causes.

Obviously, opportunities for collaboration go far beyond the examples listed here. The advantages include 1) better strategic planning and communication among causes; 2) cross-pollination of resources and interest between causes; and 3) greater understanding of the issues across the Canadian public.

Legal Mechanisms and Protections to Pursue the Cause

Although the PSM's adversaries will continue to try to intimidate it, the PSM is in a very good legal position to pursue its mandate. Canada's criminal code and Charter of Rights and Freedoms give the PSM all the leeway it needs to criticize Israeli government policy, boycott Israel and publicize Israel's human rights abuses. Although political parties trying to curry favour with the pro-Israel lobby may pass motions that put a chill on open debate around Israel, such motions have no legal import. The February 2016 parliamentary motion to condemn groups promoting the BDS movement is one such example. Nevertheless, despite being dared and taunted to condemn BDS activists following the passage of the motion (Canadians for Justice and Peace in the Middle East 2016), the Liberal government wisely never took any action.

The PSM movement should be vigilant for any steps on the part of the government or other players to curtail its right to raise issues about the Israeli government's human rights abuses. Even when they have no legal teeth, such political acts may discourage or intimidate all but the most sophisticated members and organizations in the PSM. Should the PSM be prevented from promoting its human rights message, its various leaders should not hesitate to consider legal action.

A Large Population of Fair-Minded Canadians

While most Canadians remain disengaged on the issue of Palestine/Israel, this does not mean that they have no opinions. Two professional surveys on Canadian attitudes around Palestine/Israel — one conducted in 2017 (Ralph et al. 2017) and the second in 2020 (Bueckert et al. 2020) make clear that Canadians generally want Canada to remain impartial in the Palestine/Israel conflict and expect bad international players — like Israel — to be held to account for their violations of international law. In the 2017 survey, respondents overwhelming reported believing (91 percent) that criticizing Israeli government policies is not necessarily antisemitic; more respondents held a negative view of the Israeli government (46 percent) than have a positive view (28 percent), and most (66 percent) said that sanctions and boycotts are reasonable measures to defend Palestinian rights. (Supporters of the Liberals and NDP were on average even more supportive.) In the 2020 survey, 86 percent of respondents did not think Canada should overlook the alleged human rights violation of Israel, even if Israel is considered an ally, and a strong majority (82 percent) oppose having Canada recognize Jerusalem as exclusively Israel's capital. Given that successive Conservative and Liberal governments have maintained a decidedly pro-Israel stance, the PSM has fertile ground among average Canadians for its human rights message.

These survey results should give the PSM confidence that the Canadian public is generally open to its human rights message and that it should continue its efforts to sensitize average Canadians to the issues. In parallel, the PSM should use these survey results to remind policymakers of the broad Canadian sympathy for Palestinian human rights.

A Growing Interest and Acceptance of Economic Pressure against Israel

The BDS movement is extremely important and strategic for the PSM because it gives members of the PSM a way to direct their anger at Israel's abuses. Founded in 2005, it came after decades of failed attempts to achieve justice for Palestinians through international condemnation, United Nations resolutions, the negotiations process and an ICJ advisory opinion. While an exhaustive review of the successes of the BDS movement is beyond the scope of this document, the BDS movement has had many notable successes in its first fifteen years (Visualizing Palestine n.d.). As a nation which benefits substantially from globalization and prides itself on its achievements in the arts and education, Israel stands to be greatly penalized by the economic, cultural and academic boycott proposed by BDS. Rooted in international law, the justifications of BDS are on very solid and defensible ground.

For the PSM, the BDS movement is a legitimate, inherently democratic means of protest and pressure. It was initiated by the Palestinians themselves, is specific in its goals and is deliberately non-violent. The PSM must embrace the BDS movement, strategically choose its targets, collaborate internationally and promote widespread participation from the grassroots. The pro-Israel establishment considers the BDS movement to be one of the greatest threats to Israel's right-wing political aims.

BDS provides effective and practical tools to force Israel to respect the human rights of Palestinians. As the PSM leverages these tools over a sustained period, the successes and milestones of the BDS movement will continue to accrue.

Threats to the Palestine Solidarity Movement in Canada

When speaking of threats, we refer to things that can distract or derail the PSM from capitalizing on its potential strengths and opportunities. Some of the threats described below may come as a surprise and are at risk of materializing due to missteps by PSM leaders. Others are long-simmering phenomena that have harried and impeded the movement for years. Members of the PSM must remember that these "threats" are not a foregone conclusion. With wise and visionary leadership, the PSM in Canada can mitigate or avoid these threats. Nevertheless, the PSM's degree of future success or failure will be strongly influenced by the movement's ability to navigate them.

Getting Distracted from the Core Objectives of the PSM

As described earlier, the PSM is constituted of many different segments of the Canadian public. Some of these segments may have the best of intentions for Palestinians but may put a less-than-strategic spin on their campaigns and actions in support of Palestinian rights. Such missteps may result from inexperience, lack of maturity, racism or other sources, but they can become a threat to the movement. The opponents of the PSM can be quick to jump on such blunders to undermine the work of the broader movement, and such missteps can create confusion around the moral and ethical justifications for the aims of the PSM.

The first most common pitfall is the failure to distinguish between the abuses of the government of Israel and the Jewish community at large. Usually because of inexperience or sloppiness, members of the PSM occasionally turn their frustration against the Jewish people, rather than staying focused on the human rights abuses of the Israeli government. Certain Israeli leaders and members of the Jewish community make statements which encourage confusion between the two (Pfeffer 2015). When inexperienced members of the PSM lash out against Jews, instead of the crimes of the Israeli government, the PSM can quickly get mired down in emotional public debates as to whether the movement is antisemitic. It also detracts from the critical role Jewish Canadians have played as leaders building the PSM, such as Nestel and Ralph in this collection; and the growing numbers of members from their community who feel compelled to speak up contrary to Jewish Canadian organizations that deliberately conflate Judaism with Israel or offer unflinching support to Israel to trample on Palestinian human rights (Cohen 2020; Allen 2020; Sucharov 2017).

A second pitfall is the tendency to confuse Palestinian nationalism with Palestinian solidarity. It is not surprising that elements of the PSM may occasionally project elements of Palestinian nationalism. The right to self-determination is, after all, a human right owed to Palestinians. Nevertheless, it is easier to garner sympathy among Canadians for the day-to-day human rights of the Palestinians than to get Canadians to care about Palestine as an independent state. Another reason that Palestinian nationalism can be a pitfall is that Palestinians may one day have a "state," yet still be prevented from enjoying their human rights. In that eventuality, those who are mobilized by Palestinian nationalism may consider their job complete, while Palestinians themselves continue to struggle in an Israeli-concocted Bantustan and marginalized segments of Palestinian society for their broader rights.

While the use of nationalism as a motivator can sometimes have its own issues, Palestinian nationalism strongly galvanizes many Palestinians. Nevertheless, the general Canadian population is not mobilized by symbols and acts of Palestinian nationalism, such as flying Palestinian flags or presentations of Palestinian culture. They may respond much more enthusiastically to strategies that put an emphasis on human lives and universal ideas of life and liberty.

The complexity of Palestinian politics is also a challenge. The two major political parties in Palestine right now are Fatah and Hamas, which have variously worked in unity, ignored each other or been at war; they have unique histories and vastly different political philosophies. In addition, the role of the Palestinian Authority (PA), the provisional governing authority of the Palestinians established by the Oslo Accords, creates a certain "fog" around the position and aspirations of the Palestinian people.

Members of the PSM must remember that their target is the Israeli government for its human rights abuses. They must not allow their leanings in Palestinian politics to distract from their focus or prevent them from cooperating with other members of the PSM, and they are not required to defend the statements or positions of those parties or the PA, which may have objectives that do not align with those of the PSM. The foundation of the PSM is in the immutable principles of international law and not in the evolving and self-perpetuating positions of a Palestinian political party or the Palestinian Authority.

The Increased Weaponization of Antisemitism in Canada

Jewish communities around the world have suffered from antisemitism for centuries, and it is important for governments to guard against this form of prejudice. As I have mentioned, this is also a concern for the PSM. Nevertheless, in Canada and elsewhere, pro-Israel groups will often use accusations of antisemitism to discourage open dialogue about the human rights violations of Israel. Over the past several years, there have been numerous campaigns launched by pro-Israel groups seeking to obstruct and derail PSM initiatives suggesting they were antisemitic. Examples include the campaign against "Israeli Apartheid Week" initiatives on university campuses across Canada. More recently, pro-Israel groups have sought to tar the international BDS movement as antisemitic.

The most dangerous initiative along these lines of recent years, however, is the campaign in support of the IHRA definition (International Holocaust Remembrance Alliance n.d.) of antisemitism. The IHRA definition seems virtually tailor-made to come across innocuously while nevertheless putting a damper on freedom of expression around criticism of Israel. Independent Jewish Voices Canada — a leading member of the PSM — states: "This definition is vague, imprecise and does not draw on the ample, existing scholarship on antisemitism. As such, it will not help identify instances of antisemitism, nor is it useful in educating about or fighting against this form of racism" (2019) and has extensively documented its shortcomings (n.d.). What is even more concerning is that seven of the eleven illustrative examples accompanying the definition cite criticism of Israel or Zionism.

The psm has anticipated the arrival of the ihra in Canada for some time, and members of the psm have worked hard to avert widespread adoption in Canada. However, the resources available to the movement have thus far been overwhelmed by the much greater resources of pro-Israel groups and the connectedness proponents of the ihra have with the Canadian political elite, which is discussed broadly throughout this edited collection.

The ihra definition of antisemitism is clearly meant to discourage criticism of Israel and will most certainly have a chilling effect on psm activism in the years to come. The pro-Israel lobby's broad and vigorous attempts to get the definition (with the illustrative examples) adopted federally, provincially and in many cities will no doubt create greater obstacles to organizing by the psm. In response, the psm will need to keep its rhetoric carefully focused on Israel's human rights abuses and will need to be ready to defend itself — potentially in court — against spurious and defamatory accusations.

Issue Fatigue Given the Longevity of the Palestine/Israel Conflict

For many people unaware of the details, the Palestine/Israel conflict seems to drag on with no apparent end in sight. For a casual observer, a "never-ending" conflict suggests that both sides are digging their heels in unnecessarily and if both sides would just "compromise a little bit" the conflict would be solved.

Indeed, pro-Israel groups argue that the conflict continues because the Palestinians are unwilling to compromise and will not accept a negotiated settlement (Morris 2002, Cotler 2012). People who understand the specifics of Israel's tactics can grasp why the conflict remains unresolved (Thrall 2017), but it is hard for many people to understand why the international community still needs to support Palestinian refugees after seventy years or why the Palestine/Israel conflict requires so much space in the public conversation. This makes it easier to believe false Israeli narratives such as it has been going on "for millennia" and the Palestinians "never miss an opportunity to miss an opportunity."

Barring an extraordinary development, the Palestine/Israel conflict is not going away any time soon. The PSM must understand that time is not necessarily working in its favour and that "issue fatigue" may force its supporters and allies to turn their attention elsewhere. Indeed, the normalization by powerful Gulf Arab states with Israel, effectively sanctioning Israeli rule over the Occupied Palestinian Territory (OPT), is emblematic of this concern among sectors which once demonstrated significant sympathy for Palestinian national aspirations.

The Normalization of Israeli Abuses and "Facts on the Ground"

Time also works against the Palestinians in the way that Israel's abuses and advances "on the ground" become normalized over time. The best example of this is Israel's attempt to annex East Jerusalem. Virtually no countries recognized Israel's Jerusalem law in 1980, by which it laid claim to Jerusalem as its unified capital. Successive United States administrations talked about moving the United States embassy to Jerusalem, and President Trump followed through with the move in 2018. A few other countries have followed suit, and as they do so, Israel's annexation of Jerusalem becomes progressively normalized.

Other examples are abundant: the route of Israel's "separation wall," the isolation of Gaza, the isolation of East Jerusalem, the establishment of new Jewish-only settlements. The passage of time makes it more and more difficult to argue against, let alone reverse, many of Israel's abuses. The PSM must do all it can to make Israel's attempts to create "facts on the ground" as difficult and as objectionable as possible.

A Dangerous Temptation to Employ the Tools of the Opposition

For the reasons mentioned in the strengths and opportunities sections above, the PSM must try to keep its focus on human rights and international law. Nevertheless, its various pro-Israel adversaries employ all manner of strategies to discredit and derail the PSM, including accusations of supporting terrorist groups, promulgating antisemitic ideas, inciting hatred and other nefarious actions. Pro-Israel groups try to get PSM events cancelled, prevent politicians from meeting with members of the PSM and have PSM initiatives smeared or delegitimized in the media. Because such dirty attacks sometimes appear to bear fruit, the PSM can be tempted to use similar underhanded techniques in the battle for public opinion.

Yet such attempts can very easily backfire. A dramatic back-and-forth between pro-Israel and PSM groups that leads to disruption undermines the right to free expression overall in Canada: sometimes universities ban campus groups or events related to Palestine/Israel just to avoid the headache of such confrontations. The PSM, with its need to educate and inform, is far more dependent on freedom of expression than the pro-Israel groups, which seek to obstruct open debate on the topic. Similarly, intense emotional, angry or irrational-seeming expression of positions undermines efforts for the PSM's arguments to be understood as reasonable and humane. This is unfortunately enwrapped within mainstream racist and Islamophobic "Othering," where the colonized Palestinians are already portrayed as inherently irrational, emotional and uncivilized. Other important social issues also merit time in public forums, and their proponents deserve to be heard. It is tempting to monopolize conversations with the urgency of justice for Palestinians, but the PSM can lose important allies if it makes no room for other causes to have their moment in the limelight.

Finally, the PSM must work against the perception that the issue is dominated by two sides bickering. The general public often tunes out when it perceives two sides are each trying to shout the other down. Success for the PSM depends on open, informative public spaces and articulate spokespeople to take advantage of such forums. As such, the PSM and its representatives must ensure that open dialogue on its issues is maintained and must then keep a laser-sharp focus on Israeli government policy, international law and the damning "facts on the ground."

Concluding Thoughts

The lists above may not be comprehensive, but they lay out some of the major themes in each of the four SWOT categories for the PSM. While there may not be complete agreement around the items listed, leaders within the PSM are encouraged to debate the ideas and to formulate better strategies for more effective advocacy. Hopefully, the discussion above has uncovered new possibilities for the movement and will give leaders greater confidence that history will vindicate their cause and justify their labours.

References

Allen, Jon. 2020. "Canada Votes at the UN: A Response to the CIJA, B'nai Brith Canada and Friends of Simon Wiesenthal Center." *Canadian Jewish Record*, November 25. <https://web.archive.org/web/20201125184824/https://canadianjewishrecord.

ca/2020/11/25/canada-votes-at-the-un-a-response-to-the-cija-bnai-brith-canada-and-friends-of-simon-wiesenthal-center/>.

Azarova, Valentina. 2017. "Israel's Unlawfully Prolonged Occupation: Consequences under an Integrated Legal Framework." Policy brief, European Council on European Relations, June. <ecfr.eu/publication/israels_unlawfully_prolonged_occupation_7294/>.

Baldassare, Mark, Dean Bonner, Alyssa Dykman and Lunna Lopes. 2018. "Immigrants and Political Engagement." *Public Policy Institute of California*, March. <ppic.org/publication/immigrants-and-political-engagement>.

Bueckert, Michael, Thomas Woodley, Grafton Ross, et al. 2020. "Out of Touch: Canada's Foreign Policy Disconnected from Canadians' Views." Part 1 of a national opinion survey of Canadians conducted June 5–10, 2020. Survey conducted by EKOS Research Associates, co-sponsored by Canadians for Justice and Peace in the Middle East, Independent Jewish Voices Canada, and United Network for Justice and Peace in Palestine-Israel. <www.cjpme.org/survey2020_r1>.

Carbado, Devon W., Kimberlé Williams Crenshaw, Vickie M. Mays, and Barbara Tomlinson. 2013. "Intersectionality, Mapping the Movements of a Theory." *Du Bois Review: Social Science Research on Race* 10, 2.

Centre for Israel and Jewish Affairs. n.d. "Frequently Asked Questions." <cija.ca/about-us/frequently-asked-questions/>.

CJPME (Canadians for Justice and Peace in the Middle East). 2016. "Trudeau Government Unable to Follow Through on Anti-BDS Motion." March 31. <www.cjpme.org/pr_2016_03_30>.

___. 2017. "In Visionary Move, Bloc Asks Canada to Recognize Palestine." May 30. <www.cjpme.org/pr_2017_05_30>.

___. n.d. "Pledge Endorsements." <https://mppledge-cjpme.nationbuilder.com/pledge_endorsements>.

Cohen, Andrew. 2020. "Unelected, Unaccountable, Untroubled: CIJA Says What It Wants, Then Says It Speaks For Us." *Canadian Jewish Record*, December 16. <https://web.archive.org/web/20201216191852/https://canadianjewishrecord.ca/2020/12/16/unelected-unaccountable-untroubled-cija-says-what-it-wants-then-says-it-speaks-for-us/>.

Cotler, Irwin. 2012. "Today Could Have Been Palestine's 65th Birthday." *Haaretz*, November 29. <haaretz.com/opinion/.premium-today-could-have-been-palestine-s-65th-birthday-1.5299993>.

Friesner, Tim. 2008. "History of SWOT Analysis." *Marketing Teacher,* September 3. <marketingteacher.com/history-of-swot-analysis/>.

Independent Jewish Voices Canada. 2019. "IJV Urges the Canadian Government to Reconsider its Use of the IHRA Definition of Antisemitism." <ijvcanada.org/ijv-urges-the-canadian-government-to-reconsider-its-use-of-ihra-definition-of-antisemitism/>.

___. n.d. "Fight Antisemitism and White Supremacy, Not Palestine Solidarity." <noihra.ca/>.

International Holocaust Remembrance Alliance. n.d. "The Working Definition of Antisemitism." <https://www.holocaustremembrance.com/resources/working-definitions-charters/working-definition-antisemitism>.

Kenton, Will. 2021. "Strength, Weakness, Opportunity, and Threat (SWOT) Analysis." *Investopedia*. <investopedia.com/terms/s/swot.asp>.

Morris, Benny. 2002. "Arafat Didn't Negotiate — He Just Kept Saying No." *Guardian,*

May 23. <theguardian.com/world/2002/may/23/israel3>.

Munayyer, Yousef. 2019. "Opinion: The Fight Over Ilhan Omar Is About Something Much Bigger." *Buzzfeed,* March 11. <buzzfeednews.com/article/yousefmunayyer/fight-over-ilhan-omar-about-something-bigger/>.

Pfeffer, Anshel. 2015. "Netanyahu Speaks for All Jews Whether They Like It or Not." *Haaretz,* February 12. <haaretz.com/.premium-netanyahu-speaks-for-all-jews-1.5306070>.

Pletcher, Kenneth. n.d. "Jallianwala Bagh Massacre: Causes, History, & Significance." *Encyclopedia Britannica.* <britannica.com/event/Jallianwala-Bagh-Massacre>.

Ralph, Diana, Murray Dobbin, Dimitri Lascaris, and Thomas Woodley. 2017. *Disconnect: Canadians' Views of the Israeli Government vs. Canadian Government Policy toward Israel and Palestine.* A report on a Canadian national opinion survey conducted January 25 to February 2, 2017, by EKOS Research Associates. Issued by Independent Jewish Voices Canada, Canadians for Justice and Peace in the Middle East, Murray Dobbin, and Dimitri Lascaris. February 16. <d3n8a8pro7vhmx. cloudfront.net/cjpme/pages/2537/attachments/original/1488331789/EKOS_Poll_Results_Report_-_2017-02-16-Final-v3.pdf?1488331789>.

Statistics Canada. 2016. "Canadian Demographics at a Glance, second edition." <https://www150.statcan.gc.ca/n1/pub/91-003-x/91-003-x2014001-eng.pdf>.

___. 2017. "Visible Minority (Arab), Both Sexes, Age (Total), Canada, Provinces and Territories, 2016 Census — 25% Sample Data." <www12.statcan.gc.ca/census-recensement/2016/dp-pd/hlt-fst/imm/Table.cfm?Lang=E&T=41&Geo=00&SP=1&vismin=8&age=1&sex=1>.

___. 2019. "2011 National Household Survey: Data Tables." <www12.statcan.gc.ca/nhs-enm/2011/dp-pd/dt-td/Rp-eng.cfm?TABID=2&LANG=E&APATH=3&DETAIL=0&DIM=0&FL=A&FREE=0&GC=0&GID=1118296&GK=0&GRP=0&PID=105396&PRID=0&PTYPE=105277&S=0&SHOWALL=0&SUB=0&Temporal=2013&THEME=95&VID=0&VNAMEE=&VNAMEF=&D1=0&D2=0&D3=0&D4=0&D5=0&D6=0>.

Sucharov, Mira. 2017. "Why I'm Resigning My CJN Column." *Canadian Jewish News,* June 2. <cjnews.com/perspectives/opinions/mira-sucharov-cjn-column>.

Thrall, Nathan. 2017. "Israel-Palestine: The Real Reason There's Still No Peace." *Guardian,* May 16. <theguardian.com/world/2017/may/16/the-real-reason-the-israel-palestine-peace-process-always-fails>.

UN News. 2012. "General Assembly Grants Palestine Non-Member Observer State Status at UN." November 29. <news.un.org/en/story/2012/11/427052-general-assembly-grants-palestine-non-member-observer-state-status-un>.

United Nations. 2020. "Two Years On: People Injured and Traumatized During the 'Great March of Return' Are Still Struggling." *Question of Palestine* [blog], April 6. <un.org/unispal/document/two-years-on-people-injured-and-traumatized-during-the-great-march-of-return-are-still-struggling/>.

Visualizing Palestine. n.d. "Growth of a Movement." <visualizingpalestine.org/collective-action-timeline>.

World Population Review. n.d. "Countries That Recognize Palestine 2021." Last updated July 2019. <worldpopulationreview.com/country-rankings/countries-that-recognize-palestine>.

Chapter 9

Campus Palestine Activism in Ottawa from the 1970s to the 2010s

Hassan Husseini

The idea of writing this chapter was born out of observing with awe the high level of Palestine solidarity activism at Carleton University during the period of 2008–12 while writing my PhD. I was impressed with the level of engagement, mobilization, articulation of political demands, creativity and diversity of the activists. While I saw a lot of similarities with the campus Palestine solidarity movement I was active in during the 1990s during my first degree, it also seemed to have some marked differences that I believed were worth investigating. More than anything else, I was looking to understand the factors that played a role in the evolution of the Palestine solidarity movement on Canadian campuses.

In this chapter, I focus on campus Palestine solidarity activism at the University of Ottawa and Carleton University during three distinct time periods: 1975–90; 1990–2005; 2005–10s. I examine the campus movements in a chronological order through the three distinct time periods. In each section, I discuss the main characteristics of the movement, its composition, political orientation, key political campaigns and how effective it was in achieving its goals. All this, of course, is set in the context of international as well as regional events that had an impact on the overall trajectory of student activism in Canada and in this case on the two campuses in Ottawa. It should be treated as a modest contribution to this important national topic, with the hope that it will spark interest for further research.

My research involved primary as well as secondary sources. The key primary source was information generated from questionnaires, interviews and discussions I had with former Palestine solidarity student activists at the University of Ottawa and Carleton University dating back to 1975–76. In total, I interviewed or received answers to a questionnaire from twelve former student activists. This information was supplemented with leaflets, publications, websites, blogs, videos and statements of student organizations from both universities. Secondary information was primarily in the form of articles published online about campaigns undertaken during certain periods of time, as well as books that helped me to frame the findings in the context of the changing geopolitical picture in the region.

While conducting research for this chapter, the main challenge encountered was the gap in information for certain years during the past four decades. I had easy access to former activists as well as publications for certain periods and very little, other than names of groups and organizations, for other years. As such, this chapter should be treated as a broad overview rather than a detailed account of the history of campus Palestine solidarity activism on the two campuses in Ottawa.

It is important to recognize that what makes student activism distinct from other forms of political activism, such as labour activism for example, is that student activism is transitory, cyclical and constantly changing and renewing itself. This is primarily because students graduate, leave campus, join the labour force and may transfer their activism to another sector. Furthermore, student politics is unique because the student movement is a multiclass movement which carries within it multiple sets of contradictions and potentially conflicting interests. Nonetheless, campuses are not islands, isolated and disconnected from broader society, but are influenced by the social and political struggles taking place in their communities and society at large.

While investigating and assessing the evolution of campus Palestine activism from 1975 to 2015, I focused on three main determinants: a) composition and type of organizations; b) political orientation and goals; and c) impact these organizations/campaigns had on campus, the community and Canadian society. All this is set against the context of the geopolitical situation in the Middle East and internationally.

1975–1990: Arab Students' Activism

The Palestinian struggle for liberation from colonialism and occupation dates back to the turn of the twentieth century. During this period, the Zionist settler-colonial project established itself in historic Palestine with the support of British colonialism, officially beginning with the 1917 Balfour Declaration, which has since "formed the juridical basis of Zionist claims to Palestine" (Said 1979: 15). This ultimately resulted in the creation of the State of Israel in 1948 but not before 80 percent, or "at least 780,000 Palestinians," were ethnically cleansed from their homes and lands in "77.8% of Palestine's territory" (Sa'di 2007: 289; Farsoun and Aruri 2006: 105) through a systematic process that "resulted in the destruction of 420 Palestinian towns and villages" (Sa'di 2007: 297) in what became known as the Nakba (or "catastrophe" in Arabic). The remaining Palestinians inside Israel lived under martial law until 1966 and currently exist as marginalized, second-class citizens in their own ancestral home.

The year 1967 marked a turning point for the Palestinian people and their national liberation struggle when Israel occupied the remaining 22 percent of historic Palestine (the West Bank, including East Jerusalem, and the Gaza Strip). Since the 1948 Nakba, the West Bank and the Gaza Strip had been under control of the Jordanian and Egyptian military authorities, respectively. The Arab defeat in the June 1967 war (or Six Day War as it became known) led to a radicalization of the Palestinian national liberation movement and led to the movement's independence from the control of Arab regimes under the leadership of the Palestine Liberation Organization (PLO) (Farsoun and Aruri 2006). This independence and radicalization manifested itself as conflict between the PLO and the Jordanian monarchy of King Hussein, which led to the PLO's expulsion from Jordan to Lebanon following the September 1970 Jordanian assault on it. In the subsequent period, the PLO not only continued its armed struggle against Israeli occupation from Lebanon until the 1982 Israeli invasion, but also became a party in the Lebanese Civil War, which lasted from 1975 until 1990.

The conflict in the Middle East, like in other regions of the world during this period, played itself out in the shadow of the Cold War between the Soviet Union/Socialist Bloc and the United States as the leader of the capitalist world. While the Socialist Bloc and the Soviet Union supported national liberation and anti-colonial movements, including the PLO as the legitimate representative of the Palestinian people, the United States and its Western allies provided diplomatic, military and financial support for Israel, as they did for other authoritarian and dictatorial regimes in the Middle East, Africa, Asia and Latin America. During this period of war, conflict and national liberation struggles, a wave of immigrants came to Canada from the various Arab countries, including many Lebanese and Palestinians who were fleeing the war in Lebanon. Many of these new immigrants continued or began their university studies in Canada, during which time they became politically active in the growing Palestine solidarity movement on Canadian campuses (Husseini 2020).

It appears that between the two campuses, Carleton University and the University of Ottawa, Palestine solidarity activism during the period from 1975 to 1990 was centred at the University of Ottawa. In conversations with former student activists, it was explained that although Palestine solidarity activism was present at Carleton University at the time, the stronger organizational and political presence was to be found at the University of Ottawa, which for a period of time became the hub for student Palestine solidarity activism, along with Palestine solidarity activism community-wide in Ottawa.

The primary Palestine solidarity organization at the University of Ottawa was the Arab Students' Association (ASA). It was made up of young male students who were first-generation immigrants to Canada from Middle Eastern countries including Palestine, Syria, Lebanon, Iraq and Jordan. According to information from activists from that time, the political orientation of the ASA was left nationalist (socialist, communist, Arab nationalist — Nasserist and Baathist — and Syrian nationalist). The political consciousness of these activists was very much guided by the (sometimes intense) political education they received prior to emigrating to Canada. In many respects, their political allegiances were formed in their native lands and informed their engagement in Palestine solidarity activism at the University of Ottawa.

The General Union of Palestinian Students (GUPS) was established at the University of Ottawa at some point in the late 1970s, but the primary vehicle for campus Palestine solidarity work remained anchored in the ASA. The ASA was a member of the North America–wide Organization of Arab Students (OAS) which encompassed Arab student associations across Canada and the United States. As with individual Arab student organizations, the OAS was headed by activists affiliated, to one degree or another, to political parties such as the Iraqi Baath Party, Fateh (the party of current Palestinian Authority President Mahmoud Abbas) and the Popular Front for the Liberation of Palestine (PFLP). The internal politics of the OAS was influenced by the external rivalries of these political organizations.

According to activists Ahmed Husseini, Mohamad Awada and Kassem Cheatani, Arab student activism on the University of Ottawa campus was an extension of broader Arab community activism.[1] According to Cheatani, "We [students] also played the role of leading and guiding our community and there is no doubt that the conditions were very favourable to such type of activism at the time" (Cheatani 2020). Husseini agrees and stresses that at the University of Ottawa, "one of the goals of the ASA was to unite all Arab students under one roof as a first step to uniting Arab community members across the city, as students were more politically advanced members of the community and were active on campus as well as the broader community" (Husseini 2020). According to these activists, the main goal of Arab student activists during this period was to "raise awareness of the broader student and community of the oppression in Palestine by the Israelis" (Awada 2020).

To achieve their goals, Arab student activists organized campaigns and events that were always open to the broader community. Some of the campaigns that Arab students engaged in during this period included guest speakers, primarily on the struggle of Palestinian people; cultural events such as the Arab day/week, which included music and art shows in addition to exhibitions of various Arab countries; commemorations of significant dates such as Palestine Land Day and the International Day of Solidarity with the Palestinian People; and organizing conferences in cooperation with other groups. All these events were open to Arab community members as well as Canadian allies, who were the primary targets for awareness raising.

Ahmed Husseini argued that student activism in Canada was influenced by student and community activism in the United States, including the work of the ADC (Arab Anti-Discrimination Committee), which was starting to be active in the United States at that time. However, the ASA started to forge relationships with Canadian academics, including Professors Baha Abu-Laban, James Graff, Atif Kubursi, Tarek Ismail and John Sigler, who were starting to engage in more research and activism that was critical of the Israeli occupation.

At that time, there were very few non-Arab anti-Zionist activists that were close to the ASA. There were no relationships with any unions or other mass democratic Canadian organizations or political parties. However, the ASA had friendly relationships with other student groups on campus and in some cases organized joint events. This is particularly true with Latin American student groups, which was not surprising considering that many Latin American students had immigrated to Canada to escape the brutality of pro-US authoritarian regimes such as Pinochet military rule in Chile.

The ASA remained active at the University of Ottawa throughout the 1980s and played an important role in mobilizing students and community members in opposition to the 1982 Israeli invasion of Lebanon and the subsequent occupation of the country. It seems, too, that Arab student activists at University of Ottawa in the 1970s–80s consider that their activism was successful. They were able to unite Arab students around Palestine solidarity and to carry out successful awareness raising campaigns, events and conferences and to play a leading role in doing the same in the Ottawa Arab community broadly.

1990–2005: Anti-Occupation/ Anti-War Student Activism

Monumental changes occurred in the late 1980s and early 1990s with the unravelling of the Soviet Union and the Socialist Bloc. This had a major impact not only on Communist parties and movements around the world, but also on national liberation movements, like the Palestine solidary movement, which lost the support of a major superpower in what became a unipolar world dominated by the United States.

In its dying days, the Soviet Union joined the United States to usher in the peace process between Israel and the Palestinians (with the presence of Jordan, Lebanon and Syria in the initial multilateral talks) by co-sponsoring the Madrid Peace Conference in the fall of 1991. While the Madrid Peace Conference itself did not result in a peace agreement, the subsequent bilateral negotiations between Israel and the Palestinians led to the Oslo Accords (Oslo I in 1993 and Oslo II in 1995), the first of which was signed on the lawn of the White House on September 13, 1993. Instead of resulting in an independent, viable and sovereign Palestinian state sitting alongside Israel (a two-state solution), as had been anticipated, the peace process delayed and put that outcome to the side indefinitely through a process of unending negotiations and the de-prioritization of critical political issues (like the status of Jerusalem). It further fragmented Palestinian society into regions of occupation, with some under Palestinian autonomy or shared control with Israel, and most Palestinian land left under sole Israeli authority. This contributed directly to the "bantustanization" of the promised state. Administering the limited areas of Palestinian autonomy, which were mostly urban enclaves of the West Bank and Gaza — but not Palestinian East Jerusalem — was a newly created Palestinian Authority (PA) led by PLO Chairman Yasser Arafat as president (Farsoun and Aruri 2006; Tilley 2005). This resulted in the sidelining of the PLO as the legitimate voice of the Palestinian people and a weakening of the Palestinian national liberation movement.

It is critically important to remember that the peace process between Israel and the Palestinians took place less than a year after the Gulf War against Iraq for its August 2, 1990, invasion of Kuwait. On January 17, 1991, a coalition of forces led by the United States drove the Iraqi army out of Kuwait and subsequently established permanent military bases in the region. The first Gulf War opened the door to the imposition of brutal and harsh sanctions against Iraq until the second Gulf War in 2003, which ended in the invasion, occupation and dismemberment of Iraq as a state.

The blow to the political unity of the PLO and its institutions had a far-reaching impact on the international solidarity movement and on campuses right across the world including in Canada. The disunity and the lack of political direction that resulted from the Oslo peace process led to attempts to replace Palestine solidarity activism (in the community and on campuses) with dialogue between Palestinians and their supporters, and the supporters of Israel. While most student activists shunned these initiatives, many however bought into the "peace" euphoria unleashed by Oslo. Activists recall walking out of meetings organized by Palestinian and Israeli supporters of the peace process who had a goal of working together. These activists saw this as an attempt to whitewash and sanitize the Israeli occupation and its crimes, and they wanted nothing to do with it (Abou-Dib 2020; Khouri 2020).

Given the above context, Palestine advocacy activism on the two Ottawa campuses slowed down in the mid- to late-1990s as activists focused more of their energy on the Gulf War and sanctions on Iraq. This, however, changed with the failure of the peace process and the beginning of the Second Intifada in September 2000, which reinvigorated on-campus Palestine solidarity activism, save for one exception.

The political chill that characterized the period following the 9/11 attacks was palpable among activist circles generally and had an impact on Palestine solidarity activism on Canadian campuses. For a short period following the 9/11 terrorist attacks, the Western war on Afghanistan and a crackdown on civil liberties here at home, campus activism stalled. This all started to change, however, as Israel intensified its attacks on Palestinians in the West Bank with increasingly brutal measures that included home demolitions, extra judicial killings, land grabs, ethnic cleansing in main population centres in the occupied West Bank and the acceleration of apartheid-like measures, which include the building of the separation wall that snaked hundreds of kilometres throughout Palestinian territory in violation of UN resolutions and international law.

At the University of Ottawa, the main vehicle for campus Palestine solidarity activism during this period continued to be the ASA. As with the previous period, the majority of activists in the ASA were new immigrants to Canada, including myself. I had immigrated to Canada in 1985. After finishing high school in Ottawa, I started my studies in January 1989 and immediately became an active member of ASA. As with the previous period, new immigrants came from countries such as Lebanon, Syria, Palestine, Jordan and Egypt, along with an increasing number of Maghrebi students from Morocco, Libya and Tunisia. During this period, an increasing number of second-generation immigrants and women became more active and held leadership positions within the ASA.

Although more women had become active in the ASA, "a gender dynamic was still in place where the liberation of women, Palestinian and other Arab women, was seen by the majority of fellow male Arab activists as second to national liberation, as opposed to intrinsically tied to it" (Abou-Dib 2020). This dynamic, according to activist Mariam Abou-Dib, led some women activists on campus to establish the Middle Eastern Women's Association (MEWA) as a vehicle to provide a safe space for women activists to engage in anti-occupation and Palestine solidarity activism, while also raising gender equality issues on campus. This very issue was identified by Abdo and Yuval-Davies as "a basic tension … between tendencies, on the one hand, to totally subsume women's struggles into the 'general national interests' and, on the other, to express the subjective and collective frustrations of women about their positioning both in the family and in the national struggle" (1995: 312). This was particularly evident during the first Intifada, which witnessed a growth in women's participation in the uprising and led to a "massive politicization process" (Abdo and Yuval-Davis 1995: 315) among Palestinian women and in turn may have shaped the position of women Palestine solidarity activists in the Canadian context.

Campus Palestine solidarity activism at Carleton University continued to lag behind activism at the University of Ottawa but began to pick up quickly in the early 1990s as mobilization against the Gulf War increased sharply. The Pro-Palestine Club was established in the late 1980s by a group of activists, including many Caucasian activists and second-generation Arab immigrants. The Pro-Palestine Club became the main student group at Carleton University working on Palestine solidarity for the next few years, although its composition changed to mostly new Arab immigrants. Cooperation and collaboration between the ASA and the Pro-Palestine Club increased during this period, and it was common to see activists organize joint events on both campuses.

Politically speaking, the orientation of most activists, especially those in the leadership of the student groups on both campuses was left, left of centre and left nationalist (socialists and communists, pan-Arab and Syrian). As such, this period witnessed greater cooperation with left-wing student organizations as well as left activists in the main student federations at both campuses.

The ASA and Pro Palestine Club were fairly effective at building broader alliances on their respective campuses with diverse student activist groups, such as the Caribbean student club, Latin American club, Ontario Public Interest Research Group (OPIRG) and Quebec Sovereignty club. Activists at the University of Ottawa clearly recall that during an intense period of political organizing on campus in 1991–92, complaints were made to the administration by Zionist students who were offended by the slogan "Zionism is Racism" that appeared on ASA banners. In response to these complaints, the university administration tried to restrict ASA's capacity to book space and hold events on campus. However, student activists were able to fight back and prevail with the support of a broader alliance of student and community groups that included the Student Federation, Quebec Sovereignty Club, leftist/Marxist student formations and Muslim student groups. This was an important campaign as it demonstrated the effectiveness of bringing a diverse group of students to work together on a common cause. One year later, at Carleton University there was a similar outcome when the Pro-Palestine Club fought back with a coalition of student and community groups.

Campus Palestine solidarity activists, like their predecessors in the 1970s and 1980s, organized a myriad of events that were geared toward raising awareness of the Palestinian struggle for liberation by exposing Israeli war crimes in occupied Palestine. This was done through a speakers' series of academics and activists on the Palestine question, as well as conferences, film showings, outreach to students through information tables and leafleting. One of the main events organized by students during this period was the "Arab day" (in some years "Arab week") as a social, cultural and political event to demonstrate the unity of Arab peoples and countries. Arab day/week included central events dedicated to Palestine solidarity. Also, students on both campuses often protested Zionist/pro-Israel speakers on campus on the basis that public spaces should not be provided to war criminals, apologists for a racist state and those who were attempting to whitewash Israel's crimes.

A qualitative organizational step forward was taken in 1990 when a number of Arab student organizations, including the ASA at the University of Ottawa, launched ANSAR (Arab Network of Students) at its first annual conference on June 22–24 in London, Ontario. The Pro-Palestine Club at Carleton University joined the organization at the second annual conference in Toronto the following year.

The need for such an organization arose out of the realization that "in order to achieve and sustain a credible degree of effective lobbying on campuses, Arab student groups and campus Palestinian solidarity organizations must synchronize their efforts and form a comprehensive and viable national network of action" (*Al-Mizan* 1990: 23). Although the mandate of ANSAR spoke about campus Palestine solidarity organizations, its work remained anchored with Arab students; as it stated in its mandate, "Such a network should stimulate and inspire activity, awareness, efficacy and efficiency with respect to the promotion — by Arab students — of the situation in the Middle East as seen from an Arab-Canadian perspective" (*Al-Mizan* 1990: 23).

ANSAR's politics as outlined in its Code of Principles and Conduct were, "consistent with progressive norms of morality … [and] operate in accordance to the principles of non-racist, non-sexist and secular politics." This meant that the organization, and its members, maintain an "anti-Zionist and an anti-Apartheid foundation ... where peace in the Middle East will only prevail when justice is served to the dispossessed people of Palestine" (*Al-Mizan* 1990: 23). Unfortunately, ANSAR did not survive past the end of 1993, due to political and personal differences between some of its key activists. Member student organizations continued to function after ANSAR ceased to be.

ANSAR published a semi-annual periodical called *Al-Mizan* with a circulation of five thousand throughout Canada and the United States. It featured articles, opinion pieces and analyses written by professors and graduate students about the politics and culture of the Arab world, as well as reporting on actions and events organized by its member groups (*Al-Mizan* 1992: 30).

Aside from the common political agenda collectively set by the ANSAR leadership, member organizations benefited from pooling resources for major events, including speakers' tours. ANSAR members also organized local, regional and national conferences, film nights and discussions, social events and Arab day/week events, as well as social, cultural and political events to demonstrate the unity of Arab peoples and countries. In this context, Arab student activists played a leading role in mobilizing the broader Arab communities against the United States war in Iraq, and against the occupation of Palestine and of Lebanon.[2]

According to activist Wael Afifi, "the linkage or 'intersectionality' between solidarity with Palestine and support for the Iraqi people's struggle against the imperialist vicious attack was fairly evident in the Arab community at large which provided an excellent opportunity for a dialectical rich exchange between the student movement and the community at large" (Afifi 2020). As such, strong participation by the community in campus events — and vice versa — was an important characteristic of this period of Canadian student activism at both campuses in Ottawa. In fact, student activists at the time saw themselves and their organizations, such as ANSAR, as having "the promise to become an important and permanent pillar of the Arab community" (*Al-Mizan* 1990: 23).

Notwithstanding the above, relations between campus Palestine solidarity groups and the community went through an ebb and flow during this period. This relationship was collaborative, competitive and at times even confrontational, especially when some of the more conservative members of the community felt students were being too radical. In most cases, however, community organizations worked well with student groups on common campaigns and events. When the University of Ottawa administration attacked the ASA for the 1992 "Zionism Is Racism" campaign, the community openly rallied in support of the ASA. However, some "prominent" members of the community, who were also employed by the university, chided the ASA for supposedly jeopardizing community relations with the university.

In the mid- to late-1990s and into the 2000s, there was a proliferation of new organizations at Carleton University. These organizations reflected the focus of key issues facing peoples of the Arab world, including war, sanctions and occupation. This was especially true after the 2003 invasion and occupation of Iraq. Some of these organizations included the Arab Student Union (1995–97); the Canadian-Arab Students Association (2000–02); Solidarity for Iraqi and Palestinian Children (2000–02) and Solidarity for Palestinian Human Rights (SPHR) (2001–02).

The composition of the members of student groups during this period did not change dramatically from the early 1990s. Key activists and members were drawn from the ranks of new immigrant Arab students. This included an increasing number of second-generation Canadians and women relative to the early 1990s, and most definitely compared to the period from 1975 to 1990.

The focus of SPHR on Palestine solidarity reflected the new stage in the Palestinian people's struggle with the start of the Second Intifada in the fall of 2000. The increasing Palestine solidarity actions on campuses during this period were met with objections and complaints by Jewish and Pro-Israel student groups and, as in previous periods, SPHR and other Palestine solidarity groups had to deal with unsuccessful attempts by university administrators to curtail their actions and even shut them down (Masrieh 2020).

There is no doubt that campus Palestine advocacy from 1990 to 2005 went through many ebbs and flows. Although this is intrinsic to student political activism, it was even more pronounced during this period due to the events that these student activists were having to respond to, especially as events in the region were constantly changing.

We can already see during the period that the composition of campus Palestine solidarity groups began to change slowly from being predominantly male and new immigrants to one that was slightly more inclusive of women, second-generation Canadians and non-Arab (mostly "white") allies. This is especially true when we compare 1990–2005 to the previous period, 1975–90.

Notwithstanding the ebbs and flows of campus Palestine solidarity activism at the University of Ottawa and Carleton University, the period from 1990 to 2005 appears to have been impactful. The student Palestine advocacy movement carved out a space for Palestine solidarity activism on campus: keeping Arab students united around key campaigns; engaging with the university community broadly; countering the propaganda of Israeli apologists on campus; working with the community outside campus on common campaigns; and raising critical awareness of the broader student population on the Palestinian peoples struggle for liberation. By 2005, the changing situation in occupied Palestine gave rise to new forms of organizing Palestine solidarity work on campuses.

2005–2010s: BDS Student Activism.

In 2005, Palestinians were more fragmented than ever between the West Bank, East Jerusalem, the Gaza Strip, inside Israel (1948 lands) and *ash-shatat*[3] across the globe. Israel had recognized the high cost of its direct occupation and illegal settlements in Gaza and decided to withdraw from the Strip in August 2005. While Israel ended its direct occupation of Gaza, it maintained a complete air, sea and land siege on the 1.9 million Palestinians living there in what came to be known as "remote control occupation" of the "biggest open-air prison" in the world (Stead 2019). Palestinians in Gaza continued to be subjected structurally to various forms of human rights violations on the entire population, such as food deprivation and massacres from attacks by internationally prohibited weapons, as happened with great intensity during the 2008–09, 2012 and 2014 aggressions.

These aggressions against Gaza exposed Israel to Canadians generally, and activists on campuses and in the labour movement specifically, who increasingly saw Israel as an aggressor state maintaining a repressive, racist and brutal occupation in violation of international law. More importantly, they also began to see Canadian political elites and the corporate media as complicit in the crimes committed against the Palestinian people. The change in Canadians' attitudes on Israel-Palestine can best be seen in the results of a 2020 EKOS Poll where "a significant majority (74%) of Canadians want the government to express opposition to Israeli annexation in some form [and] … 42% want Canada to impose economic and/or diplomatic sanctions against Israel" (Bueckert et al. 2020).

The Oslo peace process was long dead and the two-state solution a rhetorical tool keeping the peace industry alive at a time when Israel continued to impose facts on the ground through land grabs, settlement expansion and ethnic cleansing. Israel accelerated the building of its illegal settlements in the West Bank by "doubling their population in the 1990s" and creating a settlement grid that became an "immovable object" both physically and politically (Tilley 2005: 19–20). This rendered the "territorial basis for a viable Palestinian state" non-existent (Tilley 2005: 1). Another prime example of these facts on the ground was the separation wall (Apartheid Wall) built in the West Bank, primarily on Palestinian lands as a de facto annexation, in contravention of international law. In July 2004, the International Court of Justice (ICJ) issued a non-binding advisory opinion deeming the construction of the 750-kilometre wall to be illegal.

It became apparent during the years of the peace process that Israel was becoming more entrenched as an apartheid state. According to Omar Barghouti, "Israel's legalized, institutionalized system of racial discrimination fits the UN definition of the crime of apartheid in the 1973 International Convention of the Suppression and Punishment of the Crime of Apartheid and the 2002 Rome Statute of the International Criminal Court." For Barghouti, "Israel operates a more sophisticated, evolved, and brutal form of apartheid than its South African predecessor" (2012: 31–32). Even former US president Jimmy Carter, in his 2006 book *Palestine: Peace Not Apartheid* acknowledged the eminent failure of the peace process. He argued this was due, in part, to Israel having "embarked on a series of unilateral decisions.... Utilizing their political and military dominance, they are imposing a system of partial withdrawals, encapsulation, and apartheid on the Muslim and Christian citizens of the occupied territories" (2006: 189).

This was the situation on the ground in occupied Palestine on the eve of the 2005 Palestinian call for Boycott, Divestment and Sanctions (BDS). The call was initiated by "170 Palestinian unions, refugee networks, women's organizations, professional associations, popular resistance committees and other Palestinian civil society bodies" (BDS Movement n.d.). Professors Abu-Laban and Bakan explain that "civil society here refers to non-state organizations, including trade unions, faith-based communities, student organizations, social movement organizations, academic professional organizations and political parties" (2020: 158). The Palestinian BDS call urged nonviolent pressure on Israel until it complies with international law by meeting three demands:

1. Ending its occupation and colonization of all Arab lands and dismantling the Wall;

2. Recognizing the fundamental rights of the Arab-Palestinian citizens of Israel to full equality; and
3. Respecting, protecting and promoting the rights of Palestinian refugees to return to their homes and properties as stipulated in UN Resolution 194 (Palestinian Civil Society 2005).

The launch of the Palestinian Campaign for the Academic and Cultural Boycott of Israel (PACBI) in 2004 and the Boycott, Divestment and Sanctions (BDS) campaign in 2005 proved to be critical steps in the Palestinians' struggle for freedom, justice and equality. The official BDS movement website states that the movement was inspired by the South African anti-apartheid movement (Palestinian Civil Society 2005). The importance of the BDS movement rests in its capacity to galvanize support for Palestine across the globe.

In Palestine itself, the BDS movement occupies a space that has long been abandoned by the now dysfunctional PLO and discredited PA. Abu-Laban and Bakan quote BDS founders Omar Barghouti and Rafeef Ziadah that the "achievement of a unified response among Palestinian organizations challenged divisions that had developed particularly since Oslo" (2020: 158). "After decades of disappointment and fragmentation in the aftermath of the failed Oslo Accords, the BDS movement has united Palestinians across borders, political factions, and generations" (2020: 171).

BDS has become a powerful tool, centred on a clear call that was rights-based and solidly anchored in international law. The movement is particularly appealing to a new generation of activists, especially on campuses, including at the University of Ottawa and Carleton University. For Abu-Laban and Bakan, the "increasing influence of the movement among students and labour and human rights activists since the pivotal moment of the 2008–09 war on Gaza is indicative of its combined strategic and educational capacity" (2020: 171).

Palestine solidarity activists during this period state unequivocally that "student organizing in Canadian universities, including Carleton University, was mainly focused on the Boycott, Divestment and Sanctions Movement (BDS) with the goal of strengthening international solidarity with Palestine through advancing and emphasizing the call for BDS that came out in 2005" (Jarrar 2020; Kmail 2020 and Levitan 2020 made similar comments). Palestine student activism on campuses in Ottawa remained uneven, as it was in the case of the previous two periods. The significant change in campus Palestine solidarity activism occurred at Carleton University when a diverse group of students formed Students Against Israeli Apartheid (SAIA) in 2007.

SAIA came together in response to the July 2005 Palestinian civil society call for BDS. According to SAIA's website:

> Students Against Israeli Apartheid (SAIA) Carleton works in support of the global call from Palestinian civil society for Boycotts, Divestments, and Sanctions. On Carleton campus, our work aims to raise awareness about Palestinian human rights and promote a socially ethical investment policy for the university. We are a non-hierarchical, anti-oppressive group that functions on consensus. Specifically, our programming consists of academic and cultural events focused on our mandate, in particular, our annual "Israeli Apartheid Week." (SAIA 2014)

SPHR continued to exist on the University of Ottawa and Carleton University campuses. SPHR Carleton was more focused on cultural events whereas SAIA was more overtly political, with a clear position in support of BDS. University of Ottawa SPHR, on the other hand, appeared to be less active than SAIA but more political than its sister organization at Carleton. SPHR Carleton was mostly made up of Arab students while at University of Ottawa it was more diverse. The fact that SPHR Carleton was more oriented to cultural and social events attracted more Arab students, perhaps longing for a cultural connection. Being more political, University of Ottawa SPHR and SAIA worked together on joint events and campaigns.

SAIA Carleton was led by a diverse group of activists in addition to Palestinian Arabs. What is particularly important in its composition, however, is the fact that, from its inception, women were in leadership roles. SAIA attracted activists from diverse political backgrounds within the left as well as within the broader student community. According to activist Yafa Jarrar, "We had members from the [2SLGBTIQ] community, immigrant students, Indigenous students, Black students, Anti-Zionist Jewish students, and Caucasian students" (2020).

One of the key events that was organized on both campuses in Ottawa was Israeli Apartheid Week (IAW). This continues to be an international series of events that seeks to raise awareness about Israel's apartheid regime over the Palestinian people and build support for the growing BDS movement. IAW began in Toronto in 2004 and has since "spread to over 200 cities in more than 20 countries" (Abu-Laban and Bakan 2020: 167).

IAW events were so successful and threatening to the mainstream narrative on Israeli apartheid that Israel apologists denounced it and actively tried to malign it. This included Conservative and Liberal Party politicians in the provincial legislature at Queen's Park, as well as the House of Commons in Ottawa. While the New Democratic Party (NDP) never supported official legislative motions condemning BDS, the NDP under federal leader Tom Mulcair opposed BDS and the party blocked BDS supporters and activists from running for election on an NDP ticket (House of Commons of Canada 2016; Arnold 2013; Baglow 2015). Rafeef Ziadah wrote in 2010:

> Israeli Apartheid Week in Canada was denounced by official government bodies.... Conservative Member of the Ontario Legislature Peter Shurman put forward a motion condemning the week in the provincial parliament, the motion was passed. MPP Shurman stated that the term apartheid is "poisonous" and "odious." Former Liberal Party leader Michael Ignatieff spoke out against the IAW saying "Israeli Apartheid Week is part of a global campaign of calls for divestment, boycotts and proclamations, and it should be condemned unequivocally and absolutely."

In March 2015, would-be prime minister Justin Trudeau also attacked campus Palestine solidarity activists at McGill University, where a vote on divestment was taking place. Trudeau wrote on Twitter that "the BDS movement, like Israeli Apartheid Week, has no place on Canadian campuses." Ziadah (2010) called the reaction of Canadian politicians in the House of Commons and at Queen's Park "unwarranted hysteria over a week of educational events organized on a university campus by students." There is no doubt that "the severity of the attack is an admission that IAW is effective in reaching a wide audience and in exposing apartheid Israel" (Ziadah 2010).

SAIA's main campaign during this period was launched to pressure the university to adopt a divestment policy in keeping with the principles and goals of the BDS movement. The campaign itself involved a great deal of research on corporations and their involvement in Israeli occupation. As per the BDS movement, SAIA was inspired by the South African anti-apartheid struggle and the success it had at Carleton when, in 1988, the Carleton Anti-Apartheid Action Group forced the university to divest from South African apartheid. SAIA garnered a great deal of support for its divestment campaign from student groups, including the Graduate Students' Association, which adopted a resolution in March 2012 calling on the university to divest from companies complicit in Israeli occupation. In its statement celebrating this important victory, SAIA (2012) stated:

> Graduate students at Carleton University overwhelmingly voiced their support for the Palestinian people, by voting for the university's pension fund to divest from four companies that are complicit in the occupation of Palestine ... This marks the first time in the world that a referendum question on divestment has passed on a university campus, and it is one of many results of nearly four years of intensive campaigning by SAIA. The graduate students' will to divest adds further strength to SAIA's growing divestment campaign, which consists of 2500+ petition signatories and the endorsements of over 25 student clubs, academic workers' unions, and university service centres in an expanding student movement across campus.

The success of Palestine solidarity activism on campuses across Canada during this period is, in part, related to the heightened awareness of the Palestinian people's struggle for liberation, including among labour activists and unions generally. In fact, one can see that an organic, dialectical relationship was built between various struggles on campuses (and outside) that linked Palestine solidarity, anti-racism, Indigenous, 2SLGBTIQ and labour struggles together. This was evident in the fact that Palestine solidarity campus activists were also either academic labour activists or worked closely with on-campus unions and activists who were supportive of Palestinian people's struggle for liberation. This was especially true for Canadian Union of Public Employees (CUPE) campus locals such as Local 3903 at York University, which was a key sponsor of the BDS motion, Resolution 50, at the CUPE (ON) convention in Ottawa in May 2006. This was also evident in the important and active role that Queers Against Israeli Apartheid (QUAIA) played in the mobilization in support of BDS in Toronto between 2008 and 2015.

Outside campus, SAIA also played a leading role in organizing Palestine solidarity actions around the city. Campus activists reported that they were supported by the community as they engaged in their Palestine advocacy. The community that these activists referred to, however, was not the Palestinian and Arab community that we witnessed in previous periods. Rather, community in this case included organizations like Independent Jewish Voices, labour unions and locals, academics and university professors and campus groups such as the PIRGS. This is the community that Yafa Jarrar and other activists say supported SAIA when "our Israeli Apartheid Week poster was banned by university administrations in 2009" (Jarrar 2020).

As for the Palestinian and Arab communities in Ottawa, SAIA activists reported that not much tangible support was provided, save for passively providing some funds during Israeli Apartheid Week. It seems that the voice of the off-campus community was somewhat absent during attacks by the university administration and politicians when it was needed most. Some reported that it was even a struggle to get events circulated through community mailing lists (Jarrar 2020; Kmail 2020). SAIA activists stated that while the Palestinian community was somewhat passive in its support, SAIA had no relationship and received no support from PA officials in Ottawa. In fact, "the Palestinian General Delegation in Canada actively worked to suppress our BDS organizing." In meetings between SAIA activists and the PA Representative Office, activists were told to "calm down" on the BDS campaigning (Jarrar 2020).

With the success of the BDS and anti-Israeli apartheid work on campuses across the world, including in Canada, the State of Israel went into overdrive with its Brand Israel campaign clearly devised to "show Israel's prettier face" (Barghouti 2012: 34) and distort and demonize the Palestine solidarity movement, and BDS in particular. This included spending millions of dollars on countering the growing BDS movement across the world, a big chunk of which went to campus organizing. In 2013, the Israeli Ministry of Foreign Affairs organized a three-day conference in Jerusalem "to discuss ways of combating the different manifestations of current Antisemitism," especially on campuses (Small 2013).

According to the Preamble of the 2013 conference, "There is a war being waged against Israel and the Jewish people, an integral element of that war is taking place on university campuses throughout the western world" (Small 2013). Participants in the conference, including Charles Asher Small, a Canadian academic who currently heads the Institute for the Study of Global Anti-Semitism and Policy, called on Israel and its Ministry of Foreign Affairs to increase the resources as well as "create a single body to coordinate the struggle against anti-Semitism," which among its many tasks would be responsible for examining "the political structure surrounding the academic boycott globally and the boycott movement more generally ... and to provide students with greater organizational support to combat anti-Semitism [read: Palestine advocacy] on campuses" (Small 2013).

At Carleton, SAIA's success angered the administration, which was the target of the divestment campaign, as well as the Conservative/Zionist alliance of student groups, which was believed to be part of the larger Brand Israel campaign by the Israeli government to counter the efforts of Palestine solidarity activists on campus. According to activist Yafa Jarrar, "Because of the backlash and constant attacks from university administrations and other racist student groups, who [we believed] were funded and supported by the Israeli state and to a certain extent by Liberal and Conservative Canadian politicians, we needed to get active in student governments. We had members running for student council and executive positions. We passed BDS resolutions that forced student councils to support our BDS campaigns" (Jarrar 2020).

SPHR activists at the University of Ottawa faced a similar backlash from university administration and pro-Israel student clubs working in tandem with Conservative and Liberal student groups. This included attempts by the university to deny them space to hold events on campus, as well as threats to cancel IAW events that the university was investigating following complaints by Jewish students who were offended by them (Abunimah 2012).

Although SAIA ultimately failed to convince the university to divest from Israeli corporations who benefitted from the illegal occupation, there is no doubt that campus Palestine solidarity activism reached new heights during this period. This demonstrated its success in its capacity to organize, engage and mobilize large numbers of students on both campuses in Ottawa in support of BDS. It further indicates a growing effectiveness in Palestine solidarity activism on Ottawa campuses over the periods in question, since 1975, despite the clear ebbs and flows and constant evolution in its character. By the final period, Palestine advocacy had become much more pluralistic than ever before, forged broader alliances, and become deeply intertwined with broader social justice, anti-colonial and anti-oppression struggles in Canada.

Conclusion

In reviewing campus Palestine solidarity activism at Carleton University and the University of Ottawa from 1975 to 2015, one would be hard pressed not to recognize the significant positive developments that the movement underwent over four decades. In the course of my research for this chapter, I recognized that I am only scratching the surface and that much study and research needs to be undertaken to fully appreciate the contribution of the campus Palestine solidarity movement and its impact on altering the narrative of Palestine on Ottawa campuses, campuses across Canada and within Canadian society broadly. Nevertheless, my limited research over the past few months has led me to arrive at four key observations on the evolution of campus Palestine solidarity on Ottawa campuses between 1975 and 2015.

First, after accounting for the cyclical nature of student activism generally, the ebb and flow of campus Palestine solidarity activism on campuses in Ottawa was organically tied to the changing conditions and events on the ground in Palestine and the region.

Second, the composition of campus Palestine solidarity groups changed over the four decades in question. These organizations gradually moved from being predominantly new immigrant Palestinian/Arab students to ones that are diverse and include second- and third-generation Palestinian/Arab students, in addition to increasing numbers of anti-Zionist Jews and other Canadians of all backgrounds. A critical change also saw these organizations become led by women as the activist base became predominantly made up of women in the period of 2005 through the 2010s.

Third, the political focus, orientation and narrative of these campus associations transformed from one anchored in the political rhetoric/ program of a Palestinian/Arab nationalist project, to one that is more responsive and speaks to international law as articulated by the BDS movement, all of which are part of the broader umbrella of the national liberation struggle of the Palestinian people. In my estimation, it is this changing focus that attracted many non-Arabs, as they saw themselves in a movement that nurtures an intersectional and solidaristic form of activism.

Lastly, the type of actions and campaigns undertaken by campus Palestine solidarity groups during the BDS period became far more effective at exposing Israeli crimes and challenging Israeli apologists on Canadian campuses and the community at large — so much so that BDS campaigns and their organizers were condemned by pro-Israel university administrators as well as Canadian politicians. These campaigns attracted increasing numbers of diverse Canadian students to take up the call for BDS and Palestine liberation and exposed the fissure between Canadians and the ruling political class in Canada, which tends to be closely aligned with the Israeli settler-colonial project in Palestine.

Notes

1. The Arab community in this chapter refers to a broad and diverse group of formal and informal organizations as well as prominent Arab-Canadian individuals in Ottawa.
2. Israel's attacks on Lebanon began during the 1948 Palestinian Nakba. In 1978, Israel occupied large parts of South Lebanon and installed a surrogate collaboration force called the South Lebanon Army. Once again, in 1982 Israel invaded Lebanon, besieged and occupied the capital Beirut with the goal of driving the PLO out of the country and securing a peace agreement with a friendly Lebanese government. Israel's occupation of South Lebanon lasted until 2000, when they were driven out by the escalating armed resistance of the Lebanese people.
3. *Ash-shatat* in Arabic means diaspora and refers to Palestinian refugees who were driven out of Palestine in 1948 and 1967.

References

Abdo, Nahla, and Nira Yuval-Davis. 1995. In *Unsettling Settler Societies: Articulations of Gender, Race, Ethnicity and Class*, edited by Daiva Stasiulis and Nira Yuval-Davis. London, Thousand Oaks and New Delhi: Sage Publications.

Abou-Dib, Mariam. 2020. Questionnaire on Palestine Solidarity Student Activism.

Abu-Laban, Yasmeen, and Abigail B. Bakan. 2020. *Israel, Palestine and the Politics of Race: Exploring Identity and Power in a Global Context*. London & New York: I.B. Tauris.

Abunimah, Ali. 2012. "Students React to University of Ottawa Threat to Cancel Israel Apartheid Week Event." *The Electronic Intifada*, March 7.

Afifi, Wael. 2020. Questionnaire on Palestine Solidarity Student Activism.

Al-Mizan, Newsletter of ANSAR/The Arab Network of Students. 1990. Vol. 1, No 1. Toronto: September.

___. Fall 1992. Vol. 3, No. 1. Toronto.

ANSAR/The Arab Network of Students. 1992. *Marcel Khalife and Al Mayadine Concert Booklet*. Ottawa: October 24.

Arnold, Janice. 2013. "NDP Gov't Would Be Mideast Player, Mulcair Says." *Canadian Jewish News*, November 15. <cjnews.com/news/ndp-govt-would-be-mideast-player-mulcair-says>.

Awada, Mohamad. 2020. Questionnaire on Palestine Solidarity Student Activism.

Baglow, J. 2015. "Mulcair's Orange Purge of Pro-Palestinian Candidates Will Come Back to Haunt Him." *Rabble.ca*, August 12. <rabble.ca/blogs/bloggers/j-baglow/2015/08/mulcairs-orange-purge-pro-palestinian-candidates-will-come-back-to-h>.

Barghouti, Omar. 2012. "The Cultural Boycott: Israel vs. South Africa." In *The Case for Sanctions Against Israel*, edited by Audrea Lim. London and New York: Verso.

BDS (Boycott, Divestment and Sanctions) Movement. n.d. Main webpage. <bdsmovement.net/>.

Bueckert, Michael, Thomas Woodley, Grafton Ross, et al. 2020. "Out of Touch: Canada's Foreign Policy Disconnected from Canadians' Views." Part 1 of a national opinion survey of Canadians conducted June 5–10, 2020. Survey conducted by EKOS Research Associates, co-sponsored by Canadians for Justice and Peace in the Middle East, Independent Jewish Voices Canada, and United Network for Justice and Peace in Palestine-Israel. <www.cjpme.org/survey2020_r1>.

Carter, Jimmy. 2006. *Palestine: Peace Not Apartheid*. New York: Simon and Schuster.

Cheatani, Kassem. 2020. Questionnaire on Palestine Solidarity Student Activism.

Farsoun, Samih K., and Naseer H. Aruri. 2006. *Palestine and the Palestinians: A Social and Political History*. Boulder, CO: Westview Press.

House of Commons of Canada. 2016. "Debates (Hansard) No. 20." February 18. <ourcommons.ca/DocumentViewer/en/42-1/house/sitting-20/hansard>.

Husseini, Ahmed. 2020. Questionnaire on Palestine Solidarity Student Activism.

Jarrar, Yafa. 2020. Questionnaire on Palestine Solidarity Student Activism.

Khouri, Malek. 2020. Interview on Palestine Solidarity Student Activism.

Kmail, Mujahed. 2020. Interview on Palestine Solidarity Student Activism.

Levitan, Tyler. 2020. Interview on Palestine Solidarity Student Activism.

Masrieh, Youssef. 2020. Questionnaire on Palestine Solidarity Student Activism.

Palestinian Civil Society. 2005. "Palestinian Civil Society Call for BDS." Open letter. July 9. <bdsmovement.net/call>.

?Sa'di, Ahmad H., and Lila Abu-Lughod (eds.). 2007. *Nakba: Palestine, 1948, and the Claims of Memory*. New York: Columbia University Press.

Said, Edward W. 1979. "Zionism from the Standpoint of Its Victims." *Social Text* 1.

SAIA (Students Against Israeli Apartheid Carleton University). 2012. "Carleton University Divestment — Join the Movement." Ottawa: January 22. <youtube.com/watch?v=xke7SiXjFP4&feature=youtu.be>.

___. 2014. "Welcoming to SAIA Carleton!" <saiacarleton.com>.

Small, Charles Asher. 2013. "GFCA 2013 — Action Plan — Antisemitism on the Campuses." Jerusalem: Israel Ministry of Foreign Affairs and Ministry for Jerusalem and Diaspora Affairs. May 28–30. <youtube.com/watch?v=NMmZGvgw_GE>.

Stead, Rebecca. 2019. "Remembering Israel's Disengagement from Gaza." *Middle East Monitor*, August 15. <middleeastmonitor.com/20190815-remembering-israels-disengagement-from-gaza/>.

Tilley, Virginia. 2005. *The One-State Solution: A Breakthrough for Peace in the Israeli-Palestinian Deadlock*. Ann Arbor: University of Michigan Press.

Ziadah, Rafeef. 2010. "A View From Toronto — A Hub of 'Israel Delegitimization.'" *The Bullet*, March 10. <https://socialistproject.ca/2010/03/b322/>.

Conclusion

Emily Regan Wills, Nadia Abu-Zahra,
Michael Bueckert & Jeremy Wildeman

-40 C in Winnipeg
Palestinians and Indigenous children wave placards
Stop killing children in Palestine
Free Gaza
My tears freeze on my face
My daughter is there
Just as she was there 35 years ago
Chanting Free Palestindians
My frozen tears are cutting pain lines on my face
(Maracle 2012: 182)

The history on Turtle Island of advocacy for Palestine seems, sometimes, like a tightly woven series of highs and lows, of startling actions of solidarity in the face of multiple expressions of racism, violence
and oppression. In this book, we have tried to focus attention on the
complexity and strengths of this advocacy, even amidst the challenges
advocates have encountered. A part of this complexity is understanding
the role of settler-colonialism in both Turtle Island and Palestine, and
how that connection produces the political realities in which advocates
operate. The colonial states of Canada and Israel are often claimed to be
morally justified on the basis that the settler population is (uniquely)
deserving of refuge, self-determination and security (Massad 2018). But
settler-colonial politics cannot provide refuge, self-determination and
security to the colonized, and they codify their oppressive structures
through racist hierarchies, displacement and structural and physical
violence that can go beyond "merely" the Indigenous Other to suppress
anyone who deviates from the ideal settler narrative.

With or without the understanding that all elements and beings are interconnected, we see today that settler violence against the peoples, lands, waters, animals, plants and all beings within colonized places is fostering new forms of harm and perpetuating old ones. In this conclusion, we want to underline the push and pull between these highs and lows through a close examination of how racialized oppressive hierarchies are enforced on all who live within them, whether they are supposed to be at the top or the bottom. Hierarchies repress, silence and suppress, and they cannot simply be turned off or avoided. Oppressive hierarchies are broad and can collapse the space between places and mirror each other across the oceans.

But irrespective of people's identities and where they "should" be located on those hierarchies, their perspective on that hierarchy is not predetermined. Who you are can never answer the question of what you believe. Advocates for justice and change can be located anywhere within the hierarchy and work from their own position to undo the harms done by racist hierarchies. Solidarity is powerful and essential to creating real change, whether inside or outside formal political institutions.

Although these insights are derived specifically from the experience of advocates for Palestine living in and advocating on Turtle Island, they can find mirrors in many different struggles. In this conclusion, we trace these insights through the arguments of the authors in this volume and close by discussing why advocacy for Palestine can serve as an essential "canary in the coal mine" for all social justice advocates on Turtle Island.

Racialized Hierarchies at Work

Many of the Palestinian and Arab authors in this volume describe experiences of racialized repression — such as being forced to listen to variations of the "higher grade race" argument and endure acts of overt and subtle exclusion, as Nyla Matuk so clearly describes. Hassan Husseini points to the silencing effect of the post-9/11 period, just as Matuk gestures to the ways in which Palestinians are told not to "shut down conversation" and not to use terms like racism or apartheid. As Rana Nazzal Hamadeh says in her chapter, much of the racism Palestinians experience is embedded in a fundamental categorization of Arabs as essentially violent — a stereotype that writers in Arab American and Arab Canadian studies have analyzed for decades (Elia 2017; Regan Wills 2014, 2019; Said 1994).

Not only Palestinians experience these limits, however. For instance,

Mastracci gives an eye-opening overview of how journalists, be they Palestinian or not, are given strict limits on work pertaining to Palestine. Other writers have noted these limits, including the simple fact that the public Canadian Broadcasting Corporation (CBC) style guidelines say that the name "Palestine" should not be used because "there is no modern country of Palestine" and that "Palestinian territories" should be used instead only to refer to the territories governed by the Palestinian Authority (Nagler 2021). In fact, in May of 2021, as Palestinians in Jerusalem resisted eviction, Palestinians in Gaza endured another round of bombing, Palestinians in Israel were subject to police and settler mob violence and Palestinians in the West Bank were prevented from protesting by the Palestinian Authority, Canadian journalists circulated an open letter calling for fair reporting and criticizing the censorship and limits that were placed on what they could report. Some of their employers, in retaliation, then removed these journalists from covering Palestine as an alleged conflict of interest (Krishnan 2021).

Journalists are not the only ones to experience this form of silencing: major Canadian non-governmental organizations, research funders and academics continue to face attacks, job loss and revocation of funding for supporting Palestinian organizations or documenting Israel's violence against Palestinians or Palestinian autonomy; as attested by the stories of organizations like Rights and Democracy and IRFAN-Canada, and scholars like Valentina Azarova and Faisal Bhabha (Cheadle 2010; Wildeman 2016; Wildeman 2018: 163–64; Labelle 2019; Friesen 2020; Bhabha 2021). Being an advocate for Palestine within electoral politics is as risky as anywhere else (Foreword, this volume; Dyer 2021).

Jews who speak out on behalf of Palestinian rights face silencing and intracommunal violence, as Nestel describes from her own experience. Nestel is not alone, as shown in the survey data Ralph discusses: Jews in Canada actually have fairly diverse opinions with regards to Israel. The bargain of whiteness that Nestel describes for Jews in Canada demands participation in the suppression of Palestinians; those who deviate from it are reminded that their status can be conditional and that bargaining with white supremacy is always risky business. Regardless of your position on the hierarchies of power, you remain subject to them. Speaking out on behalf of Palestinians comes at a price, and you cannot avoid that price even if you are not racialized.

Activism on behalf of Palestinians is often smeared as aggressive, hostile or discursively connected to white supremacy, Holocaust denial and neo-Nazism, as Nazzal Hamadeh, Ralph and Keefer all discuss in their chapters. This kind of inversion, when supporters of racist hierarchies attempt to malign human rights defenders as human rights abusers, has precedent in debates over apartheid South Africa, as Bueckert shows. It also means that advocates for Palestine must constantly be ready to defend themselves against accusations, as Woodley describes in his chapter. This preparation for the inevitable attack takes time and energy away from mobilizing and makes it harder for advocates for Palestine to be heard. And this sort of attack is neither meaningless nor merely discursive; when the government of Canada not only officially adopts the IHRA definition of antisemitism, which names criticism of Israel as a form of antisemitic speech (Bueckert, this volume), but also allocates $45 million to promote its acceptance and implementation by all levels of settler governance — federal, provincial and municipal (Ralph, this volume) — fear of the consequences of advocating for Palestine is powerful.

Solidarity Can Transcend Hierarchy

The counter to the intensity of the racialized hierarchies to which advocates for Palestine find themselves subject is the strength of the solidarity and political commitment from people at many different points on those hierarchies. Woodley's chapter offers a dizzying list of communities who can find convincing reasons to support Palestine that align with their ethics, values and principles. But the key insight running through this book's stories about mobilizing for Palestine is that solidarity can come from anywhere. All of us have the option to choose whether and how we show up for justice in Palestine.

Many of the organizers on behalf of Palestinian rights are themselves of Palestinian origin. Solidarity, however, neither derives from some kind of "automatic" nationalism inherent in Palestinians nor — as is sometimes alleged — some form of parental indoctrination. Instead, it comes from the fact of being deeply moved by oppression in Palestine, through personal experience and the stories of family members. Not all Palestinians choose to engage in political work for Palestine; as Matuk describes, sometimes they even encourage their family members not to, out of fear of the consequences. But those who do become engaged may invariably anchor their advocacy in their own experiences and what they have witnessed.

Advocates for Palestine who are Jewish often feel a particular moral duty to solidarity with Palestinians. They recognize that the Israeli state and the Zionist movement make claims in the name of the global Jewish community, and advocates for justice want to refuse their own implication in that process (Regan Wills 2019). Organizations like Independent Jewish Voices trace a moral position, rooted in Jewish ethics and history, which gives them a strong standpoint from which to advocate for justice. Anti-occupation or anti/non-Zionist Jews may not be the whole of the Jewish community on Turtle Island, but their voices matter, and the work they put into the movement is essential.

Woodley lists other categories of people who might feel a particular tie to the Palestinian cause — those who care about the freedom of Muslims to pray freely at Al-Aqsa or Al-Ibrahimi Mosques, Québec sovereigntists who care about a nation denied statehood, land and water protectors who recognize the parallels between settler-colonial practices in Palestine and on Turtle Island, and human rights and justice advocates concerned with "systematic Israeli domination and oppression" in Palestine (Human Rights Watch 2021: 3). As we mentioned earlier, solidarity is not naturally occurring; it must be strengthened and nourished like any living thing. But it can transcend oppressive racialized hierarchies; the Palestine solidarity movement as described in this book is at its core an inclusionary movement closely linked to anti-apartheid, anti-colonial and anti-racist values, resonating with people seeking social justice and basic human rights.

One of the primary factors that keeps people out of advocacy for Palestine is fear, including a deeply rooted fear that they will be threatened, harassed or attacked, possibly from their own communities. Many struggle with the fears implanted by Zionist narratives — that Palestinian existence and demands for justice are inherently antisemitic — and are unsure how to take action that will not make them subject to attacks of that basis. These fears are a part of a social system that aims to discourage people from taking action to seek justice. But what we see are how many people are overcoming multiple fears, binding together the joint intentions to combat antisemitism and structural inequalities and prejudices of all kinds, and thereby demonstrating how our movements for justice come together.

Grounding movements for justice in joy, connection and freedom is a way to address and overcome fear and build community. As we wrote in the introduction to this book, building community and healing from inner fears are mutual activities. One reason for this book is to understand how — in our personal struggles against fear — we may transcend and address racialized hierarchies rather than seek to fit in to or move up in them. We refuse to control our fears by enabling systems that control others. Instead, as we stated in the opening to this book, movements for justice and those within them seek liberation through solidarity and healing.

Listening to Canaries

In their 2002 book, critical race theorists Lani Guinier and Gerald Torres argued that racialized communities in North America serve as "canaries in the coal mine" for core issues of democracy:

> Miners often carried a canary into the mine alongside them. The canary's more fragile respiratory system would cause it to collapse from noxious gases long before humans were affected, thus alerting the miners to danger. The canary's distress signaled that it was time to get out of the mine because the air was becoming too poisonous to breathe.
>
> Those who are racially marginalized are like the miner's canary: their distress is the first sign of a danger that threatens us all. It is easy enough to think that when we sacrifice this canary, the only harm is to communities of color. Yet others ignore problems that converge around racial minorities at their own peril, for these problems are symptoms warning us that we are all at risk. (2002: 11)

In closing this book, we want to emphasise that one of the reasons to pay attention to advocacy for Palestine is that it serves as a miner's canary. When advocates for Palestine face repression and suppression, the problem is not theirs alone, but represents a broader challenge to all of us to ensure that political space remains open for the pursuit of justice. When advocating for Palestine produces risks for future employment, this naturalizes the idea that being an advocate for justice is outside the bounds of political speech. When legal principles related to freedom of expression or the content of hate speech are applied differentially to advocates for Palestine and Zionist activists, this makes it harder for all advocates for justice to find space for their work. If the news media is unable to provide honest reporting on Palestine, the trustworthiness of the media as a whole is undermined. And when these tactics work to subjugate and silence, then repressive forces of all kinds will know it and will not hesitate to use them again.

This is not merely theoretical. The same discourses and abuses of power targeting advocacy for Palestine on Turtle Island are used against Indigenous land and water defenders (e.g., Forester 2021; Kanji and McSorley 2021; Desai 2021; Naber 2017). After all, as many scholars have noted (Abu-Laban and Bakan 2008, 2020, Bahdi 2019, Labelle 2019, Wolfe 1999, 2012, Veracini 2010, 2013, Waziyatawin 2012, Krebs and Olwan 2012, or Hamzah 2020), Canada and Israel are both settler states that benefit from a situation where the "veneer of reconciliation or peace replacing the focus on the colonial relationship [works to] keep each settler-capitalist economy thriving through continued resource extraction, land confiscation, and dispossession" (Desai 2021, 16). As stated by the Gender Studies Departments in Solidarity with Palestinian Feminist Collective (2021), signed by seventeen Canadian Women's and Gender Studies Departments along with dozens in the United States and elsewhere: "From Angela Davis we understand that justice is indivisible; we learn this lesson time and again from Black, Indigenous, Arab, and most crucially, Palestinian feminists, who know that 'Palestine is a Feminist Issue.'" The limits and challenges to advocacy for Palestine must be taken seriously; sacrificing the canary is not just morally wrong for the canary's sake but strategically wrong for all of us.

The Way Forward

Despite the very real challenges put in the path of advocates for justice in Palestine, we do not want to end this book only with a canary's distress signals. We see fresh air in Indigenous and anti-racism struggles and advocacy for Palestine coalescing in movements for change on the streets, in the classrooms and in the homes of people across Turtle Island. Speaking for the Ottawa Black Diaspora Coalition at a thousands-strong rally in 2021, Khadija El Hilali shared:

> From unceded Algonquin territory … to Palestine, we are witnessing state sanctioned violence.… Hashtags like #BlackLivesMatter and #FreePalestine are not trends/They are demands. Our lives are not a thing of the moment. These are

constant pleas because we cannot know real peace until we are all free....

We must stand together in solidarity, love and rage to condemn, challenge and dismantle all systems of oppression.... We recognize that the fight against injustice occurs at an intersection where elements of our identity — whether it be race, sexuality, class or faith — converge to inextricably bind us together in the struggle for freedom.

As a community the liberation of Black people means the liberation of all people. We cannot and will not ever be silent and therefore complicit with genocide. We may not live in Palestine but Palestine lives within all of us. (El Hilali 2021)

We see the growth of advocacy worldwide against racism, colonialism, extractivism, patriarchy and violence. We see solidarity in action: in focusing on people-to-people mobilizing, mutual aid and building structures to support others and create new ways of living; in drawing on the democratic and grassroots power of unions, communities and non-profits to effect meaningful change; and in advocating for formal political change and decolonial governance.

One of the lessons of this book, then, is that the solidarity that can be formed among those who care about justice in Palestine is central to the strength of movements for Palestine, as well as movements for justice elsewhere. Healthy relations can serve to overcome the fears at the root of so much prejudice and overcome the inertia that drags down movements. The more that these healthy relations can be cultivated, the stronger our movements for justice will be.

When we speak of freedom
we must also speak of our freedom
to be kind
to be just
and to be in love
when we speak of freedom
this is what we
must speak of
(Groulx 2019, 7.4)

References

Abu-Laban, Yasmeen, and Abigail B. Bakan. 2008. "The Racial Contract: Israel/Palestine and Canada." *Social Identities* 14, 5.

___. 2020. *Israel, Palestine and the Politics of Race: Exploring Identity and Power in a Global Context.* London: Bloomsbury Publishing.

Bahdi, Reem. 2019. "'All Arabs Are Liars:' Arab and Muslim Stereotypes in Canadian Human Rights Law." *Journal of Law and Social Policy* 31, 1.

Bhabha, Faisal. 2021. "Smearing, Silencing and Antisemitism." *Obiter Dicta* [blog], January 20. <obiter-dicta.ca/2021/01/20/smearing-silencing-and-antisemitism/>.

Cheadle, Bruce. 2010. "Tory Appointees 'Unfit' for Rights Agency Board, Staff Says." *Toronto Star*, January 12. <thestar.com/news/canada/2010/01/12/tory_appointees_unfit_for_rights_agency_board_staff_says.html>.

Desai, Chandni. 2021. "Disrupting Settler–Colonial Capitalism: Indigenous Intifadas and Resurgent Solidarity from Turtle Island to Palestine." *Journal of Palestine Studies* 50, 2.

Dyer, Evan. 2021. "Violence in Gaza and Israel Has Left Behind a Changed Political Landscape in Canada." *CBC News*, May 29. <cbc.ca/news/politics/israel-palestinian-gaza-canada-1.6044837>.

El Hilali, Khadija. 2021. Unpublished transcript of a speech to the Protest for Palestine on Parliament Hill, May 23.

Elia, Nada. 2017. "Justice Is Indivisible: Palestine as a Feminist Issue." *Decolonization: Indigeneity, Education & Society* 6, 1.

Forester, Brett. 2021. "Top Spy Agency Tracked Caledonia Land Dispute as Possible Threat to National Security: Secret Document." *APTN*, June 29. <aptnnews.ca/national-news/spy-agency-tracked-caledonia-land-dispute-as-possible-threat-to-national-security-secret-document>.

Friesen, Joe. 2020. "Canadian University Teachers Begin Process to Censure U of T over the Azarova Law School Affair." *Globe and Mail*, October 15. <theglobeandmail.com/canada/article-canadian-university-teachers-begin-process-to-censure-u-of-t-over-the/>.

Gender Studies Departments in Solidarity with Palestinian Feminist Collective. 2021. Open letter. <genderstudiespalestinesolidarity.weebly.com/>.

Groulx, David. 2019. *From Turtle Island to Gaza.* Edmonton: Athabasca University Press.

Guinier, Lani, and Gerald Torres. 2002. *The Miner's Canary: Enlisting Race, Resisting Power, Transforming Democracy.* Cambridge, MA: Harvard University Press.

Hamzah, Dyala. 2020. "'Something Is Rotten in the State of Denmark:' An Open Letter to Justin Trudeau Regarding Palestine." *Mondoweiss*, October 2. <mondoweiss.net/2020/10/something-is-rotten-in-the-state-of-denmark-an-open-letter-to-justin-trudeau-regarding-palestine/>.

Human Rights Watch. 2021. *A Threshold Crossed: Israeli Authorities and the Crimes of Apartheid and Persecution.* Report, April 27. <hrw.org/report/2021/04/27/threshold-crossed/israeli-authorities-and-crimes-apartheid-and-persecution>.

Kanji, Azeezah, and Tim McSorley. 2021. "Islamophobia in Canada: Submission to the National Action Summit on Islamophobia." July 22. <islamophobia-is.com/wp-content/uploads/2021/07/Islamophobia-Summit-2021-report-final.pdf>.

Krebs, Mike, and Dana M. Olwan. 2012. "'From Jerusalem to the Grand River, Our Struggles Are One:' Challenging Canadian and Israeli Settler Colonialism." *Settler Colonial Studies* 2, 2.

Krishnan, Manisha. 2021. "CBC Journalists Told They Can't Cover Israel-Palestine after Demanding Fairer Coverage." *VICE World News,* May 21. <vice.com/en/article/5db398/cbc-journalists-told-they-cant-cover-israel-palestine-after-demanding-fairer-coverage>.

Labelle, Maurice J. 2019. "Jameel's Journal: Jim Peters, Anti-Orientalism, and Arab Decolonization in 1960s Canada." In *Undiplomatic History: The New Study of Canada and the World,* edited by Asa McKercher and Philip Van Huizen. Montreal and Kingston: McGill-Queen's University Press.

Maracle, Lee. 2012. "Remembering Mahmoud 1986." *Decolonization: Indigeneity, Education & Society* 1, 1.

Massad, Joseph. 2018. "Against Self-Determination." *Humanity Journal* 9, 2.

Naber, Nadine. 2017. "'The U.S. and Israel Make the Connections for Us:' Anti-Imperialism and Black-Palestine Solidarity." *Critical Ethnic Studies* 3, 2.

Nagler, Jack. 2021. "An Awkward Apology." CBC/Radio-Canada Ombudsman, March 4. <cbc.radio-canada.ca/en/ombudsman/reviews/Awkward_Apology>.

Regan Wills, Emily. 2014. "Polemics, Political Racism, and Misrecognition: Naming and Analyzing Prejudice Against Arab-Americans." *Constellations* 21, 1.

____. 2019. *Arab New York: Politics and Community in the Everyday Lives of Arab Americans.* New York: New York University Press.

Said, Edward W. 1994. *Culture and Imperialism.* New York: Vintage.

Veracini, Lorenzo. 2010. *Settler Colonialism: A Theoretical Overview.* Houndmills, Basingstoke, New York: Palgrave Macmillan.

____. 2013. "The Other Shift: Settler Colonialism, Israel, and the Occupation." *Journal of Palestine Studies* 42, 2.

Waziyatawin. 2012. "Malice Enough in Their Hearts and Courage Enough in Ours: Reflections on US Indigenous and Palestinian Experiences under Occupation." *Settler Colonial Studies* 2, 1.

Wildeman, Jeremy. 2016. "'Either You're with Us or against Us:' Illiberal Canadian Foreign Aid in the Occupied Palestinian Territories, 2001–2012." PhD dissertation, University of Exeter.

____. 2018. "Donor Aid Effectiveness and Do No Harm in the Occupied Palestinian Territory." *Aid Watch Palestine,* December 10. <uottawa.academia.edu/JeremyWildeman>.

____. 2021. "Assessing Canada's Foreign Policy Approach to the Palestinians and Israeli-Palestinian Peacebuilding, 1979–2019." *Canadian Foreign Policy Journal* 27, 1.

Wolfe, Patrick. 1999. *Settler Colonialism and the Transformation of Anthropology the Politics and Poetics of an Ethnographic Event.* London; New York: Cassel.

____. 2012. "Purchase by Other Means: The Palestine Nakba and Zionism's Conquest of Economics." *Settler Colonial Studies* 2, 1.

Index